Dialectics of Liberation

D1521477

Dialectics of Liberation

The African Liberation Support Committee

Abdul Alkalimat

AFRICA WORLD PRESS

Trenton | London | Cape Town | Nairobi | Addis Ababa | Asmara | Ibadan | New Delhi

AFRICA WORLD PRESS
541 West Ingham Avenue | Suite B
Trenton, New Jersey 08638

Copyright © 2022 Abdul Alkalimat

Book design: Dawid Kahts
Cover design: Ashraful Haque

Library of Congress Cataloging-in-Publication Data may be obtained from the Library of Congress.

ISBNs: 978-1-56902-778-3 (HB)
       978-1-56902-779-0 (PB)

To my sister Aysha/Sandra
Sibling, Comrade, Friend

Table of Contents

Table of Contents

Introduction

This book is about the African Liberation Support Committee (ALSC), a pivotal organization in the Black liberation movement from 1971 to 1975. In just five years, ALSC, which began as part of the anti-imperialist movement in support of the national liberation struggles in Africa, became the preeminent context for debates about the development of revolutionary vanguard cadre organizations. This featured a full national debate between the adherents of Black nationalism and Marxism. The ALSC experience enables us to examine the dialectics of how a mass social movement process can transition into an organizational process debating the possibility of revolutionary ideological unity.

Dialectics is an important concept. It is the process by which differences within and among different phenomena interact and produce the change by which new developments take place. This is a process of opposites contending and in the process being transformed into something entirely new. This is a universal process, and one that applies to the historical development of ALSC.

This study reveals the strong connection that African Americans have to Africa. The fight for liberation in the United States impacts Africa and what happens in Africa impacts the Black liberation movement in the United States. The long history of this dialectical relationship is both manifested and extended by the practice of ALSC in support of the six armed struggles that were finally to end direct European colonial rule in Africa.

The major event that launched the organizational process of ALSC was the African Liberation Day conference and demonstration that took place on May 24-25, 1972. It is time for a major summation of ALSC, since we now have fifty years of subsequent experience in the struggle for Black liberation.

We have the crisis of generational transition, as the activists involved in ALSC have been passing away. Among those who have gone on home are Amiri Baraka, John Warfield, Ron Walters, Kwame Ture, Elombe Brath, Jitu Weusi, Tim Thomas, Walter Rodney, Tim Hector, Ron Washington, Rod Bush, Tanya Russell, Florence Tate, Mike Hamlin, and Jeanette Walton. Activists in every stage of the movement are responsible for remembering those who have preceded them and for calling their names. Hopefully, this analysis will help others to call more names.

There is still time to learn from the experience of those who remain active as elders: Milton Coleman, Gene Locke, Howard Fuller (Owusu Sadaukai), Mark Smith, Randall Robinson, James Turner, Carl Turpin, Nelson and Joyce Johnson, Bill Sales, Sam Anderson, Pat Wagner, Benda Paris, Phyliss Jones, Faye Coleman, John Mendez, Viola Plummer, Bertie Howard, Walter Aaron, Malcolm Suber, Cleve Sellers, Saladin Muhammad, Carl Redmond, Omali Yeshitela, Mickey Dean, Muhammad Ahmad, Haki Madhubuti, Julialynn Walker, Walter Searcy, and Abdul Alkalimat. But there are many more, so, if you are reading this and are a veteran of ALSC, please get in touch.

As one of these elders, I have accepted the responsibility of initiating the summation to find the key lessons from the ALSC experience. During that time of ALSC, I was director of Black Studies at Fisk University and chair of the research sub-committee of the ALSC executive committee. Since then, I have continued as both an academic and an activist. My personal bias will likely be seen in some instances, but not without an attempt to provide documentation that can be used to advance an alternative interpretation as well. The goal is to stimulate a discussion in today's movement so that the ALSC experience can be a source of lessons.

Most scholars have chosen to focus on why ALSC declined in importance. The most common analysis targets the left for making extreme dogmatic errors (Johnson 2007, 131–72; Plummer 2013, 276–81). We will present a different interpretation. Any analysis that targets errors assumes that there is clarity about how history ought to have happened. Further, in this case, this analysis is from the perspective of the sustainability of the Black protest that actually took place, extending the practice of the first African Liberation Day (ALD) in 1972. What this book will do is present an analysis from the point of view of the activists and chart the change, both intended and unintended, over a period of five years. So, I will demonstrate that the radical Black left was grappling with the same dialectics as was the left across United States and throughout the world, including Africa

There is much to be learned from ALSC. Of course, we remember the maxim by George Santayana that those who fail to learn the lessons of history are doomed to blindly repeat its mistakes. Today we have the wonderful rebirth of mass forms of resistance, especially under the slogan "Black Lives Matter." This spontaneous movement is beginning to face its own dialectical divides between a well-financed wing and a more grassroots wing. The grassroots wing is coming to the conclusion that more study is needed to clarify a path forward, a path that has to lead to societal transformation. As with ALSC, the critical task is to determine what to believe and what to do, both in theory and in practice. More specifically, what's up is to deal with ideology as the basis for revolutionary strategy and tactics and for cadre organization to serve as the staff for the mass movement. Cadres are needed by the movement to be its scaffolding and its brain trust.

The present ALSC analysis will have two results. The first is this book, which cites both published material and archival material in my possession. The second will be the creation of an archive in a public repository, as well as an online digital collection. This is so that activist researchers will have full access to the ALSC experience.

The two main questions about ALSC are the following: The

objective question is: What happened? The subjective question is: What does it mean? To answer the objective question, the analysis will use seven sources: my personal experience, interviews with other ALSC activists, ALSC organizational documents, movement documents from Africa and the United States, media reports about the movement, academic scholarship, and general revolutionary theory.

To answer the subjective question will require the application of theory to the ALSC experience to extract lessons, in this case concerning whether there are comparable experiences in global and/or national movements. In the summation of meaning, we will provide lessons for today's movement. Drawing on my experience as both an academic scholar and a movement activist, my interpretation will be a major part of this analysis.

The book's chapters are organized by the key years of 1972, 1973, 1974, and 1975. Each year saw changes in the theory and practice of ALSC. Each year is placed in the context of national and international events that place ALSC within a larger historical development of revolutionary forces.

Chapter 1–1972: United Front is about the first ALD in 1972. We begin by tracing the development of the six countries in Africa then engaged in armed struggles, as well as the historical context of the Pan-African solidarity movement that defined how African Americans have supported self-determination struggles on the African continent, a movement born of a united front of diverse forces across ideological tendencies and class positions.

Chapter 2–1973: Black Liberation takes up how ALSC developed after 1972. The focus is on how ALSC became a focal point for the political development of the Black liberation movement. The outcome included a new composition for national leadership as well as mass mobilization and coalition building for local demonstrations throughout the country.

Chapter 3–1974: Class Struggle is about how the ideological debates generated by ALSC policy decisions led to a historic Marxist-nationalist debate in 1974. This led to key nationalist leaders withdrawing not only from ALSC but also from the Congress of African People as it moved to the left.

4

Chapter 4–1975: World Revolution places the ALSC intensification of ideological debate between organizations in the context of world and national revolutionary developments. These debates led to multiple fractures within the Black left after ALSC ended its previous two years of active struggle.

Chapter 5 focuses on the **lessons and legacy** of the ALSC experience. This is the main purpose of historical analysis: what we can learn for our use today and in the future.

Our target audience is diverse. We most want this analysis to be discussed and debated by activists in the Black liberation movement today. We hope this will be in dialogue with the veteran activists from the ALSC experience. We have tried to develop a narrative analysis with general trends as well as details about who was involved, to honor local activists as models for today.

We also hope that the faculty and students in Black Studies programs will accept this as a case study for their focus on the fight for Black liberation. Finally, we hope that our counterparts in Africa will accept this as documentation of the solidarity that has always existed between African Americans and the fight for liberation in Africa. We look forward to collaboration in our struggles going into the future.

Abdul Alkalimat
August 13, 2021

Chapter 1

1972: United Front

Chapter 1 is about the first African Liberation Day (ALD), celebrated on May 27, 1972. As such, since pivotal historical events reflect a historical process, we will begin with the background that led to ALD. This memorial day should be seen in relationship to the historical development of the African liberation struggles and the support for African liberation provided by African Americans. The main political lesson is how the politics of a United Front were successfully realized.

Part 1 of this chapter is about the African Liberation efforts that took the form of armed struggle. This took place in two kinds of countries, Portuguese colonies (Guinea-Bissau, Angola, and Mozambique) and white settler colonies connected to England and the Netherlands (South Africa, Namibia, and Zimbabwe). The history of each country shows a pattern of middle-class forces—mainly ministers, teachers, government employees, and students—making attempts to negotiate reforms. The colonial powers were driven by economic imperatives, namely, the building of the economic base of the home country on colonial exploitation, whether in the case of the Portuguese or the white English and Dutch settlers turning the colony into a permanent home for themselves while serving their country of origin.

7

Peaceful protests were met with murderous repression, forcing the freedom fighters to move from nonviolence to armed struggle based on the mobilization of workers and peasants. Both stages were based on building a unity process.

Part 2 of this chapter is about the Pan-African movement in the United States, leading up to the ALD 1972 demonstrations. The two dominant tendencies of Pan-Africanism in the United States go back to the beginning of the twentieth century and have been associated with Marcus Mosiah Garvey and W. E. B. Dubois, mainly rooted in major Black communities like Harlem and Chicago. In the 1960s, two youth movements were major forces: veteran Student Nonviolent Coordinating Committee (SNCC) forces based in Washington, DC, and organizations in North Carolina (Malcolm X Liberation University and the Student Organization for Black Unity). A key Pan-Africanist leader who emerged was Howard Fuller (Owusu Sadaukai).

Part 3 of this chapter is about the first ALD, which was held in Washington, DC. The goal of this major demonstration was building a large-scale Black united front. In addition to this demonstration, there were demonstrations in Canada and the Caribbean. This day of protest redefined the relationship between the African Liberation movements and the Black liberation movement. Unity events that set the stage for ALD included Black Power Conferences (1967, 1968, 1970), the Congress of African People (1970), and the National Black Political Convention (March 1972).

Africa

For centuries, the entire African continent has been a primary target of global capital for colonization and imperialist plunder. This has been a fundamental concern of progressive forces throughout the African Diaspora. This section will discuss the suppression of African people and their efforts to liberate themselves. This is a twentieth-century freedom narrative. Its high points are marked by key conferences at each stage of the struggle. The African Liberation Support Committee (ALSC) is best viewed in relation to these struggles for the liberation of Africa. ALSC was formed to

8

support and emulate the organizations that carried out these struggles.

The complete colonization of Africa was advanced in a European conference convened in Germany in 1884. George Padmore sums up what happened as a result of the conference:

> The German Chancellor convened the Conference in Berlin in November 1884, at which the powers with colonial ambitions in Africa were invited to regulate their claims peacefully. After the General Act of the Berlin Conference was signed on February 26, 1885, the three great Western European Powers—Britain, France, and Germany—started in real earnest to annex colonies and protectorates all over the continent. (Padmore 1956, 79)

This process of colonization was based on how capitalism was developing into its globally oriented imperialist stage. In 1916, Lenin (1973) defined imperialism as monopoly capitalism:

> Imperialism is capitalism at that stage of development at which the dominance of monopolies and finance capital is established; in which the export of capital has acquired pronounced importance; in which the division of the world among the international trusts has begun, in which the division of all territories of the globe among the biggest capitalist powers has been completed. (Lenin 1973, 106)

Wars defined how imperialism expanded around the world, including both World Wars I and II. Once the world was divided up by the imperialist powers, those powers then fought each other in search of greater shares. Du Bois laid this out in his insightful 1915 article "The African Roots of War," in which he anticipates Lenin's analysis by describing the economic interests driving the imperialist World War I and the fight for African plunder between the nations involved. About the nature of the war to expand colonial control, he asked "What was the new call for dominion?" and followed up with "The answer to this riddle we shall find in the economic changes in Europe . . . , the divine right of the few to determine economic income and distribute the goods and services of the world" (Du Bois 1973, 28-40).

African agency fought back. There has always been resistance on the African continent to foreign aggression. In a global context, there were Pan-African congresses beginning in 1900 that involved people from throughout the African Diaspora carrying liberation politics forward. The critical turning point was the Fifth Pan-African Congress, held in Manchester, England, in 1945. Delegations came from all parts of Africa and the Caribbean, as well as the United States and Europe. Key future political leaders were there, including Kwame Nkrumah (Ghana), Jomo Kenyatta (Kenya), Hastings Banda (Malawi), and Obafemi Awolowo (Nigeria). Key leaders from the African Diaspora who were at the congress included George Padmore (Trinidad), W. E. B. Du Bois (USA), Amy Ashwood Garvey (Jamaica), and Ras T. Makonnen (Guyana) (Adi, Sherwood, and Padmore 1995, 125–49).

Kwame Nkrumah returned home and, at the head of the Convention Peoples Party, led Ghana to its independence twelve years later, the first African country south of the Sahara Desert to achieve this. At the independence celebration, the U.S. government was represented by Vice President Richard Nixon and Congressman Adam Clayton Powell. As an expression of Nkrumah's affinity with the African Diaspora, Nkrumah invited Martin Luther King to the 1957 Ghana independence celebration, one year after King had led the successful Montgomery bus boycott. Upon reflection, this is how King interpreted the historical event in Ghana:

> And if Nkrumah and the people of the Gold Coast had not stood up persistently, revolting against the system, it would still be a colony of the British Empire. Freedom is never given to anybody. For the oppressor has you in domination because he plans to keep you there, and he never voluntarily gives it up. And that is where the strong resistance comes. Privileged classes never give up their privileges without strong resistance. (Bolling 2017)

The following year, Nkrumah organized the All-African Peoples Conference. Whereas the Berlin conference was known as the "Scramble for Africa," this conference adopted the slogan "Hands Off Africa!" It was organized by a team from across the African Diaspora that included George Padmore, Bill Sutherland, and St.

Clair Drake.

Key participants included Sekou Toure (Guinea), Patrice Lumumba (Congo), Kenneth Kaunda (Zambia), Joshua Nkomo (Zimbabwe), and Frantz Fanon (Algeria) (Adi 2018, 144–45). As Nkrumah's biographer observed,

> this conference represented freedom fighter movements, nationalist parties, as well as trade unions, co-operative and youth movements from all over Africa. Some three hundred delegates attended. It was the first time that members of freedom movements from British, French, Portuguese, Spanish and the racist minority regimes had met together to discuss common problems and to formulate plans (Milne 2000, 86–87).

At this conference, Patrice Lumumba emerged as a formidable leader. He captured the significance of the 1958 conference, stating, as it concluded, that

> This historical conference, which puts us in contact with experienced political figures from all the African countries and from all over the world, reveals one thing to us: despite the boundaries that separate us, despite our ethnic differences, we have the same awareness, the same soul plunged day and night in anguish, the same anxious desire to make this African continent a free and happy continent that has rid itself of unrest and fear and of any sort of colonial domination (Lumumba, quoted in Adi 2018, 146).

Out of this conference, two kinds of struggle developed, one based on nonviolent mass protests and the other on armed struggle. The nonviolent protests initially proved extremely effective, as they led to seventeen countries' becoming independent in 1960, which the UN acknowledged by naming it the "African Year" (Hofmann 1960). But more needed to be done.

A key theorist who challenged the independent countries to realize a Pan-African revolution was Frantz Fanon (Fanon 1965; 1964; 1967). As leader of the Algerian delegation representing the National Liberation Front, he was firm in his support for armed struggle: "If Africa is awakening it must not make apologies or entreaties. We must wrest by force what belongs to us. No African must regard himself as demobilized from the struggle as long as any foreign nation dominates any part of Africa. All forms of struggle must be adopted, not excluding violence" (Fanon, quoted in Adi 2018, 145).

The conference delegates responded by passing a resolution supporting the armed struggle in Algeria.

Following the African Year 1960, it became clear that Fanon was on point, as armed struggle was adopted as the main method to rid Africa of the last vestiges of direct colonial rule. The final battles were beginning, organizations had been formed, and the whole world was drawn into the historic process of Africa's fighting to free itself. Table 1 lists the years in which armed struggle began in several countries:

Table 1. Armed struggles in selected countries

Date	Country
1961	South Africa
1961	Angola
1963	Guinea-Bissau
1964	Mozambique
1966	Zimbabwe
1966	Namibia

South Africa

South Africa was a classic case of settler colonialism, beginning with the Dutch settlers' invasion in 1652. They survived, but the African kingdoms of the Zulu, the Xhosa, and others remained free and independent for over two hundred years until defeated by British troops who had come to the aid of the Dutch, who had by then been transformed into South African Boers. The drive for this colonial domination intensified after the Boers discovered diamonds in 1867 and gold in 1886.

After the British military defeated the African kingdoms (1878–1900), they granted independence to the white settlers, British and Boer, creating the Union of South Africa. This was merely a new form of imperialist domination, as the South African

Communist Party noted in 1962:

> South Africa is not a colony but an independent state. Yet masses of our people enjoy neither independence nor freedom. The conceding of independence to South Africa by Britain in 1910 was not a victory over the forces of colonialism and imperialism. It was designed in the interests of imperialism. Power was transferred not into the hands of the masses of people of South Africa, but into the hands of the white minority alone. The evils of colonialism, in so far as the non-white majority was concerned, were perpetuated and reinforced. A new type of colonialism was developed, in which the oppressing White nation occupied the same territory as the oppressed people themselves and lived side by side with them. (The South African Communist Party, quoted in Callinicos and Rogers 1978, 11)

After the British, by establishing the Union of South Africa in 1910, ignored the demands of the African leadership for necessary reforms, a new stage of the struggle developed. The African National Congress (ANC), formed in 1912, was the first organization that united all the peoples of South Africa:

> "Every tribal group was represented: intellectuals and chiefs, workers and peasants. Zulus, Xhosas, Twanas, Sothos, Vendas, Shangaans, Tongas and other who had hitherto looked on each other with suspicion were for the first time united on a common platform" (African National Congress 1971, 4).

South African capitalist development took place in three stages. The first was the proletarianization of the peasantry into mine workers (African National Congress 1994, 4–5). The second was the taking of the land by means of the 1923 Land Act, which gave 87 percent of the country's land area to the white minority, followed by the transformation of the country's small-scale farms into large-scale operations to produce crops for export using landless farm workers (Callinicos and Rogers 1978, 25). The third stage was the development of an industrial base producing for the local market. Industrial production became more important than mining by the mid-sixties (Callinicos and Rogers 1978, 67).

In response to the intensification of capitalist development, the

Industrial and Commercial Workers Union was organized in 1919, followed by the South African Communist Party (SACP) in 1921 (Lerumo 1987, 52–53, 41–47). A major problem with the SACP was the continuation of the practice of limiting its membership to whites while ignoring the masses of Black people. This became a major issue during the Communist International's deliberation on the South African national question and led to criticisms of the SACP and practical intervention by the International Trade Union Committee of Negro Workers (Bunting 1986, 14–42; Adi 2013, 365–400). The 1928 Comintern resolution laid out a clear policy:

> South Africa is a black country, the majority of its population is black and so is the majority of the workers and peasants. The bulk of the South African population is the black peasantry, whose land has been expropriated by the white minority. Seven eighths of the land is owned by the whites. Hence the national question in South Africa, which based on the agrarian question, lies at the foundation of the revolution in South Africa. The black peasantry constitutes the basic moving force of the revolution in alliance with and under the leadership of the working class. (Lerumo 1987, 129)

The crisis of fascism and the onset of the inter-imperialist World War II led to many political changes in the world, including in South Africa. The ANC, led by Black elites, took a moderate approach to change. This resulted in a generational challenge with the formation of the ANC Youth League in 1944, key members of which included Nelson Mandela, Walter Sisulu, Olive Tambo, and Robert Sobukwe, who brought a more militant outlook to the freedom struggle. The youth began to move into the top leadership positions of the ANC: Sisulu became general secretary of the ANC and Mandela became general secretary of the Youth League. This wave of militancy saw the formation in 1943 of the Trotskyist Non-European Unity Movement, led by I. B. Tabata.

The Boers reacted by forming their Nationalist Party, which took power in 1948 and formally installed their policy of apartheid. The new African militancy made its move in a massive Defiance Campaign that began in 1952, during which mass rallies and protests, energized by protest freedom songs, defied the apartheid laws. The Nationalist Party then instituted draconian measures to control the physical movement of Black people, most notably extending the pass laws (requiring a document to be carried at all times) to apply to both men and women. Over 250,000 Black people a year were arrested for pass law violations.

The militant push for mass civil disobedience led to the building of a broad-based united front that included the ANC, the South African Indian Congress (SAIC), the South African Congress of Trade Unions (SACTU), the Coloured People's Congress (CPC), the South African Congress of Democrats (COD), the Federation of South African Women (FSAW), and the South African Communist Party (SACP). The political policy of this alliance, adopted in 1955, was termed the "Freedom Charter." This policy statement did not give priority to Black South Africa, but stated the following:

> We, the people of South Africa, declare for all our country and the world to know: that South Africa belongs to all who live in it, black and white and all shall have the right to occupy land wherever they choose. (Bragança and Wallerstein 1982, 81, 82)

By 1959, a militant wing of the ANC Youth League led by Sobukwe had broken away and formed the Pan Africanist Congress of Azania (PAC). The PAC was more oriented towards the Native Republic thesis of the Comintern than to the ANC-led Freedom Charter. The government used the 1950 Suppression of Communism Act to ban the organizations of the alliance, claiming that the Freedom Charter was a communist document. They had banned the SACP and went on to ban the PAC as well.

Anti-pass–campaign activities were suppressed, most extremely by the murder of sixty-nine protesters in the Sharpsville Massacre of 1960. This event triggered the adoption of armed struggle by both the ANC and the PAC. The ANC launched its armed wing, Umkhonto we Sizwe (Spear of the Nation), in December 1961, with Nelson Mandela as its commander in chief. The PAC's equivalent armed wing, called "Poqo" (Alone), was formed in February of 1960 by Robert Sobukwe. The first phase was a series of antigovernment bombing attacks inside South Africa, and the second phase was sending recruits out of the country to train in order to form a revolutionary army.

Before long, the government arrested Mandela and several other key leaders and convicted them in the infamous Ravonia Trial:

> On 30 October 1963 ten defendants appeared in the Pretoria Supreme Court charged on two counts of sabotage. The specific charges the accused faced were: (1) recruiting persons for training in the preparation and use of explosives and in guerrilla warfare for the purpose of violent revolution and committing acts of sabotage; (2) conspiring to commit the aforementioned acts and to aid foreign military units when they invaded the Republic; (3) acting in these ways to further the objects of communism; and (4) soliciting and receiving money for these purposes from sympathisers in Algeria, Ethiopia, Liberia, Nigeria, Tunisia, and elsewhere. (South African History Online n.d.)

They were sentenced to life imprisonment in Robbin Island Prison.

Following this, another major thrust of the freedom struggle emerged in the form of the Black Consciousness movement. As in the United States and elsewhere, young people in South Africa rejected the institutional racism of higher education, and of white liberals in general, and advanced a South African version of a Black Power movement. The first such organization, formed in 1968, was the South African Student Organization (SASO), of which the main leader was Bantu Steve Biko. This action was a continuation of the Comintern resolution and the formation of the PAC (Woods 1979; Adi 2018, 173–78; Biko 1979).

These political developments in South Africa informed activists in the United States, inspiring us to focus on African liberation. There were two main demands that gave focus to the global antiapartheid movement:

1. Free South Africa!
2. Free Nelson Mandela and all political prisoners!

Angola

Portugal reached its golden age when Vasco da Gama made voy-

16

ages to India in 1488 and to Brazil in 1500. It became a major power based on trade, and then Spain invaded Portugal and took over, ruling for sixty years. After Portugal gained its independence from Spain in 1668, gold was discovered in Brazil and that led to a new period of economic expansion. Back in 1455, Pope Nicholas V had granted the Portuguese the right to run the slave trade out of Africa. Initially, slaves were imported into Portugal due to a demand for labor there, but the demand for slaves in Brazil eventually became the basis for economic growth from the late seventeenth through the eighteenth century. After Napoleon invaded Portugal in 1807, the economy was ruined and Portugal became a poor country. The Portuguese colonial system got a boost from the Berlin Conference in 1884–1885 by gaining control of three colonies in Africa (Guinea-Bissau, Angola, and Mozambique). When Antonio Salazar rose to power in 1928, he set in motion a fascist dictatorship over Portugal's three colonies that would last into the 1960s.

The Portuguese were the first European country to benefit from the rape of Africa. In Angola they began by running an extensive slave trade. Centuries later, they set up a colonial state to exploit Angolan labor and natural resources. As everywhere in Africa, there has always been some kind of resistance (B. Davidson 1972; Chilcote 1972). One great example is Queen N'Zinga Mbande (1583–1663), who at first negotiated with the Portuguese and then fought them for thirty years (Heywood 2019). But the persistence of the Portuguese invasion and the great demand for slaves in the New World was irresistable.

> The slave trade was the most significant factor in the history of Angola until the twentieth century. The major items of Afro-Portuguese trade were slaves and ivory, supplied from deep in the interior by means of the highly organized and tightly controlled trade routes of powerful African states, such as Mbundu and Kongo. . . . For 300 years, until the final abolition of the slave trade in 1878, Angola was the "Black Mother" of the New World. . . . Angola became the major source of slaves for the Portuguese in Brazil, whose need of plantation labor led them to dominate the South Atlantic trade. (Herrick et al 1967, 32)

The colonial state was the tool used to exploit the Angolan people. A government committee in 1898 stated their evil policy clearly:

> The state, not only as a sovereign of semi-barbarous populations, but also as a depository of social authority, should have no scruples in *obliging* and if necessary *forcing* [the italics are the committee's] these rude Negroes in Africa . . . to work, that is, to better themselves by work, to acquire through work the happiest means of existence, to civilize themselves through work. (First 1972, 3)

The new system, despite cosmetic changes, maintained the previous structure of oppression:

> It became obvious that the Portuguese of 1929, in spite of the march of time, was still the slave dealer who depopulated Africa to satisfy the needs of the Americas. Now the system has changed and the people of Angola are slaves in their own country. (Chilcote 1972, 54–55)

The economy of Angola became mainly a plantation system of agricultural production for export to Portugal. It started with coffee in the 1930s, with Angola eventually becoming the fourth-largest producer in the world. In the 1950s oil was discovered, and by the 1970s oil had surpassed coffee in value. Oil propelled the Portuguese colony of Angola right into the heart of the global economy. In addition, industrial mining for diamonds had begun in 1912 and Angola later became one the world's biggest sources of industrial diamonds.

All along, the Angolan people were fighting back. After the Portuguese were successful in gaining European approval, at the Berlin conference, of their taking possession of the colonies mentioned above, they tried to take control of Angola by military force. An example is the war against the Dembos people. It took fifteen successive expeditions to suppress the people, which did not occur until 1919 (Chilcote 1972, 186). Following their initial hard approach of war, the Portuguese, led by their Premier António de Oliveira Salazar, took the soft approach in adopting a policy of allowing a few Black people to become assimilated into Portuguese culture. So, the struggle became a dialectical relationship between the African masses of rural peasants and the cities comingling workers and *assimilados*. The liberation fight followed these two bases of mass support.

The emerging Angolan intellectuals began to use culture as a revolutionary tool, starting a journal in 1948, *Mensagem* (Message):

> Under conditions in which all political activity was ferociously suppressed, poetry reflected and propelled the growing ferment of rebellion. It was intrinsic to that struggle. . . . The colonial authorities were soon to persecute and ban *Mensagem*, which had so forthrightly challenged the myths underpinning slavery. The poets had to go into clandestinity. (Neto 1974, xx–xxi)

There were no institutions of higher education in Angola, so aspiring middle-class elite *assimilados* had to make their way to Portugal. They had learned the language so they could navigate their way. A few of them landed in Lisbon, where:

> . . . this work continued . . . [as] a group of student and intellectuals . . . founded a Centre of African Studies in the early 1960's. The founders of the Centre were Agostino Neto, Francisco-Jose Tenreiro (a poet from Sao Tome who died in Portugal in 1963 under mysterious circumstances), Amilcar Cabral, and Mario de Andrade. The purpose of the Centre of African Studies, to quote Mario de Andrade, was "to rationalize the feelings of belonging to a world of oppression and to awaken national consciousness through an analysis of the continent's cultural foundations." (Neto 1974, xxiii)

These intellectuals also received clandestine education from the Portuguese Communist Party. This is so very much like our experience in the United States, with Black Studies and the radical Black tradition anchored in Marxism. The difference is that the fascist Portuguese closed the center after two years, while in the United States the institutionalization of Black Studies survived, being transformed along with a decline in the radical sector of the Black liberation movement.

Three main organizations developed in the Angolan National Liberation Struggle: the Popular Movement for the Liberation of Angola (MPLA) and the National Front for the Liberation of Angola (FNLA) in the 1950s and the Angolan Revolutionary

Government in Exile (GRAE) in the 1960s.

The MPLA was founded by the merger of several organizations and then joined by several others. These included the underground Angolan Communist Party, the Party for the United Struggle for Africans in Angola, the People's Movement for the Liberation of Angola, the Movement for the National Independence of Angola, and the Democratic Front for the Liberation of Angola.

Taking up the fight against Portuguese fascism had its consequences:

> In Angola, the MPLA spent its first five years on clandestine political agitation and organizing in the capital city of Luanda, sinking roots in the swelling, proletarian shantytowns ringing the city. In 1960 Neto, having returned to Angola to lead the liberation movement, was arrested by PIDE [the Portuguese secret political police], flogged publicly, and imprisoned. A thousand people of his home village of Bengo and the neighboring village of Icolo assembled peacefully at the district office of Catete to demand Neto's release. The Portuguese armed forces fired into the crowd, killing 30. The next day, the Portuguese soldiers arrived at Bengo and Icolo, killing and arresting everyone they could find there, and then setting both villages on fire. (Fogel 1982, 221)

The FNLA, originally called the United People of Northern Angola (UPNA), eventually merged with other groups in 1962 to become GRAE, all under the leadership of Holden Roberto. This was a movement based in the traditional area of the Angolan Kongo Kingdom, mainly active in rural parts of the country. Roberto attended the All-African Peoples' Conference in 1958 in Accra called by Nkrumah. He made contacts with key leaders like Fanon and Patrice Lumumba, but in the end he became involved with the U.S. Central Intelligence Agency (CIA):

> The CIA chose a man by the name of Holden Roberto, the brother-in-law of General James Mobutu of Zaire (formerly the Congo) as "a future leader of Angola." For seven years, from 1962 to 1969, the CIA supplied Roberto with money and arms but, according to the *New York Times* account, "to no avail." Roberto was "deactivated" and placed on "retainer." (Green 1976, 86)

Early on, Jonas Savimbi was a leader with Roberto of the GRAE, but he broke away to found the National Union for the Total Independence of Angola (UNITA) and become its president. UNITA operated on the eastern front with a base in Zambia. It received aid from the Organization of African Unity's liberation committee as did the MPLA, but in the end it allied itself with the CIA and opposed MPLA.

All of these forces were engaged in armed struggle by the early 1960s. Military training was supplied by many countries, based on the policy that if you were fighting on the ground in Angola, you deserved support. The goal was the unity of the liberation organizations; efforts were made to achieve this, but none was ever achieved.

Guinea-Bissau

The Portuguese used the Cape Verde Islands as a refueling station for the slave trade, whence they extended their settlement into Bissau on the Guinea mainland. There were no plantations, as in Angola, and no industrial development. In 1960, 60 percent of foreign trade was based on groundnuts, 70 percent of which were for export (Chaliand 1971, 6).

The policy of Portuguese colonialism was grossly hypocritical. Pointing to the fact that during the entire colonial period only fourteen Africans from Guinea-Bissau graduated from college, Cabral states:

> Portugal has pretended to assimilate the African people. This is a lie. In my country, during 500 years of the Portuguese coastal presence and more than 100 years of full colonial exploitation, they have assimilated, according to their own statistics, only 0.3% of the population. . . . But to become assimilated you have to have had four years at primary school. . . . In Portugal itself the situation is very bad. From official figures, 46% of the people there are illiterate, but I myself have worked in some regions of Portugal where 70% were illiterate. (Amilcar Cabral 1972, 5)

Cabral went to Portugal in 1945 at the age of twenty-one to study at the Agronomy Institute at the Technical University of Lisbon on a scholarship. A number of Africans from the colonies who were able to get to Lisbon began to meet and plan their future march to freedom, influenced by the recent Pan-African Congress in Manchester. Meanwhile:

> In Lisbon, . . . Cabral and his friends, such as Augustino Neto and Mario De Andrade, felt that it was time to set up an independent organization bringing together the citizens of 'Portuguese speaking' colonies, away from the control of the euro-centric Left. It is against this backdrop that Cabral and his friends began their political education with the aim of national liberation. Influenced by the emergence of 'Negro-African' literature, they were convinced that only a 'return to the roots' would enable the movement to be in total symbiosis with the deepest aspirations of the peoples of Africa. (Ameth LO, quoted in Manji and Fletcher 2013, 65)

After Cabral earned his degree, he went to work for the Ministries for Overseas Territories based in Lisbon, which assigned him to conduct an agricultural census of Guinea Bissau. He became intimately familiar with the people in his country, which enabled him to make an analysis of the social organization and class structure (Cabral 1969). He started by comparing the rural areas with the towns. In the rural areas were two different groups, the Foulas and the Ballantes; the former had a hierarchal feudal society that worked with the colonial state, whereas the latter were communal with councils of elders as the leadership. The Foulas was the hardest group to win over to the struggle.

Cabral identified three main classes in the towns: (1) the petty bourgeoisie, who could be divided into three tendencies, those tied to colonialism, nationalists, and the vacillators; (2) the wage earners; and (3) the marginalized, called the declassed. The key wage earners were the dock workers, and:

> . . . another important group were the people working in the boats carrying merchandise, who mostly live in Bissau itself and travel up and down the rivers. Those people proved highly conscious of their position and of their economic importance and they took the initiative to launch strikes without any trade union leadership at all. We therefore decided to concentrate all our work on this group. (Amílcar Cabral 1969, 438)

But in general, the organizing of the movement was a protracted process. The first step was designing an education process for the development of cadres, trained organizers who could immerse themselves in mass work and gradually win people over.

> Cabral made many political contacts with both Cape Verdeans and Guinea-Bissauns. Many initially outright rejected his ideas on decolonization, but after he discursively provided examples, often with empirical and irrefutable evidence (e.g., disenfranchisement, deprivation, starvation, lack of education, and violent government repression), usually over a prolonged period of time (i.e., usually several weeks or months), they were persuaded to seriously contemplate radical political alternatives as solutions to the problem(s) of Portuguese colonialism. . . . To this end, in 1954 he formed a sports, recreational, and cultural club for local youngsters, with the aim of using it as a front to promote nationalism, political education, and anticolonial consciousness-raising. (Reiland Rebaka, quoted in Manji and Fletcher 2013, 116–17)

The colonial authorities were aware that while Cabral could be used by them, he had had to be watched since his student days in Lisbon. Under their noses, however, he had been building a vast network of contacts and strengthening his social capital with them, as he had been consistent in his vision for the future of the country based on a commitment to the well-being of the people. The time for action soon came. He made the organizational move:

> Our party was formed in 1956 by six Africans from Guinea and the Cape Verdes. We set up an underground party in Bissau, and extended it to other urban centres. We believed at that time that it was possible to fight by peaceful means. With the help of an underground trade union organization we launched some strikes against the Portuguese and we held some demonstrations, but the Portuguese always answered us with guns. On 3rd August 1959, during a workers' strike in Bissau, they killed 50 African workers and wounded more than 100 in 20 minutes. That finally taught us a lesson: in the face of Portuguese colonialism, and, we think, imperialism in general, there is no question of whether you use armed struggle or not. The struggle is always armed because the

colonialists and imperialists have already decided to use their arms against you. We decided, at an underground meeting in Bissau in September 1959, to stop our demonstrations, to retain our underground organization but to move it to the countryside to mobilize the people, and prepare ourselves for armed struggle. (Cabral 1972, 6)

They formed the African Party for the Independence of Guinea and Cape Verde (PAIGC), which after 1959 focused on cadre development of militants prepared for both armed combat and for being political representatives of the party, and as such focused on organizing and mobilizing the masses of people. They were not merely training soldiers, they were training freedom fighters.

Portugal had such a poor economy that the country was not able to fight the war by itself. The Portuguese had to become the agents of global imperialism, receiving military support from NATO. They stationed their troops in the towns and on the borders, thinking that PAIGC would be invading.

They were wrong. PAIGC did not take that approach, but started the armed struggle in the center of the country and worked out into the towns and the countryside. By 1965, PAIGC had liberated half of the country and was forming the foundation of a new nation, which included organizing the people for health care, education, security, and increased food production, especially without with the war of liberation underway.

> The years 1970 and 1971 introduced the Guinean people to the use of Napalm and herbicides by desperate Portuguese troops. In the spring of 1971, the enemy began to launch fragmentation bombs which destroy houses, foliage, trees, and everything within thousands of feet from the center of explosion. Villages, bridges, schools, camps, hospitals, all are wiped out, but only until they can be rebuilt or moved to another place within the country. Nothing is a permanent setback; always you can hear the call "No Pintcha!"—"Forward"—it is the only way to go. (Chicago Committee for the Liberation of Angola, Mozambique, and Guinea 1974, 11)

Guinea-Bissau grabbed the attention of the world because it was building a new nation while it continued fighting. Its success made the PAIGC leader Cabral a leading voice among world revolutionary leaders.

24

Mozambique

As with the other African nations discussed above, the Berlin conference was the springboard for Portuguese colonialism in Mozambique. Eduardo Mondlane sets the historical time frame:

> After the partition of Africa at the Berlin Conference of 1884–85, Portugal was impelled to capture and control what had been assigned to her. . . . At the beginning of the twentieth century, the Portuguese began to set up their system of administration, although it was not until the early 1920s that armed resistance from the African population [of Mozambique] was finally crushed in all areas of the country . . . [and] the main characteristics of Portuguese colonialism were established: a centralized net of authoritarian administration; the alliance with the Catholic Church; the use of companies, frequently foreign, to exploit natural resources; the concession system; forced labour, and the extensive export of workers to South Africa. (Mondlane 1969, 26–27, 33–34)

The Third Pan-African Congress, organized by Du Bois and Padmore, was held in 1923 in two sessions, one in London and the other in Lisbon. Delegates at the congress represented eleven African countries, including the Portuguese colonies. The main local host was Liga Africana, an umbrella group representing organizations throughout the Portuguese colonies. Du Bois said at the time that Liga Africana "knows how to express to the government in no ambiguous terms but in a highly dignified manner all that should be said to avoid injustice or to bring about the repeal of harsh laws" (Adi, Sherwood, and Padmore 1995, 70).

Nothing about Portuguese colonialism was dignified. They set up an economy with six types of labor: prison, forced, contract, voluntary, forced cultivation, and export. The first two were forms of slavery, the next two were forms of capitalist wage work, and the last two forced farm work and then export of labor to South Africa. This was used to ramp up cotton production:

> By the middle 1950s, the number of Africans engaged in the cultivation of cotton had risen to half a million, and production in Mozambique alone had reached 140,000 tons.

> The Portuguese textile industry, which employs a third of Portugal's industrial labour force and accounts for a fifth of the value of total exports, took 82 per cent of its raw materials from the colonies. (Mondlane 1969, 83)

Mozambique was tied to South Africa, as demonstrated by the building of the Cabora Bassa Dam in the Zambezi Valley in 1968. At the time this was the largest dam in Africa; its stated purpose was to provide electricity to South African farms, factories, and cities. In fact, it took farmland away from the local people and did not supply them with any electricity!

The people were not happy under colonialism and took action to get free from it:

By the late 1940's three groups of Africans were struggling against Portuguese colonialism through secret political organizing and actions.

> The first of these groups was the intellectuals (especially those few who had been to Portugal), who had come to regard the Portuguese nation of "national unity" between Portugal and the colonies as hypocritical. Their political consciousness took the form of cultural expression, since overt political organization was illegal. Through poetry and prose they played on three main themes: 1) reaffirmation of Africa as their mother country and cultural heritage; 2) the call to revolt of black people all over the world; 3) the sufferings of ordinary black people throughout the world.

The second group was composed of secondary school students who formed an organization called NESAM; they worked to build a sense of pride in their African heritage and Mozambican nationhood. NESAM was banned in 1964 but from it have come many of the nationalist leaders who are today fighting the Portuguese.

Workers from the towns and plantations formed the third of these groups. In 1947 and 1948 they conducted a series of strikes on Mozambican docks and plantations. Several hundred people were deported to a small island off the coast of West Africa in retaliation. In 1956 Portuguese police killed 49 striking African Dock workers. (Bengelsdorf and Roberts 1971, 3)

The terms of the struggle were set by the brutality of the Portuguese. At a major peaceful demonstration in Mueda in 1960 at which several thousand people gathered to protest, the Portuguese armed forces shot down and killed five hundred people in cold blood. This was the turning point: people who had believed in nonviolence now vowed to never again be without arms to defend themselves (Mondlane 1969, 117).

From that point on, political organizations started to form, especially in neighboring countries out of reach of PIDE, the Portuguese secret police. The first, the Mozambique National Democratic Union (UDENAMO) in 1960, was based in Rhodesia. The next year the Mozambican African National Union (MANU) was established in Kenya and the African Union of Independent Mozambique (UNAMI) in Malawi. After Tanganyika gained its independence in late 1961, all three movement organizations relocated their headquarters to Dar es Salaam, where in 1962 they merged into one organization, the Front for the Liberation of Mozambique (FRELIMO) (Herrick et al. 1969, 165; Mondlane 1969, 119).

The first president of FRELIMO was Eduardo Mondlane. After starting his education in Mozambique, South Africa, and Portugal, he finished his undergraduate degree at Oberlin College in 1953 and his doctorate at Northwestern University in 1960. After working for the United Nations and teaching at Syracuse University, Mondlane returned to Mozambique to join the freedom movement. Mondlane's close comrade, Samora Machel, became head of the FRELIMO army. Together they held the top leadership positions until Mozambique's independence in 1975.

FRELIMO was based on the development of cadres, militants trained to provide leadership:

> Cadres are decisive to the implementation of our political line, our ideology. . . . Intensifying our work among the cadre means, in fact, creating the conditions for stepping up ideological work among the masses, to further unite the masses and make the war advance even more. Our task is to raise the cadres' level of political consciousness and knowledge, uniting them even more with the masses and the fighters. This can only be achieved through the method of always combining the practice of combat and production with study, ensuring regular discussion, criticism and self-

criticism, not allowing them to fall into a routine, ensuring study with practice. (Machel 1975, 14)

Zimbabwe

The precolonial history of Zimbabwe features a series of kingdoms. Great Zimbabwe was a major city-state:

> The settlement on the hill was surrounded by a high wall made of granite blocks. This stone wall was built in about AD 1200. . . . For over 200 years, Great Zimbabwe was probably the largest city anywhere in Africa, outside Egypt. It was the capital of a well-organized, wealthy, powerful and long-lived state. (Garlake and Proctor 2010, 82)

> Great Zimbabwe had an economy based on the mining of gold and copper and the trading of ivory far and wide, including with China. ("Great Zimbabwe" 2020)

The European invasion began establishing settlements in Zimbabwe at the end of the nineteenth century, when Cecil Rhodes moved from South Africa seeking to increase his mining fortune. He negotiated mining rights from the Ndebele in 1888. Following this, and British military actions, his company, the British South African Company, gained control of the country and ruled it from 1890 to 1923; the country was named Rhodesia in 1895. The First Chimurenga (a Shona word meaning "revolutionary struggle") was carried out in 1896–1897 by the Ndebele and Shona, but ended in defeat.

In 1922, by an agreement with the British government, Zimbabwe became a self-governing British colony, although Britain retained the right to veto any policy it deemed not in its interest. The settler colony took permanent shape in 1930 with the Land Apportionment Act. This set aside 87 percent of the country's area for white settlers and deprived large sectors of the African population of their land, forcing them to seek employment with the white settlers on farms and in the mines. This demonstration that colonialism was theft astonished the people. Joshua Nkomo argued that, from the perspective of the Zimbabwean people:

> . . . the land belongs to the people. The farmers and the

cattle ranchers can use the land they need, but nobody can expropriate the land that has traditionally belonged to everybody. When I was a boy, signs saying 'Trespassers will be prosecuted' sprang up all over Rhodesia. I suddenly became a trespasser on the land where I was born and where my family had lived for years. There is something wrong with a system like that. The product of your labor, your house and your crops, are rightfully yours. But the land itself belongs to the people. (Joshua Nkomo, quoted in Scott 1979, 7)

The people began to organize against this colonial madness. Trade union organizing that had begun in South Africa in 1919 took hold in Rhodesia when the same union established a branch called the Rhodesian Industrial and Commercial Workers Union (RICWU) in 1927:

RICWU was the first organization which tried to get African workers to forget their tribal and religious differences, and to unite as a working class to challenge the capitalists. It also helped to unite workers in the towns with the peasants. (Garlake and Proctor 1992, 110)

The Europeans discovered copper in the early 1900s and began to coopt and proletarianize Africans as labor for the mining industry in what eventually became a dominant transformative process for these workers (Powdermaker 1965, 87–104). This common experience ended up being the basis for a profound sense of national unity, because all the major ethnic groups in the country were involved.

In 1934 a national organization, again modeled on one in South Africa, took shape: the Rhodesian African National Congress (RANC). This was a moderate group of Black elites who believed that they could negotiate change. Twenty-one years later, frustrated by the lack of improvement in the country, a more militant group was formed, called the City Youth League, that within two years had taken over the leadership in the RANC. In the wake of mass arrests, the National Democratic Party (NDP), which brought together leaders of several groups, including both Joshua Nkomo and Robert Mugabe, was founded.

The government had put in place legal measures to suppress any resistance. The Unlawful Organizations Act (1958) was used to ban organizations for fomenting disaffection, ill will, or hostility. The Law and Order Act (1960) imposed strict limitations on all forms of political activity. The Emergency Powers Act (1965) allowed the government to arrest and hold people for indefinite periods of time; in addition, capital punishment was sanctioned (Amnesty International 1976).

After NDP was banned, the militants formed the Zimbabwe African People's Union (ZAPU) in 1961, electing Nkomo as president. ZAPU was banned the next year. After a disagreement in the leadership, Nkomo suspended four people from the executive. These four then left and formed the Zimbabwe African National Union (ZANU) in 1963, led by Robert Mugabe. In 1964 ZANU was banned (Garlake and Proctor 1992, 135–36).

The white minority government of Rhodesia, led by Ian Smith, decided to break with the United Kingdom and promulgated a Unilateral Declaration of Independence (UDI) in 1965. This granted total control of the country to the white people, who were 5 percent of the total population. The United Kingdom did not object, as it continued to rake in profits from its neo-colony. But for Africans this represented a further fascist clampdown that rejected the legitimate African leadership and formed councils of bribed tribal elders to falsely represent the African population.

This led to the Second Chimurenga, which began several months after the UDI:

> On 28 April 1966, the first real battle of the liberation war took place outside Chinhoyi. Seven young guerillas from ZANU fought a large number of Rhodesian soldiers who were armed with heavy weapons and helicopters. The guerillas were all killed. Other ZANU guerillas who entered Zimbabwe with them were captured.

> In July 1967, a joint force of guerillas from ZAPU and ANC of South Africa crossed the Zambezi River and entered Zimbabwe. They moved into Hwange National Park. They fought a number of battles there with the Rhodesian army over the next two months. Eventually this group, and others who entered the country at the same time, were defeated by the superior numbers and weapons of the Rhodesian army. (Garlake and Proctor 1992, 137)

Both ZANU and ZAPU learned from these forays that small gue-
rilla forces would not win unless they had the active participation
of the masses of people. A successful national liberation struggle
requires a people's war. This lesson helped them to redefine the
struggle and become victorious.

Namibia

With the local peoples being successful in keeping the early Portuguese explorers from settling in Namibia, the Berlin Conference
of 1884–1885 granted the territory to Imperial Germany, thereby
creating German South West Africa. The peoples of Namibia then
faced a genocidal war of conquest:

> By 1907, fewer than 20,000 of the original 80,000 Hereros
> survived, and more than half of the Nama and Damara
> were also dead. Altogether, the German war machine had
> exterminated some 60% of the population of Central and
> Southern Namibia. Many more were to suffer the same fate
> in the German concentration camps and labour gangs as the
> colonial government imposed a savage forced labour system
> on the survivors. (South-West Africa People's Organisation
> of Namibia 1987, 13–14)

The kind of demonic action Germany started in Africa was repeat-
ed under Hitler's fascism in Europe. Medical experiments were
conducted on Africans, alive and dead. In fact, as part of this, 300
African skulls were sent to Germany for examination ("Herero
and Namaqua Genocide" 2020).

Germany occupied South West Africa for thirty-five years,
until the former's defeat in World War I and the Treaty of Versailles
in 1919 resulted in the loss of its colonies, with the control of
South West Africa being transferred to South Africa.

South African colonial capitalist ventures in South West
Africa were concentrated in agriculture, fishing, and mining. As
capitalism developed in South Africa, development went forward
in South West Africa, but never without investment (mainly) from
the United Kingdom and the United States:

> The growth of capitalist production in the 60 years of South
> African occupation falls into three broad stages. During the

inter-war period, between 1915 and 1945, there was only limited investment and output as all sectors stagnated and suffered periodic catastrophic collapses. After the Second World War, both investment and output expanded at a high rate, with only short-lived minor interruptions. But, in the mid-1970s, the advances of the liberation struggle throughout Southern Africa, and above all in Namibia itself, combined with the effects of the world recession in the industrial West, halted growth and dried up most new investment. (South-West Africa People's Organisation of Namibia 1987, 23–24)

Another aspect of the impact of imperialist investment is that as much as 36 percent of the Namibian GDP had been sent abroad by the 1970s, as reported by the United Nations (South-West Africa People's Organisation of Namibia 1987, 43). Similar to the war-time effect on the country's economy,

The Second World War marked a turning point in the Namibian people's struggle for freedom. . . . The late 1940s and the 1950s were the formative phase in the building of the modern national liberation movement in Namibia. Opposition to colonialism emerged in four main fields of active resistance: within the traditional leadership, in the churches, amongst educated people and intellectuals and workers in the main urban and mining centres. During this period (1946–1960), the strategy of struggle was transformed from weak and localized attempts at self-defense against the excesses of colonial oppression to a widespread commitment to national liberation by revolutionary armed struggle. (South-West Africa People's Organisation of Namibia 1987, 166–167)

Organizational development started in 1957, when the Ovamboland People's Congress was formed, which was later renamed the Ovamboland People's Organization (OPO). This was followed by the South West African National Union (SWANU) in 1959. These formed a united front with traditional leaders and began to launch action. They led a protest in Windhoek, the capital city, in opposition to a large-scale resettlement scheme. On December 12, 1960 the police opened fire on the protesters, killing thirteen and wounding over fifty. This was the Namibian counterpart to the Sharpsville massacre in South Africa.

The united front broke down in the face of this heightened repression, and the OPO reorganized itself as the South West African People's Organization (SWAPO), electing Sam Nujoma president in 1960. Two years later, the SWAPO central committee decided to prepare for armed struggle. They sent militants to friendly countries for military training; these militants began returning in 1964 to set up an underground organization and train more recruits. The armed struggle formally began in 1966.

What we have done so far in this chapter is describe the development of the national liberation struggles up to the time of the first ALD in the United States and the founding of ALSC. It is important to point out that there are patterns of similarity in these struggles. They have moved in certain "typical" phases, though at different times and with their own national characteristics:

1. From tribal initiatives to struggle based on national unity
2. From a class focus on peasants to one based on urban workers
3. From nonviolent protest to armed struggle
4. From public activities to underground and secret forms of organization
5. From local support to global support
6. Development of cadres as a basis for all organizational progress

Pan-Africanism

The main focus of this section is to clarify the basis for the connection between the African American freedom struggle and the struggles for national liberation in Africa, especially the six cases of armed struggle just discussed that led to the ALD mobilization of 1972. The historical narrative involves stories of organizational development and the unique contributions of key individuals. This is the dialectical reality of the role of charisma in the context of the social forces making history.

The existence of African American people is the result of transplanting Africans into the Americas. They were taken out of Africa, but Africa was never taken out of them. This process involved people who brought a diversity of languages, religions, and forms of social organization from different parts of Africa. Even as people changed under the different conditions of oppression by one or another European settler colonial community, three common experiences cut across every situation: racist class exploitation of the African descendants; memory of Africa connected with self-defined identity; and the desire for freedom for African people the world over (Magubane 1989; Blyden 2019).

The continuity of African cultural retention has been documented in language and in material culture such as quilts, food, aesthetics, religion, music (especially the drum), and dance. The power of American racism forced assimilation of African peoples into the European Diaspora, a process facilitating upward social mobility. There was (and is) a material benefit to becoming assimilated into mainstream Euro-American culture. Delinking from Africa was associated more with middle-class status than with the masses of Black people, more with integration than the Black masses being forced into a segregated existence. The masses of poor and working-class Black people do share an African heritage, but over generations don't always think about their identity in those terms (Thompson 1984; 2011; Holloway and Vass 1993; Holloway 2005; Bower 2007).

Two Tendencies

The twentieth-century narrative of Pan-Africanism in the United States involves the organizational tendencies associated, respectively, with Marcus Mosiah Garvey (1887–1940) and W. E. B. Du Bois (1868–1963). Both tendencies were focused on the relationship between Africa and the African Diaspora, and both advocated the liberation of Africa. But there were major differences. This is often discussed as the difference between a mass-based bottom-up process versus a more elite middle-class top-down one. These tendencies were often in open public conflict, and yet many important organizations and individual leaders have been influenced by both. This demonstrates the dialectical principle of the unity of opposites (Shirokov and Leningrad Institute of Philosophy 1978, 133–44).

Chapter 1

Garvey brought his nationalist orientation from his home country, Jamaica. He founded the Universal Negro Improvement Association and African Communities League (UNIA) in 1914. The main slogan was "Africa for the Africans," based on his understanding of African identity as uniting all people in Africa as well as the people of African descent spread throughout the world who constituted the African Diaspora. The UNIA set up chapters everywhere there was a substantial Black population, especially Africa, the Caribbean, Canada, and the United States. Tony Martin (1986, 15-16) reports that at its height the UNIA had 725 branches in the United States, and 271 outside of the United States in 41 different countries.

The message of the UNIA was promoted through their newspaper, *The Negro World.* Black people working on the railroad and on ships carried this publication to the ends of the earth, making the UNIA message known at the grassroots level. This helped lay the basis for African nationalism from South Africa to Cuba.

Du Bois, a Harvard University PhD with European academic credentials, was also active at the international level promoting Pan-African unity. He began in 1900, when he joined Trinidadian attorney Sylvester Williams in the first Pan-African Congress, and would go on to play a leading role in five more: 1919 in Paris (First Pan-African Congress), 1921 in London (Second Pan-African Congress), 1923 in London and Lisbon (Third Pan-African Congress), 1927 in New York City (Fourth Pan-African Congress), and 1945 in Manchester (Fifth Pan-African Congress). Many of the African students in Europe and the United States who attended these congresses went on to be leaders of independence movements in their respective countries.

In the United States, Du Bois was active in the Council on African Affairs, organized in 1937, along with Paul Robeson, Max Yergan, Alphaeus Hunton, Ralph Bunche, Rayford Logan, and E. Franklin Frazier, among other key activists and institutional leaders:

> The Council on African Affairs articulated and promoted a fundamental connection between the struggle of African

Americans and the destiny of colonized peoples in Africa, Asia, and elsewhere in the world. Among a host of other campaigns, it lobbied the federal government and the United Nations and lent material support on behalf of Indian independence, striking trade unionists in Nigeria, and African famine relief. It publicized the connections between these campaigns and its larger critique of colonialism and capitalism via its monthly bulletin *New Africa*. The CAA's most significant work took place in relation to South Africa. It supported striking black miners and helped direct worldwide attention to the African National Congress's struggle against the Union of South Africa government and its policy of imposing racial apartheid. ("Council on African Affairs" 2020)

The members of the council published pamphlets, organized petition drives, held mass rallies, and maintained a library in their offices, open to the public, where they prepared bibliographies for study groups. The council was the major Black organization supporting the liberation of colonized African countries for two decades (Du Bois 1952, 15–19; Hill and Kilson 1969, 215–219; Alphaeus Hunton, quoted in P. Robeson 1999, 126–128).

During this same time, the Trinidad Three—C.L.R. James (1901–1989), George Padmore (1903–1959), and Claudia Jones (1915–1964) had a global impact, in addition to their impact in the United States. They linked the communist movement with various aspects of the freedom struggle throughout the African Diaspora and mentored activists in the generations following their lead (Padmore 1972; James 2012; Davies 2008).

The Garvey tendency generated multiple voices for a connection with Africa. One of the main activists was Carlos Cooks. Born in the Dominican Republic, he was a leading activist in Harlem, founding the African Nationalist Pioneer Movement in 1941. He defined it as being "an educational, inspirational, instructive, constructive, and expansive society. It is composed of people desirous of bringing about a progressive, dignified, cultural, fraternal and racial confraternity amongst the African peoples of the world" (Harris et al 1992, xiii).

Cooks created the Code Afric for members of his movement:

Chapter 1

"As a member of the African Nationalist Pioneer Movement, I will devoutly live my life in such a manner that the best interest of my race will be served. I further pledge that I shall do everything in my power to bring about the liberation of Africa from the tentacles of European colonialism. . . . When Africa strikes physically for freedom I shall volunteer as a soldier fighting my people's battle." (Harris et al 1992, 7)

Also impacted by Caribbean radicalism, this time through his mother from Grenada, was a major charismatic figure of 1960s Pan-Africanism: Malcolm X (1925–1965) (Carew 1995). Malcolm X electrified militant activists and was the main progenitor of the ideological and political paradigm shift in the Black Power movement. He networked with Africans at the United Nations and then went to Africa and met with African leaders in several countries (Sales 1994; X, Boyd, and Shabazz 2013).

Malcolm X compared the situation facing Africans and African Americans in plain language:

You can't understand what is going on in Mississippi if you don't understand what is going on in the Congo. And you can't really be interested in what's going on in Mississippi if you're not also interested in what's going on in the Congo. They're both the same. The same interests are at stake. The same sides are drawn up, the same schemes are at work in the Congo that are at work in Mississippi. The same stakes—no difference whatsoever. (Breitman 1965, 133)

Malcom X represented the organic expressions of Black nationalism and Pan-Africanism that had germinated in Harlem, the emerging political and cultural center of the African Diaspora. He embraced the main thrust of both Garvey and Du Bois, which represented the politics of Harlem and most cities. The Nation of Islam was reoriented toward Africa by Malcolm X following Garvey and Carlos Cooks, in contradiction of the Asiatic perspective of Elijah Muhammad (Essien-Udom 1962, 321). This shift in ideological orientation reflected a generational difference between those who had formulated their thinking before the African independence movements and those who embraced their African origin and were optimistic about the future of Africa (Sales 1994, 53–94).

New York City has long been a major center of Pan-Africanism, in thought and action. Since the United Nations is in New York, activists have made it the target of protest to advance Pan-African goals. One powerful example is when Abbey Lincoln and Max Roach were involved in a protest over the murder of Patrice Lumumba that implicated the UN:

> Lincoln, along with Rosa Guy, Maya Angelou and other women who had formed a group called The Cultural Association of Women of African Heritage, organized a demonstration at the United Nations on February 15, 1961, protesting the assassination of Patrice Lumumba. . . . Roach and others joined the demonstration, at which about 60 men and women burst into the Security Council Chamber shouting, "Murderers! Assassins!" Many credit this action with being the opening salvo of the Black Power movement. (Crothers 2010).

This action reflected the militant activism of the late 1960s.

Two important journals were founded in New York, *Freedomways* and the *Liberator*. *Freedomways* was Marxist in orientation, and the *Liberator* was more nationalist, but there were people, such as John Henrik Clarke, who contributed to both. At the mass level there was active discourse on Harlem street corners. Political culture was articulated by community-based intellectual activists, a.k.a. Harlem street speakers (Smith, Sinclair, and Ahmed 1995, 38–42).

The Student Nonviolent Coordinating Committee: From Black Power to Pan-Africanism

The generation that had been thrust into the educational mainstream by the 1954–1955 Supreme Court Brown decisions to integrate U.S. schools emerged in 1959–1960 to reignite mass protest through the sit-in movement to integrate public accommodations. SNCC emerged as the vanguard organization of the civil rights movement, using high school and college students to push the militancy of the protests into mass confrontations that got national attention.

James Forman (1928–2005) was the first executive secretary of SNCC. He moved from Chicago, his birthplace, down to Mississippi and then back again to Chicago. He studied at Roosevelt University under St. Clair Drake, where he gained his intellectual foundation in the study of Africa, before moving on to graduate school at Boston University (Forman 1972, 83–84, 101–102, 483). Forman then got involved with the people's sharecropping struggle in Fayette County, Tennessee (Forman 1972, 116–145).

Forman ended up in Atlanta, becoming the executive secretary of SNCC (1961–1966). SNCC leadership had a key encounter with an African revolutionary in 1963, when Forman arranged a meeting with the Kenyan Minister for Home Affairs, Jaramogi Oginga Odinga, who was passing through Atlanta. A small group met with him and he explained his country's history of armed struggle and his hope for a continuing relationship with the Black movement in the United States. Following the meeting, the group was refused service at a restaurant in downtown Atlanta, arrested, and sent to jail. In that setting, Matthew Jones of the SNCC Freedom Singers penned an important song that told the story:

> We went down to the Peachtree Manor
> To see Oginga Odinga
> The police say, "What's the matter?"
> To see Oginga Odinga
> The police he looked mighty hard
> At Oginga Odinga
> He got scared 'cause he was an ex Mau-Mau
> To see Oginga Odinga.
>
> ("SNCC Workers Meet Oginga Odinga" n.d.; Oginga Odinga 1967)

The very next year, in 1964, SNCC activists went to Africa: "Guinean President Sekou Toure had asked Harry Belafonte to invite a group from SNCC to discuss organizing techniques with Guinean youth" (Visser-Maessen 2021, 264, 266); Ruby Doris Smith contemplated establishing worldwide Friends of SNCC groups, while

James Forman dreamed of creating an African Bureau. Forman eventually achieved his goal three years later:

> I myself became director of the newly created International Affairs Commission, based in New York, a position that I held until the summer of 1969. . . . For all the people and nations with whom we would want to have international associations were against racism, capitalism, and imperialism. In addition, they were striving in the main to build socialist societies. I was never able to get SNCC to declare itself for socialism, but I did not worry about that too much at the time. To have achieved a realization that our fight was against racism, capitalism, and imperialism represented a major victory in itself. (Forman 1972, 481)

By 1969, two important leaders of SNCC had actually moved to Africa: Robert Moses to Tanzania and Stokely Carmichael to Guinea. Moses settled down and taught school, plunging deep into serving the people through education (Visser-Maessen 2021, 294–296).

Carmichael became a charismatic icon of Pan-Africanism, touring global revolutionary centers from Algeria to Cuba and being feted by heads of state and national liberation movements. SNCC had propelled him, as did his leadership role with the Black Panthers. His magnetic personality won media approval. He attached himself to Sekou Ture and Kwame Nkrumah (then living as a guest of Sekou Ture in Guinea after being ousted by a coup in Ghana). To honor them, Carmichael changed his name to Kwame Ture (Joseph 2016, 213–30, 217–21, 277–279).

His relationship with Nkrumah was problematic, as Nkrumah felt he stressed race over imperialism. However, that didn't stop Kwame Ture from taking up the Nkrumah proposal for a new political party, the All African People's Revolutionary Party (Milne 2000, 228–29; Nkrumah 1973, 486–87).

Another Pan-African project that SNCC veterans developed was a trio of organizations based in Washington, DC: the Center for Black Education, Drum and Spear Bookstore, and Drum and Spear Press. Those involved included Jimmy Garrett, Courtland Cox, Charlie Cobb, Jean Wiley, Ralph Featherstone, and Jennifer Lawson, among others (Rickford 2016, 199–203; Davis 2018).

In addition, they published a newsletter, *The Pan African*, about which they wrote:

> The major task of this newsletter lies in developing and expanding the consciousness of our people —particularly those residing in Washington, DC. Thus all features in this paper will reflect three major themes: (a) We are an African people—we have always been—and our future will be that of an African people; (b) We are at war with the Europeans—we have been since the 15th century; (c) Our struggle is one for an independent African nation. (Center for Black Education 1969)

Their publishing efforts made a major contribution to Pan-African thought by reprinting the seminal book by C. L. R. James, *A History of Pan-African Revolt*. Two of their leading members, Charlie Cobb and Jennifer Lawson, were sent to open an office of their Drum and Spear Press in Dar es Salaam, Tanzania. They targeted youth and began publishing in English and Kiswahili (Markle 2008). In 1972, heading into the first African Liberation Day, they published *African Liberation: An Analytical Report on Southern Africa* (Center for Black Education 1972).

Student Organization for Black Unity

At this same time, a new stage of the Black student movement emerged in North Carolina out of the Historically Black Colleges and Universities (HBCUs), namely, the Student Organization for Black Unity (SOBU), which was founded on May 9, 1969. SOBU developed in close collaboration with the Center for Black Education and SNCC veterans, especially Cleve Sellers. Its ideological underpinnings reflected a Black nationalist orientation that evolved into Pan-African socialism. As such, it developed cross-movement linkages with other Pan-African and Black nationalist student and youth formations in Africa and the Black Diaspora, among them the Pan African Students Organization in the Americas, the Student Movement for African Unity in Ghana, the Student Movement for the Liberation of Southern Africa, the Pan African Students Association, and the African Students Association. These linkages underscored the importance of Black transnationalism to SOBU's development and how much its international outlook was shaped by interaction with African and Caribbean independence movements.

The institutional base for the students who took the lead in the formation of SOBU was North Carolina A & T University, located in Greensboro. Nelson Johnson, vice-president of student government at A & T, was elected the first president of SOBU. This reflected the orientation of SOBU's tactical decision making to recruiting campus leaders as a step toward impacting the broad mass of Black students. Johnson, a U.S. Air Force veteran, brought experience and a level of maturity that anchored SOBU and guided it into sustainability, just like Forman had done for SNCC.

The initial leadership collective of SOBU included Mark Smith (a former student at Harvard University who helped lead the fight for Black Studies there); Tim Thomas (also a military veteran; he later became a student leader at George Washington University), Joyce Johnson (a student leader from Duke University); Ron Washington (a student leader and basketball star from Wichita State University and the University of Kansas); Claude Barnes (president of the Dudley High School Student Council); John McClendon (former student body president of Central State University); Milton Coleman (a journalist on the campus of University of Wisconsin-Milwaukeeand with the Black press); and Victor Bond (also formerly a student at Harvard University).

SOBU gained national visibility because of its newspaper, the *SOBU Newsletter*. It reported on Black students around the country and the politics of liberation in Africa and the African Diaspora.

SOBU had several programs: the SOBU Pan-African Work Program, the Pan-African Medical Program, the SOBU Development Press, and the SOBU Book Club.

In the Spring of 1971 in Frogmore, S.C., SOBU fashioned out of a national SOBU convention a new regional structure and outlined a program of work. Twelve months later in the spring of 1972, 80 dedicated young Black people from the twenty-seven states met in Epps, Alabama. These 80 people have along with many others been working within the SOBU

structure and on the program outlines in 1971. (SOBU News
Service 1972, 11)

As a leadership organization, they based their organizational recruitment plan upon the building of dedicated cadres:

> When we speak of ideology and protracted struggle, it should
> be clear to us that a particular issue, such as hunger, is not
> an ideal one on which to base a cadre. Reason being that the
> longer the immediate problem exists, the weaker is the faith in
> the cure. . . . Our cadres, on the other hand, must be organized
> around the principles, values and strategies inherent in a
> clear understanding of the ideology of Pan-Africanism. . . .
> SOBU was explicit about the characteristics a recruit should
> have: good work habits for cadre, an active logical mind, an
> honest approach, political orientation, and commitment to the
> ideology of Pan-Africanism and to the struggles of African
> people. (Student Organization for Black Unity n.d., pp. 4–5)

After one year, the organization began to transform itself. They
changed the name in 1971 from SOBU to Youth Organization for
Black Unity (YOBU); this was the name of a local group in North
Carolina, and the decision to take it reflected a shift of focus from
the college campus to one embracing the youth of the Black working class as well. They also changed the name of their newspaper
from the *SOBU Newsletter* to *The African World*, thus affirming
their Pan-Africanist orientation.

Their newspaper, along with *Muhammad Speaks* and *The
Black Panther*, were the national publications that served the Black
liberation movement. Nelson Johnson wrote a regular column
called "The Struggle in Perspective." At first their Pan-African
perspective was reflected in another regular column called "Land
is the Basis of Struggle" that featured a different country in Africa
or the African Diaspora in each issue. As YOBU moved to the
left, two new columns were added: "The Point of Production," to
explain political economy; and "The Political Cook Book," which
covered a glossary of revolutionary concepts.

After several years of development, the primary function of the
newspaper crystallized into being a vehicle for political education
and organizing of the movement, first among students and then
more broadly in society (Student Organization for Black Unity

1975). They explicitly stated that their paper was an example of the strategic line of a cadre organizing a movement advanced by Lenin in his essay "Where to Begin":

> A newspaper is what we most of all need; without it we cannot conduct that systematic, all-round propaganda and agitation, consistent in principle, which is the chief and permanent task of Social-Democracy in general and, in particular, the pressing task of the moment, when interest in politics and in questions of socialism has been aroused among the broadest strata of the population. . . . The role of a newspaper, however, is not limited solely to the dissemination of ideas, to political education, and to the enlistment of political allies. A newspaper is not only a collective propagandist and a collective agitator, it is also a collective organiser. . . . With the aid of the newspaper, and through it, a permanent organisation will naturally take shape that will engage, not only in local activities, but in regular general work, and will train its members to follow political events carefully, appraise their significance and their effect on the various strata of the population, and develop effective means for the revolutionary party to influence these events. (Lenin 1901)

YOBU programs anchored the cadre in sustainable movement initiatives. Most of the activists had come out of HBCUs and were critical of what they called colonial education, but they avoided the ultra-left position of trying to destroy the HBCU by advancing the slogan to "Save and Change Black Institutions." This political message affirmed the positive role the HBCUs had played in the post-slavery experience by providing basic educational opportunities. At the same time, YOBU pushed the HBCUs to change and serve Black people as doorways to freedom in the late twentieth century. As evidence of YOBU's close attention to HBCUs, *The African World* reported on a national conference in which sixty-seven Black colleges participated, "National Black College Conference Maps Out 'Survival Strategy'," which took place in April 1973:

> The Conference detailed a series of local and national activities to be carried out over the next 12 months designed to bring the problem of the survival and transformation of

Black schools before the entire Black community to be faced and dealt with. (YOBU News Service 1973)

The general ideological orientation of these forces initially based in university settings combined forms of Black nationalism and Pan-Africanism. The Congress of African People, founded in Atlanta in 1970, combined two slogans that sum this up: "Its Nation Time!" and "We Are an African People" (Baraka 1972).

Malcolm X Liberation University and Owusu Sadaukai

The Pan-African tendency in the Black liberation movement was manifested most intensely in one institution, Malcolm X Liberation University, and in its charismatic leader, Owusu Sadaukai (Howard Fuller), whose rise to prominence was cemented by his participation in the 1970 meeting of the Congress of African People.

This dialectical unity of organizational form and individual leadership is critical to understand. So, first, what is a charismatic leader? Charisma is the ability to inspire and attract other people to some form of action, i.e., to followership. It is possible to model this for the Black movement by examining the life and agency of Paul Robeson and identify seven characteristics associated with charismatic leadership. Not everyone has all, but some are necessary, and in each case one or more stands out. I call it the A-7 model of Black leadership:

1. Athletic performance
2. Academic achievement
3. Authoritative knowledge
4. Attractive appearance
5. Ambition
6. Audience receptivity
7. Agency for freedom

Paul Robeson had all of these qualities at the highest standards on a global level, including being an All-American football player, a

Phi Beta Kappa, and an internationally acclaimed singer. Next to W. E. B. Du Bois, Robeson was the most celebrated anti-imperialist African American spokesperson of the twentieth century. His revolutionary position placed him in opposition to the American state and its ruling capitalist economy, so he was silenced, and efforts have been made to diminish the memory of him. It is important therefore that when discussing leadership we recall this, one of the tallest trees in the forest of our humanity (P. Robeson 1999; S. Robeson 1999; Foner 1982; Ransby 2014).

Howard Fuller, who took the name Owusu Sadaukai in 1970, began to fit this model of charismatic leader when he emerged as the key organizer of African Liberation Day in 1972. His autobiography tells his story (Fuller and Page 2014a). He was raised by two women, his mother and grandmother, in Shreveport, Louisiana, and Milwaukee, Wisconsin. He became a standout basketball star in high school and college. In high school, though it was majority white, he was elected president of the student body, and in college joined a white fraternity. With a scholarship from the Urban League in 1962, he entered Case Western Reserve University to study for a master's degree in social work, where he again was elected president of student government. Two decades later, he would complete his doctorate on the sociological foundation of education at Marquette University.

His development followed the three stages outlined by Frantz Fanon for colonized African intellectual activists:

In the first phase, the native intellectual gives proof that he has assimilated the culture of the occupying power. . . . In the second phase we find the native is disturbed; he decides to remember what he is. . . . Finally in the third phase, which is called the fighting phase, the native, after having tried to lose himself in the people and with the people, will on the contrary shake the people. . . . The native intellectual nevertheless sooner or later will realize that you do not show proof of your nation from its culture but that you substantiate its existence in the fight which the people wage against the forces of occupation. (Fanon 1965, 178–179)

In both high school and college, Owusu stood out while integrating into a predominantly white situation; in fact he was the only Black person in the entire student body when he entered Carroll College in 1958. Fuller was the first Black male graduate of the college. He won the first Whitney Young Scholarship to attend Case Western Reserve University.

In graduate school he met a Black woman in one of his classes, Jean Harris, who:

> ...struck up a conversation one day in class and invited me to a party. She also introduced me to her older sister and the two of them embraced me as their little brother. It must have been obvious to them that I was a bit of a square because they guided me socially through the next year. They introduced me to their circle of friends, taught me the latest dances, and helped me hook up my wardrobe. . . . The world those two sisters brought me into was unapologetically Black, and that helped me reconnect to the part of me that I felt had been lost. (Fuller and Page 2014a, 44–45)

Owusu later became the life of the party, widely known for his collection of R&B and soul music hits. People loved being invited to his house to dance the night away based on his being a master DJ. Then he met activists affiliated with the Congress of Racial Equality (CORE) and began to connect with the civil rights movement. His take on social work was in the direction of community organizing. Based on his Urban League scholarship's requiring him to work for them for a year, he graduated and spent a year at the Chicago branch. Then he dove deep into the Black experience by going south to take a job in North Carolina. His ideological development began to turn to Black nationalism and Pan-Africanism.

The South shocked him into undergoing a paradigm shift in his thinking. He raised and began to answer the following questions:

- Black people, who are we, what is our identity?
- What is the basic nature of our situation in this country?
- What can we do to get free?
- What is the nature of the problems faced by African people, on the continent and throughout the African Diaspora?

Owusu was asking the questions that were being raised throughout the country, with the rise of Black Power in 1966 having moved the focus from civil rights to Black liberation. This section will focus on his thinking up to the 1972 demonstration, while subsequent chapters will feature ideological shifts from 1972 to 1975 and beyond.

These paradigm shifts were not merely verbal shifts, conversational ploys. These ideological developments were based on the practice of movements in the United States and throughout the African Diaspora, and most important of all the practice in which Owusu was engaged at the grassroots level. The two most important areas of practice included his work in North Carolina and his experience with FRELIMO in the liberated territory of Mozambique.

After graduate school, Owusu went to work for a community organization set up by the Office of Economic Opportunity called Operation Breakthrough. It was later supported by the North Carolina Fund. This was an antipoverty program. Owusu recalls:

> The Operation Breakthrough job sounded like just what I had been seeking. I applied and was interviewed by the program's new executive director, Robert Foust, as well as two of Durham's most influential Black men, John Wheeler, president of the Black-owned Mechanics and Farmers Bank, and attorney/civil rights activist Floyd McKissick. I must have said something right because I got the job.

> I was ready to go to war. We could win this war. I was sure of it. My weapons were simple but mighty: a little book sense, some big ideas, and a whole lot of hope. (Fuller and Page 2014a, 58–59)

The Economic Opportunity Act of 1964 had contained a key mandate that programs should be "developed, conducted and administered with the maximum feasible participation of residents of areas and members of the group served" (Fuller and Page 2014a, 63). This guided Owusu into the community with one goal in mind: to build an organization of the people themselves, organic forces from the community, for the community. He embraced the dictum of good organizers: swim among the people like a fish in water. This meant meeting with people in their living rooms, churches, and pool halls.

Digging that deep into the community for mobilization made Owusu both a hero and a villain, a respected activist in the community whom people began to trust and a challenger of power whom the ruling officials began to recognize as their enemy. He had made close connections to some students and pulled some in to work as interns during the summer of 1968. Key interns included Chuck Hopkins, a Duke University student, and Jerry Walker, later to become editor of *The African World*.

The students at Duke University, in keeping with the national rise of Black student militancy, took an aggressive position in protesting institutional racism at Duke and demanding implementation of a Black Studies program. They seized a building, and Owusu rushed to join them, subsequently becoming part of a bargaining process. They forced some change, but were disappointed at how limited it turned out to be. They began to think that in this era of Black Power, self-determination was the only way forward, so an independent Black institution had to be developed.

This led to thinking about and then the founding in October 1969 of what came to be called the Malcolm X Liberation University (MXLU). This was a self-described institute of ideological and technological training for service to African peoples. This development took place in an environment of Black self-determination that saw Black Nationalists and Pan-Africanists join forces in formal structures:

1. Congress of African People (CAP) – 1970
2. Revolutionary People's Constitutional Convention – 1970
3. Council of Independent Black Institutions (14 schools) – 1972
4. National Black Political Assembly – 1972

All four of these national organizations were versions of a united front, what we can call networks of common practice (Baraka 1972; Rickford 2016). The activists from the Center for Black Education, SOBU/YOBU, and MXLU were involved in most of these organizations, helping to shape the ideological orientation of this upsurge in social movements for Black liberation.

An example of this is that Owusu was asked to speak at the founding meeting of CAP, first to read the message to the meeting sent by Kwame Ture (Stokely Carmichael) and then to make his own remarks. In his words, he stated the core ideas of the meeting and the Pan-Africanist movement in general:

> I would like to define Pan-Africanism for you as I see it. Pan-Africanism tells us who we are, links us together around the world, and outlines our objectives as a people. In other words certain things are clear: that we are all African people, not red people, not yellow people, not brown people, but Black people. People of African descent. That number two, no matter where we are in the world, we are inseparably linked by our common heritage and out common oppression. Number three, we must govern ourselves in order to determine our own destiny and in order to determine our destiny, we must have a nation. . . . Brothers and Sisters, I am saying that nation-building is in fact what we must be about. (Howard Fuller, quoted in Baraka 1972, 63)

MXLU was planned by a network of veteran and young activists. The main planning meeting took place in Bricks, North Carolina, on May 2–4, 1969. This followed at least five meetings held in different cities around the state: Winston-Salem, Raleigh, Greensboro, Durham, and Greenville. This was a democratic process, making the planning for MXLU a collective achievement of the people, a mass-based process. They discussed the key issues—goals and objectives, composition of decision-making bodies, administration, involvement of whites, recruitment of faculty and students, funding, the military draft, parents, and curriculum.

They summed up the discussion by stating five goals and objectives:
1. To respond to the needs of the Black community and provide an ideological and practical methodology for meeting the physical, social, psychological, economical and cultural needs of Black people
2. To analyze existing political systems and institutions of colonizing societies, and how they relate to and influence Black

people
3. To develop a total understanding of the relationship between Black people in this country and the whole Pan-African liberation struggle and to establish a Black Revolutionary ideology and positive self-awareness for Black people
4. To be a real alternative for those seeking liberation from the misconception of an institutionalized racist education
5. To seek accreditation from the Black community (Fuller and Page 2014a, 101)

Initially, the organization of MXLU was being coordinated by Owusu, based on his position at the Foundation for Community Development. The first leadership group consisted of eleven people elected at the Bricks meeting. Within a year, the main leadership body expanded to thirteen and became the Council of Elders. Five people were on both: Cleveland Sellers (SOBU/ YOBU), Nelson Johnson (SOBU/YOBU), Jimmy Garrett (Center for Black Education), Kwame McDonald (Foundation for Community Development), and Owusu Sadaukai (MXLU).

The opening of MXLU was a glorious celebration that brought together people from many parts of the country:

> Malcolm X Liberation University opened its doors on Saturday, October 25, 1969. . . . Approximately 3,500 community residents celebrated the opening day ceremonies for MXLU. . . . Honored guests of the day included Sister Betty Shabazz, widow of Malcolm X. Shabazz shared the speakers platform with Nathan Garrett, executive director of the Foundation for Community Development (FCD), and Courtland Cox, director of the Washington DC Center for Black Education (CBE). (Benson 2014, 113)

As with the CAP meeting, Carmichael was not in attendance, but sent a message from Guinea, West Africa.

MXLU opened with about forty students, went through some growing pains, but continued on. Structurally, MXLU consisted of four sectors: students, staff, resource people (teachers), and the Council of Elders. They produced an ideological pamphlet, *Understanding the African Struggle*, and a monthly newspaper,

The African Warrior.

By 1972, MXLU was starting its fourth year and its ideological orientation was taking on new dimensions:

> Pan Africanism and scientific socialism is the ideological basis of the University and the technical training given is geared to meet some of the fundamental needs of African Nation building. (Malcolm X Liberation University 1972)

The influence of socialism was very significant, reflecting what was happening in the fight for African liberation. This was manifested in the thinking of key African thought leaders, mainly Kwame Nkrumah and Amilcar Cabral. MXLU's earlier material had placed ideological and technical training on an equal footing; but a new informational brochure stressed the technical engineering curriculum.

Owusu was involved with the reparations movement that was hitting the churches in the United States, having become a board member of the Interreligious Foundation for Community Organization (IFCO) headed by Lucius Walker, which was:

> ...an interdenominational 'parachurch' agency, created in late 1966 to open lines of communication between mainstream American churches and disenfranchised minority communities in the United States. Established by the United Presbyterian Church, the original membership consisted of nine religious groups and one foundation, only one of which represented a minority community. By the mid-1970s, however, IFCO had developed into the largest minority-controlled foundation in the country. (New York Public Library, n.d.)

IFCO was committed to supporting the African Liberation Movements, including providing some funding for MXLU, and would soon be an important funding source for ALSC and other organizations with a similar orientation. Lucius Walker, director of IFCO, was invited to South Africa, but Owusu opposed it in favor of creating a fund for African Liberation, something that would have been opposed by the South African Government. This was worked out as IFCO came out decisively on the side of African Liberation.

Some of the church funding had happened as a result of the civil rights movement; the bulk of the funding came as the result of an initiative called the Black Manifesto that grew out of the National Black Economic Development Conference (held in Detroit on April 26, 1969). James Forman took over the pulpit at Riverside Church in New York on May 4, 1969, and demanded reparations (Forman 1972, 543–553). This shook things up and began a new era of church and NGO funding of social justice movements and community organizing in oppressed communities.

FRELIMO and Liberated Mozambique

Owusu was asked by the National Committee of Black Churchmen to attend a conference bringing them together with their African counterparts in August 1971. In the first stage of the trip, he was joined by Ron Daniels from Youngstown, Ohio. Daniels was going to speak about community-based economic development and Owusu was going to discuss the MXLU project. In Dar es Salaam, Tanzania, following up on the MXLU commitment to support the African liberation struggle, Owusu made arrangements to visit the offices of the liberation organizations headquartered there, due to its being the location of the Liberation Support Committee of the Organization of African Unity (OAU). The critical meeting was at the FRELIMO office:

> At the headquarters for the Mozambique Liberation Front . . . I [Owusu] met Joaquim Chissano, the brother in charge. Neither of us could have known back then that fifteen years later he would become the second president of independent Mozambique. . . . He advised me that I could get the most reliable information from visiting various centers of operation, such as his organization's hospital and school at Tunduru in southern Tanzania, near the Mozambique border. If I was interested, he said, there was an opportunity for me to go inside liberated Mozambique. (Fuller and Page 2014a, 123)

So this was a decisive moment: a Pan-Africanist from the United States being invited into the heart of the struggle to liberate an African country. No more mere speculation and imagination; this was going to be the real deal, a top-secret action that would reveal some truths that could not be contested. Owusu had questions:

> I wanted to know just how the Freedom Fighters viewed their struggle: Who was the enemy? What were they fighting for? What were they trying to build? (Fuller and Page 2014a, 129)

Owusu was not alone on this trip with the FRELIMO comrades. On the same trip were two African American filmmakers, Robert Van Lierop and Bob Fletcher. They documented the FRELIMO experience in their film *A Luta Continua* (Parrott 2015). They also provided conversation, both about home, a necessary psychological relief, and about their experience abroad; the profound nature of what they were experiencing was so much more than the mere sense perceptions and challenges they faced in the African bush.

One of the contradictions that sums up the way FRELIMO hosted them was when Owusu wrote that they were welcomed as comrades, but also treated as guests. There were sacrifices for the visitors to help them survive the hard tasks of marching for miles, eating food in the bush, and sleeping when and where one could. This also involved the sacrifice of local villagers, who served the militants and their guests, sharing what little they had. Frequently, one could not distinguish militants from leaders, because everyone worked and joined in all activities.

A main aspect of understanding this trip into Mozambique was philosophical, the sorting out of the difference between idealism and materialism. Before the trip, Owusu had ideas in his head about the liberation struggle and engaged in debates with people taking positions about what they imagined was going on. The trip into liberated Mozambique was total immersion in what was actually going on, direct experience of the struggle. Were they dupes of white people, like some Black nationalists in the United States were suggesting, because they were building a socialist society? No, they weren't, because they were making their path forward by walking, by being in the reality of their country and making change as they could. Owusu recalled that:

> …during the walk, there was a great deal of discussion, fortunately in English. Time and again, Guebuza made the point that the struggle was against imperialism, worldwide imperialism. Anyone struggling against imperialism was a

friend, he said. I had personally conceived of our struggle in the United States as being against white people, who represented and controlled the forces of imperialism. But there was also no doubt in my analysis that Black people who represented the forces of imperialism had to be fought against, as well. (Fuller and Page 2014a, 130)

Another great lesson of this experience was about women, a critical issue, because patriarchy had been holding back the struggle in the United States, both in the society and in the movement:

> It was on this march that I saw why the women of FRELIMO were considered full comrades, no ifs, ands, or buts about it. Maria, for example: twenty years old, five feet two inches tall, and just one hundred pounds. In addition to the rifle draped over her shoulder, she carried a knapsack on her back and another load of over fifty pounds on her head. She seldom used her hands to steady the load, and at one point even broke into a brisk trot. (Fuller and Page 2014a, 132–133)

Finally, on the march into liberated Mozambique the issue of armed struggle became more of a reality. The struggle involved life and death, and not merely the advocacy of belief without facing the reality of acting on the belief. They were warned that this march would be in a "hot" zone, where the Portuguese could attack at any time. They got hit more than once—helicopters, planes, or just gunfire sent the militants and their comrades/guests dashing off into the bush to hide and wait. They even came across abandoned Portuguese camps where they waited to ambush and attack. And all this sometimes disrupted a meal, came with heavy rain, or broke up daily events like taking a shower, sleeping, or just hanging out in camp.

Owusu was an African American activist gathering information for us in the heat of battle on the African continent. It required him to think about the movement and himself in trying to comprehend what he was learning. This was the critical task that he struggled with on his way home:

> I saw very clearly the contradictions of my own life within our "movement" in the United States. I also saw that leadership by mouth only had no place in a revolution, or, for that matter, in a school like MXLU. Leadership comes from what you

do—by example. Revolution also was no place for ego trips, pouting arguments that have no constructive base, etc. I just hoped when I got back I could somehow turn the experience into a positive force for the university and my people. (Fuller and Page 2014a, 136)

African Liberation Day

The story of ALSC begins with the first ALD, held on May 27, 1972. This did not occur in a vacuum. As demonstrated above, the first ALD was a compressed moment of a process, a political project implemented on a global level of mass mobilization along with practical projects in many places in the country. When Owusu came back from Mozambique in 1971, he was determined to be the catalyst for what many were waiting for, a campaign that crystallized support for African liberation based on a high level of national Black unity. He was clear on his task:

> As soon as I returned from Mozambique, I began thinking of what I could do to support the liberation struggles in Africa. It didn't take long to come up with a plan: Organize a national demonstration that would draw Black people from every corner of the country to the nation's capital. My people needed to know what was happening in Africa, that America was supporting countries fighting to maintain the racist system that had colonized our brothers and sisters there. I'd seen the American made bombs used against them. A huge demonstration would draw attention to the issue, and could bring about a change in U.S. policies that supported the European regimes that denied various African nations their independence. (Fuller and Page 2014b, 149)

Origin

Owusu's first move was to pull together a small group of people he had been working with, agreed with, and trusted. Thirteen people answered his call to meet with him at MXLU. Included in this group were Gene Locke, Amiri Baraka, Cleve Sellers, Nelson Johnson, Ron Daniels, and Joe Waller (soon to be Omali Yeshitela).

They reached an agreement to organize ALD and decided on May 27 of the next year. They initially considered May 25, in order to commemorate the Organization of African Unity's African Liberation Day on that date in 1963. But, realizing that a Saturday was better than any weekday for working people and students, for 1972 the 27th was the best choice. No one seemed aware that the 1958 conference called by Nkrumah had set April 15 as Africa Freedom Day, well before the OAU decision. This demonstrated that new forces were emerging in support of African liberation, unaware of historical precedent, but nonetheless embarking on a critically important new initiative. This represented independence and initiative from the diaspora.

The first outreach was to the Black nationalist and Pan-Africanist militants who had changed the national discourse from civil rights to Black liberation following the introduction of the Black Power slogan in 1966 and then conferences in 1967 (Newark) and 1968 (Philadelphia). The young activists were not only turning their own demand for Black Power into Pan-Africanism, they were also engaging movements that had been doing Africa-related work at the grassroots level since the 1950s, which in turn had grown out of movements led by Marcus Garvey, Carlos Cooks, and Malcolm X.

New York is an example. The representatives of YOBU, Roger Newell and Bobby Johnson, were students at Columbia University. When beginning their organizing for ALD, they contacted representatives of the African Nationalist movement and were confronted by the cautious reaction of people who had been relatively isolated from the mainstream and who therefore questioned the new initiative (Alkalimat 1976). Some of the New York activists reached out to Owusu to get some understanding of how this new initiative would connect with their longstanding leadership of the Pan-African movement. This was a first meeting of northern and southern activists in the post-civil rights movement.

Sam Anderson places this in context:

> As for preALSC African Liberation Day events, in 1969-70, Bill Sales, St Clair Bourne, Carolyn Brown, Sam White,

myself and several other Sisters & Brothers formed the *Pan African Solidarity Day Committee* in Harlem that explicitly supported the unfolding African liberation struggles. We marched from Harlem to the UN one year and around Harlem the next year. We were close to ANC and SWAPO forces because they were a combination of fellow college students and living within Harlem. We had about 250-300 folk to join us. And this group was essential to forming the NYC ALSC organizing committee for the DC demo. (Anderson 1976)

Another center of Black nationalist critique was in Chicago, especially around a group based at the Center for Inner City Studies, which included Anderson, Thompson, and Conrad Worrill. Their organizational activities included the Chicago chapter of the UNIA and the Communiversity. Also included was Zimbabwean activist Ruwa Chiri. They made the criticism that some leaders of the African revolution (e.g., Amilcar Cabral) and African Americans supporting the African Liberation Day (e.g., George Wiley) were married to white women, and that, since white people were the enemy, they were suspicious and hesitant to get involved.

Stokely Carmichael (aka Kwame Ture) sent Owusu a letter arguing that the demonstration should not go forward for two reasons: the possibility of repression and the likely lack of mass response. However, he was in West Africa, without a direct leadership role in the process, and seemed not to be in touch with the grassroots surge that was taking place in support of African liberation.

In the end, these critics in New York, Chicago, Detroit, and West Africa joined in the campaign as supporters of the ALD. Everyone followed the general trend of a united front by balancing unity for the sake of the agreed-upon action with their own independence and initiative on other matters.

The African Liberation Day Coordinating Committee

The support from all these diverse sectors of Black politics represented an opportunity to build a broad united front that would bring new focus and public attention to the issue of African self-rule. As a first step, the African Liberation Day Coordinating Committee (ALDCC) was formed, which set as a goal the building of a long list of solid supporters. This took a major leap when the committee connected with elected officials, beginning with Congressman Charles Diggs from Detroit. Diggs was a founding member in 1971 of the Congressional Black Caucus, serving as its first president. He joined the House Committee on Foreign Affairs, serving as chairman of the Subcommittee on Africa. His first move was to embark on a multi-country tour of Africa, to prepare an agenda to work with as chair of his new committee. Though he was refused entry into what were then called South West Africa and Rhodesia (since renamed Namibia and Zimbabwe), he did visit several countries and, based on what he had seen, issued an Action Manifesto, portions of which follow:

> This Action Manifesto consists of a number of recommendations for United States policy resulting for the most part from my fact-finding mission to several African countries, including Guinea-Bissau, Cape Verde, and South Africa. . . . The visit to Guinea-Bissau and Cape Verde was extremely informative, particularly with respect to the stark racism of the Portuguese government and the tenuous position of the Portuguese in Guinea-Bissau. Guinea-Bissau is an armed camp, and the Portuguese there are beleaguered. . . . The basic fact which I found on the fact-finding mission to South Africa was the indomitable spirit and the unquenchable will of the people of South Africa to be free. I have returned with the conviction that majority rule in South Africa is inevitable and the rest of the world, particularly the United States, has no choice but to get on the side of freedom. I am not prepared to start predicting when or how, but the countdown has begun. (Diggs 1972, 62)

Ronald Dellums, elected to Congress in 1970 and another founding member of the Congressional Black Caucus, was another advocate for African liberation. He began his work with an antiapartheid bill he introduced in 1972, finally seeing it passed in 1986. Other key political officials stepped forward to join Diggs and Dellums in supporting African Liberation Day: Julian Bond (former SNCC leader, at that time a Georgia state representative),

John Conyers (Detroit congressman), Walter Fauntroy (congress-man representing Washington, DC), Louis Stokes (St. Louis con-gressman), Parren Mitchell (Baltimore congressman), and Rich-ard Hatcher (mayor of Gary, Indiana).

Support was also coming from civil rights movement veterans Marion Barry and H. Rap Brown (SNCC) as well as Ralph Abernathy, Walter Fauntroy, and Jesse Jackson (SCLC). Two important civil rights lawyers, Howard Moore and Margaret Burnham, stepped forward. From his jail cell, Rap sent out this message:

> African Liberation Day represents the awakening of Blacks in America to the fact that our struggle here is definitely related to that of our people on the continent. The same oppressive forces that are seeking to commit genocide against us in the United States though murder, assassination, imprisonment, population control, mind control, "behavior modification" schemes, implicit government toleration and endorsement of hunger, disease, poverty, unemployment and drug racketeering—are the same ones carrying out murderous, imperialist aims in Africa. African Liberation Day says to the world that we recognize this fact and therefore support our people's struggle for independence, wherever they are. (African Liberation Day Coordinating Committee 1972)

In academia, Black Studies was also making a major turn toward Africa. In opposition to the mainstream African Studies Association, Black scholars revolted and in 1969 formed the African Heritage Studies Association, holding its first national conference at Howard University in 1970. Leaders of this new motion included John Henrik Clarke and James Turner. This was an effort to explicitly link academic scholarship to advocacy for African liberation. Many Black Studies scholars joined the ALDCC process, including Vincent Harding (founder of the Institute of the Black World in 1969); Preston Wilcox (chairman of the Association for the Advancement of Afro-American Educators, founded in 1968); Ron Walters (Howard University professor, also representing the National Conference of Black Political Scientists, founded in 1969); and Andrew Billingsly (vice president for academic affairs at Howard University).

Religious leaders got involved, among them Leon Modeste (National Committee of Black Churchmen), Charles Spivey (World Council of Churches), Lucius Walker (IFCO), Douglas Moore (Black United Front, Washington, DC), and Ben Chavis (Commission for Racial Justice).

Perhaps the most remarkable support for the ALD proposal came from forces in the movement who were known to differ. However, they were convinced to join this united front effort. This included nationalists and Marxists of different tendencies: Huey Newton, Bobby Seale, and Elaine Brown (Black Panther Party); Angela Davis (Communist Party USA); Joe Waller (All African Peoples Socialist Party); Muhammad Ahmad (African People's Party); Stokely Carmichael (All-African People's Revolutionary Party [AAPRP]); Paul Boutelle(the Socialist Workers Party); Imari Obadeli (Republic of New Africa); Kwadwo Akpan (Pan Africanist Congress); Charles Koen (United Front of Cairo, Illinois); Gina Thornton (UNIA); Roy Innes (CORE); George Wiley (National Welfare Rights Organization); Gene Locke (Africans in America for Black Liberation, Houston); Tanya Russell (Black Workers Congress [BWC]); and the widow of Malcolm X, Betty Shabazz.

This was an amazing group of diverse organizations and leading individuals guiding streams of struggle who united for action on this day to proclaim that Africa must be free! Johnson (2007) underscores this fact:

> A measure of the ALDCC's organizing strength was its success in drawing together ideological rivals such as the Black Panther Party and Karenga's U.S. Organization around a common cause. Some of the organizations that formally sponsored the mobilization included SCLC; The National Welfare Rights Organization (NWRO); SOBU; student organizations from various historically black colleges; CORE; CAP, National Council of Negro Women; Delta Sigma Theta Sorority, Inc.; and Alpha Phi Alpha Fraternity, Inc. (Johnson 2007, 141)

This was no easy task, and everyone asked was not in agreement, but a critical mass was reached. Owusu explains:

> At the time, there were warring factions of Black folks, and

it took some cajoling to get some of them to agree to serve on the committee together, even though they never had to sit across the table from one another. In the end, though, many of them agreed that it was important to come together for the sake of Black unity. (Fuller and Page 2014b, 151)

The plan was based on having a staff responsible for implementing the national plan for mobilization. The administrative structure of any movement organization is based on cadre and an efficient and accountable division of labor. For ALD 1972, this was created by recruiting tested cadres from three organizational networks of common practice: MXLU/YOBU, CAP, and SNCC.

The director of operations in charge of the national office was Mark Smith. Mark had become the vice-chair of SOBU/YOBU after dropping out of Harvard College to become a full-time activist. He was immediately in touch with the SOBU/YOBU chapters in key cities and states and was in close contact with the *African World* newspaper staff. Cleve Sellers, the field secretary, was closely connected to Kwame Ture and the SNCC network as well as to MXLU and SOBU/YOBU. He was a key provider of information about the campaign, as he sent out announcements to local organizers throughout the country. Florence Tate, an experienced journalist, served as the information coordinator; among her contributions was taking a leading role in organizing the press conference that officially announced the launch of ALD (Benson 2014).

CAP was a national network and its political leader, Amiri Baraka, was a very well-known activist. It was critical to have their full cooperation. Baraka's base in Newark, N.J. was well organized, having both a clearly articulated leadership structure and an ample number of disciplined members available to serve as marshals for the ALD march. Out of Newark and CAP, Mwanafunzi Hekima was recruited to be the ALD logistics coordinator and Juadine Henderson to serve as secretary-treasurer.

Basic movement organizing had been going on for months by the time Owusu got back from Mozambique. SOBU/YOBU had made its newspaper the voice of Pan-African resistance and was educating a new generation of Black students. Campus struggles were underway from coast to coast. Some activists were connecting with Africa and planning to go there to provide practical assistance. There was a broad-based development of networks of common practice.

The first public announcement of ALD went out from Cleveland Sellers on March 5, 1972. A national mailing list of movement activists was generated, who were then asked to begin organizing. The text of the letter from Sellers read as follows:

> This is to inform you of the formation of the African Liberation Day Coordinating Committee which is an ad hoc broad-based national coalition to protest U.S. involvement in Southern Africa and to influence Black public opinion in support of the armed liberation struggle being waged by our brothers and sisters in Angola, Mozambique, Southwest Africa, Zimbabwe, South Africa, and Guinea-Bissau. Toward this end plans are being made for a mass protest demonstration in D.C. on May 27, which hopefully will bring at least 10,000 Black folks here on that date. (Sellers 1972)

Two weeks later, during an ALDCC leadership meeting at MXLU, a national press conference was organized by Florence Tate. At the press conference, Tate read the following statement:

> We must let the world know that we stand shoulder to shoulder with our brothers on the continent who are waging warfare to take back their land,' avowed Owusu Sadaukai, chairman of the ad hoc broad-based coalition (ALDCC) and president of Malcolm X Liberation University in Greensboro. Sadaukai and Imamu Baraka, head of the Committee for a Unified Newark, announced plans to bring 10,000 Black people to Washington for African Liberation Day, May 27. (Tate 1972)

The ALDCC decided on the theme for the ALD: "Breaking the Chains of Oppression Thru Black Unity." This was a clarion call for a united front, signaling that our strategic weapon for liberation was unity. The implication was that the African national liberation struggles were implementing this strategy, and the African American struggle should do the same. This was a slogan that could be raised in each national context of Africa and throughout the African Diaspora.

The organizers for ALD began reaching out in person to

activists throughout the country, including travelling for face-to-face meetings, sometimes with established connections and sometimes meeting new activists for the first time. Owusu was the main organizer, meeting with people to get their agreement to join the national list of supporters. One of his key advantages, in addition to his recent trip with FRELIMO into liberated Mozambique, was that, though he had attained some prominence as the leader of MXLU, he was relatively unknown.

The key reason this national touring was possible was support from religion-based social justice groups. Viola Plummer was a key staff person with the Episcopal Church and she did the legwork to make financial resources available, along with Leon Modeste. Most of the support came from IFCO and its leader Lucius Walker.

Conference

Despite the big push for unity being made by the ALD organizers, significant differences remained across the Black political spectrum. A two-day conference sponsored by the Congressional Black Caucus was convened at Howard University in Washington, DC, before the ALD demonstration. It became a site of struggle within the African American community:

> The conference at Howard University and the march on May 27 displayed two tendencies, the one by people who wanted to help U.S. capitalism in Africa which did not take a clear anti-imperialist position, and the other tendencies of the masses of people who were objectively anti-imperialist and did not want to be pawns for U.S. capitalism in Africa. . . . Indicative of the two tendencies was the composition of the conference which attracted Black Americans from the different government agencies, from the large corporations and from many Afro-American organizations. (Rogers 1972, 1)

The keynote was given by A. A. Farah, the UN Ambassador from the Republic of Somalia. He attacked U.S. imperialism, and was subsequently echoed by Henry Winston and Robert Rhodes, both speaking from the perspective of the Communist Party, as well as by Charles Diggs. Owusu spoke for the ALDCC, both to condemn U.S. imperialism as well as to ask African comrades to support the struggle here while those in the United States were supporting them over there:

> The plain fact is that the export of U.S. capital is increasing the misery of our people. It is further entrenching a racist, capitalist, illegal, illegitimate government in power. It is giving aid and comfort to the enemies of African people. It is helping to deter the liberation struggles for the time being, and even where it does give jobs it affects only a small number of African people and it ends up creating a whole new level of petty bourgeois Black people who will move to stifle the legitimate concern of the masses for democracy and self-determination. . . . Finally, to my African brothers and sisters who are here directly from the continent. The labor of love for our liberation is a reciprocal arrangement. When we demonstrate because of Sharpsville you must demonstrate to commemorate the Orangeburg massacre. When we protest the bombing of Tanzania you must protest the shooting into the Muslim Mosque. When we memorialize Nkrumah you must memorialize Malcolm. When we study Chaka you must study Toussaint. (Sadaukai 1972b)

Black workers in the United States had already drawn a line against that country's imperialism, specifically where it was counter to African self-determination. One step was to expose the role of U.S. corporations (Gershon 2015; Wilkins 2005, 156–160):

> Black employees at the Polaroid Corporation's Cambridge, MA headquarters founded the Polaroid Revolutionary Worker's Movement (PRWM) in 1970 in response to Polaroid's production and processing of film for South Africa's passbook system. PRWM briefly stimulated widespread public discussion and debate on the American corporate role in South Africa.. (Culverson 1996, 137)

Another action by Black workers was of great importance. In Burnside, Louisiana, on March 22, 1972, Black members of the International Longshoreman's Association Local 1419 refused to unload illegal exported chromium ore from Rhodesia (Wilkins 2005, 152–153). Representing the ALDCC, Owusu stated:

> In collusion with European/American investors in Rhodesia, the government has flagrantly allowed Union Carbide of New York and the Foote Mineral Company of Delaware (both of which are longtime mining industrial conglomerates with interlocking directorates) to purchase several hundred thousand tons of chromium.

The all Black AFL-CIO Longshoremen's local in Burnside must also be hailed for risking their livelihoods to honor the student-induced prevention of the planned unloading. Special praise must also go to a young Black faculty member of Southern University, Dr. Alex Willingham of the Political Science Department, who helped to provide tactical advice and assistance as well as mobilized some faculty support for the students' actions. (Sadaukai 1972a, 1,2)

This was a moment of unity against imperialism and in support of African liberation across social groups and social classes. So, in raising the demand that "Black Workers Take the Lead," the movement was basing this on practice, not merely on abstract ideology.

African Liberation Day

All of this militant resolve peaked on ALD, the day designated for the mass demonstration. The people were gathering, coming by all means of transportation and pushing the numbers way past the original goal of 10,000. Black people were reconnecting with Africa, making it clear that this was yet another awakening of an African American nationality, the deepest African penetration into the West. The spirits of Garvey, Du Bois, and Malcolm X were generating an energy flow into the Black liberation movement. The warriors in the African bush were not alone—they were being joined by their distant cousins creating battlefields of support.

The ALDCC had planned to have three centers of mass demonstration in North America: Washington, DC; San Francisco; and Toronto, Ontario. Others joined in such places as Nashville (Peoples College) and New Orleans (Black Workers Congress) (Johnson 2007, 144). The Washington, DC plan was for key stops along the march at which speakers would address specific issues connected to where the march had stopped, and then head to the main rally. There were speakers at four stops (Table 2):

Table 2. Washington, DC African Liberation Day stops and speakers

Stop	Speakers
Portuguese Embassy	Roy Innes, Ron Daniels
Rhodesian Information Center	Inez Reid, Ruwa Chiri
South African Embassy	Douglas Moore, Lucius Walker
U.S. State Department	Jitu Weusi, Dawolu Gene Locke

The speakers at each stop gave short, impassioned speeches. The sum total of these march-stop speeches constituted an anti-imperialist school of advocacy supporting the fight for African liberation. Speakers came from different regions and different backgrounds. The one glaring omission was that only one sister was scheduled to speak at one of the march stops.

The fullness of the united front was expressed in the program of the main rally. The chair was Congressman Fauntroy, after an opening invocation by Bishop John Walker, followed at the end with a benediction by Bishop Smallwood Williams. This was the stamp of approval by middle-class institutional elites. A key speech was also given by Congressman Diggs from Detroit, which included the following passage:

> It is time to set the record straight, to say that Black people in America and Black people in the Caribbean understand that our African past is intricately bound up with our African future. The revolution that we seek in the nature of our relationships to Americans is ultimately reflected in the struggle between African and European peoples in the world. We ought to put in perspective the relationship between the American Gross National Product and the origin of the corporate products which feed off African soil and African souls, and we ought to

put into proper context the development of racism in America and its export to Africa through the American foreign policy making apparatus, and between the high need for American security and the high need, it is felt in these racist quarters, to keep Africa stable and peaceful, but, yes, in white hands. (Diggs, quoted in Campanella Jr 1972)

The energy flow was enhanced by songs from the Harambee Singers and the Spirit House Movers and poetry by Don Lee (aka Haki Madhubuti). All along the three-hour march, drummers set the pace and rhythm for people to move by, as well as all during the rally.

The three major statements of political ideology that defined the present and future motion of the day's politics were given by Kwame Ture, Amiri Baraka, and Owusu Sadaukai. Ture sent a letter of support that was read at the rally. Baraka, a leading member of the Committee for a Unified Newark (CFUN) and CAP, presented his vision of where the movement needed to go:

We must be done with mere rhetorizing, we must be done with talking a good game. We must begin to organize a political structure that can transform not only our spiritual consciousness but transform our reality. We must deal with the transformation of our reality. This is the time, the seventies, that we must put together a political party, a political structure that can elect people to office, that can function as a community organization to build housing, to open hospitals, to open schools, to teach nutrition, and to teach health. A party, a structure, that can make alliances and coalitions, and a party, if necessary, that can wage armed struggle. But we must put together a structure, and it can only be done, not with only words, but with Kazi as Nyerere says, Kazi Kazi Kazi, which means [in KiSwahili] work, because Kazi is the blackest of all. If you are interested in moving past the 60s now you must think about a political structure, a political party. (Baraka, quoted in Campanella Jr 1972)

Owusu was the final speaker and guided the people to realize that the naysayers were wrong, the estimates of the turnout had fallen short, and the consciousness of the masses was underestimated. As he had often done in his speeches, he quoted Frederick Douglass:

> If there is no struggle there is no progress. Those who profess to favor freedom and yet deprecate agitation are men who want crops without plowing up the ground; they want rain without thunder and lightning. They want the ocean without the awful roar of its many waters. This struggle may be a moral one, or it may be a physical one, and it may be both moral and physical, but it must be a struggle. Power concedes nothing without a demand. It never did and it never will. Find out just what any people will quietly submit to and you have found out the exact measure of injustice and wrong which will be imposed upon them, and these will continue till they are resisted with either words or blows, or with both.
> (Sadaukai, quoted in Campanella Jr 1972)

He ended his remarks with the powerful technique of repetition, summoning the people to join in the chant of a slogan that linked African Americans to the African liberation struggle: "We are an African People!" The African liberation struggles were being reborn in the hearts and minds of those involved in the African American freedom struggle in the United States.

In addition to the main rally and march on the East Coast, San Francisco was chosen for a rally on the West Coast. San Francisco was the major city, but next to it were Berkeley and Palo Alto, centers of radical student activism, and Oakland, a Black working-class community that had given birth to the Black Panther Party. Thus, the entire Bay Area was targeted for mobilization. At the rally, the organizers duplicated the East Coast model of diverse unity and cultural performance.

In San Francisco, the ALD demonstration convened at Raymond Kimball Park, which organizers renamed "DuBois Savannah." The San Francisco ALD actions were initiated on 25 May when twelve activists staged a midday demonstration at the Portuguese consulate. The march culminated with a mass rally over which California state assemblyman (and later, San Francisco Mayor) Willie Brown presided. The speaker's platform featured addresses by Black panther Party leader Bobby Seale; Guyanese Marxist Pan-Africanist intellectual Walter Rodney; Community Party activist Angela Davis; Nelson Johnson of SOBU, Reverend

Koen; and Gary Mayor Richard G. Hatcher. The rally also featured performances by the Nairobi Messengers, The Pharaoh Sanders trio, the Umoja Dancers, and the Freddie Hubbard Jazz Band. (Johnson 2007, 144–145)

The invocation was given by Cecil Williams of Glide Memorial Church. Nelson Johnson made the following statement:

> Today, brothers and sisters . . . we have come together as the sons and daughters of Mother Africa to demonstrate our support and solidarity with the liberation struggles on the Continent of Africa. . . . Their decision to take control of their land and their destiny is intimately tied up to our freedom as Black people in the United States. . . . We must resist the United States sending arms, money, and other support through NATO (North American Treaty Organization) and other mechanisms to sustain the oppression of our people in Africa. (Robinson 1972, 1)

The third demonstration in North America was held in Toronto, Ontario, coordinated by Brenda Paris and other Toronto activists. The West Indian Diaspora community in Canada had been on militant alert since the 1968 Congress of Black Writers. Most of the speakers at the congress, co-chaired by Rosie Douglas, were supporters of ALD four years later, including Walter Rodney, Robert Hill, C. L. R. James, Harry Edwards, James Forman, and Stokely Carmichael. This was followed by the militant uprising the next year in Montreal, the George Williams University Affair, when Black students revolted and tore up the campus computing center to protest campus racism (Austin 2018; 2013; Forsythe 1971).

This set the stage for the ALD demonstration in Toronto:

> In Toronto's ALD an estimated three thousand Black people participated as a show of support for the transnational event. On Canadian soil, participants of mostly West Indian heritage "marched past the French, British, Portuguese, US, South African, Israeli and Italian consulates in protest of colonialism and in solidarity of marchers elsewhere." Activities were held in Christies Park, which march organizers later renamed in honor of Marcus Garvey. The Toronto march, which was largely coordinated by Rosie Douglas, included speeches by "Dr. Lew Sealy, Afro-Caribbean Movement, Leroy Butcher,

Augustine Mogibe/ZANU, Hidippo, SWAPO; Joyce Squires, Director, Black Education Project (Toronto); Sonia Davis; Ed Brown (Rap's Brother); Atsu Harley, Black Peoples Movement; Oliver Sampson, Afro-West Indian Organization; and Horace Campbell, Toronto ALD Committee"; former SNCC activist and lawyer Julian Bond; and John Conyers. (Benson 2014, 236)

Linked to the West Indian–based action in Toronto was the ALD motion in other Caribbean countries. ALD was being planned as a coordinated international event at several places in the Caribbean under the leadership of key activists (Table 3).

Table 3. Caribbean African Liberation Day coordinators

Country	Coordinator
Antigua	Tim Hector
Canada	Rosie Douglass
Dominica	Mabel Augustus
Grenada	Maurice Bishop

This was a calculated plan that enabled each of the Caribbean islands to ride the wave of radical politics and provided a pathway for each of these organizers to play prominent roles in the politics of their respective countries. Bishop became prime minister of Grenada in 1979, Rosie Douglas became prime minister of Dominica in 2000, and Tim Hector became a leading figure in his Antiguan-Caribbean Liberation Movement. In terms of the numbers of participants, "[the] gathering in Antigua drew around eight thousand people; the celebration in Dominica reportedly attracted five thousand; and in Grenada an estimated two thousand people demonstrated in support of the Africanist cause" (Benson 2014, 236).

Overall, the first ALD brought out nearly 60,000 people in the 6 major locations (see Table 4).

Table 4. African Liberation Day turnout by location

Location	Participants
Washington, DC	30,000
San Francisco	10,000
Toronto	3,000
Antigua	8,000
Dominica	5,000
Grenada	2,000
TOTAL	58,000

Summary

The ALDCC did not last long as an organizational structure after ALD. It was replaced by ALSC, which will be the focus for the rest of this book. Nonetheless, the first ALD was unique in many respects and must be understood on its own terms. We have been using the term "united front" to describe the diversity and broad character of those organizations and individuals who supported the action. It might have been better to use a related term, "popular front." In the fight against fascism in the mid-twentieth century, both terms were used. A popular front described multiclass unity, while a united front described the unity of diverse working-class forces, including revolutionary tendencies. In these terms, ALD 1972 was a case of a popular front, unity across class lines within the oppressed Black community. This was very much like the national liberation movements in Southern Africa. However, this was not to the extent of the class collaborationism with the capitalist class that was the popular front program advanced by the Communist Party under Earl Browder. Browderism liquidated progress, while the Black popular front advanced it, at least for a time under specific conditions (Foster 1955, 327–34; Murrell and Aptheker 2015, 68, 117).

So, in this context, what can we learn from the ALDCC experience in 1972?

The first major point is that uniting forces takes the work of cadre, dedicated militants who have unity of political line, organizational discipline, and the ability to think in motion and be flexible concerning tactics. In this sense, building unity is working to build a network of common practice. This was accomplished by individual cadre who were recruited from among SNCC veterans, CAP, MXLU, and SOBU/YOBU.

Secondly, much like the anti-Vietnam war movement, the African liberation support movement was a case of thinking global. On the ground in Africa the liberation struggles were explicitly revolutionary. They were fighting to destroy one system and replace it with another. On the global level, there was a postwar general agreement that colonialism should come to an end. In the United States, this meant that the struggle was for a reform of U.S. policy to end direct and indirect support for colonial rule in the colonies of the United States, such as Puerto Rico; in Portuguese colonies via NATO; and by white-minority settler regimes.

The third point, and an aspect related to thinking global, is acting local. In this context, the ALDCC process of reaching out to forces fighting for reforms through their institutional bases was vital to success. This included elected politicians, the Black media, and leading institutions like the church. The key was contacting grassroots organizational forces fighting for Black liberation and helping them connect their on-the-ground efforts to the struggles in Africa.

The main political skill needed is to find the developing consensus in the networks of common practice. People in the struggle will tell an organizer what they think about what they are doing. Learning how to listen in order to sum up what is developing as unity, what convergence of thought and action are organically taking place and therefore can be developed into something at a higher level of unity and action—that is what the cadre have to become expert at. This is practicing the mass line, summing up and focusing on what is possible to guide the masses, based on what can be learned from them.

Finally, in sum, there is always the contradiction between strategy and tactics, between reform and revolution. This is always a matter of principle. The usual unity-building processes for mass action focus on reform struggles, what people will fight for based on the immediate reality of their lives. In the case of support for African liberation, the unity was built by forces who were in motion around their reform issues, but were also drawn to the fight to reform U.S. policy on a global level. This was a special time, just like the peace movement to end the war on Vietnam.

The ALDCC was a major achievement. It led to a new stage of struggle, the radicalization of the Black liberation movement. In the terms we have discussed, it went from being a popular front to a united front. This is the topic of chapter 2.

Chapter 2
1973: Black Liberation

African Liberation Day 1972 was hailed as a major success. This was a revelation: individuals and organizations in the African Diaspora could be a political force rising to support the six armed struggles underway to rid the African continent of European colonization. This made the next action of the Black liberation movement even more important. Something new was possible, but what was it going to be? Who would decide? When would the decision be made? The mantle of national leadership was available, and many local leaders were being challenged to take the struggle to the next level.

The intense political climate following the first ALD formed the context for the development of ALSC following the disbanding of the ALDCC. This chapter on ALSC will cover three topics. The first is the origin and organizational development of ALSC, encompassing the early leadership meetings, the principles of unity, and the issues of discussion and debate. The second topic is ALD 1973, which was planned and carried out as local demonstrations; these will be discussed on a regional basis. The third is the main character of ALSC; because it was based on a dialectic of theory and practice, we will discuss two major cases of ideological discussion and debate, each of which was followed by major campaigns of demonstrations.

The Black media was alive with reports of support for African liberation struggles. This was especially true in the big-city Black communities of New York (*Amsterdam News*), Detroit (*Michigan Chronicle*), *Chicago Defender*, and Los Angeles (*Sentinel*). The Black movement newspapers—*The African World, The Black Panther,* and *Muhammad Speaks*—were especially full of coverage. The Black campus press was also very actively reporting on developments, especially *The Hill Top* of Howard University.

A film was made of ALD 1972. There were two versions, one in English and one in Kiswahili. It was duplicated and made available at cost (Campanella Jr 1972) . Owusu and Kwadwo Akpan took the film to Africa on July 31, 1972. Their trip was discussed in the minutes of a national ALSC meeting in Detroit on September 30:

> They discussed the showing of the ALD film and gave accounts of the meetings and responses from various liberation movements. Meetings were held with SWAPO, OAU Liberation Committee, FRELIMO, FROLIZI, PAC, MPLA, ZAPU, ZANU, and TANU Youth League. The funds raised through the efforts of the ALD Committee members (which amounted to $1,532.00) were given to FROLIZI, for which a return receipt was given. (ALSC 1972a)

FROLIZI (the Front for the Liberation of Zimbabwe) was the joint military command that for a short time united ZANU and ZAPU.

Following this, Amilcar Cabral, one of the most important theoretical leaders of African national liberation movements, made his final trip to the United States. On October 15th he was given an honorary doctorate at Lincoln University, the HBCU previously attended by Kwame Nkrumah of Ghana and Nnamdi Azikiwe of Nigeria. During this event Cabral was presented a check for $2,200, raised by the Boston ALSC committee.

Sharing the podium was Owusu Sadaukai of ALSC, who stated:

> It is an honor for me to represent Malcolm X Liberation University and the African Liberation Support Committee at this very significant event. We feel that Lincoln University is

to be congratulated for what amounts to a bold step in giving Brother Cabral this honorary degree. . . . In the final analysis, our major contribution may lie in our ability to heighten the struggle against racism and imperialism in this country, and our ability to link this struggle up with the one that Brother Cabral's people are waging in Guinea-Bissau. (Sadaukai 1972c, 12)

A few days later Cabral met with movement activists in a meeting set up by the Black activist organization Africa Information Service, which Robert Van Lierop and Prexy Nesbitt had founded (Africa Information Service 1973, 71–92):

> The AIS was also instrumental in coordinating Cabral's final visit to the United States in 1972. During the visit Cabral asked the African Information Service to set up a meeting with various leading forces in the BLM [Black Liberation Movement]. The meeting was held in New York City on the twentieth of October and involved participants from over thirty BLM organizations. The speech was entitled "Connecting the Struggles: An Informal talk with Black Americans," and had a profound and lasting impact on the BLM in all its diversity, as it clearly affirmed the interconnectedness between the African liberation struggles on the continent with those in the United States, the Caribbean, and beyond. (Kali Akuno cited in Manji and Fletcher 2013, 427)

Exactly three months later—January 20, 1973—Cabral was assassinated by the Portuguese state. This was another reminder why armed struggle was necessary to free Africa from colonial domination. Memorial events were held throughout the country by forces seeking to join a movement to support the struggles in Africa.

Origin of ALSC

On the very day of ALD 1972, after the demonstration, key activists on the ALDCC met to sum up the experience and discuss the future. Two major decisions were made: the ALDCC would be disbanded and another meeting to organize next moves would be held. Owusu initially had only planned for one major demonstration, after which people would return to their local areas of work. He was a community organizer with limited experience in national or even regional levels of activism. However, a defining moment had occurred just before the summation meeting took place. Mark Smith pulled Owusu aside and informed him that others were set on keeping the ALD motion going and that it was necessary to maintain some portion of the existing organization. This was a moment for decisiveness, an opportunity to demonstrate leadership. It was made. Owusu went into the meeting prepared to lead the developing consensus to hold a subsequent meeting that could adopt a plan for future work.

This set in motion a series of face-to-face leadership-level meetings that brought ALSC into being (see Table 5).

Table 5. African Liberation Support Committee meetings, 1972–1973

Date	Location
July 6, 1972	Chicago
July 30, 1972	MXLU
September 30, 1972	Detroit
November 4, 1972	Atlanta
December 23, 1972	Washington, DC
February 10, 1973	Chicago
March 31, 1973	Atlanta
April 28, 1973	Greensboro, NC

It is important to note the differences between organizing in the 1970s and in the 2020s. There was a technological difference: meetings could not be held by conference calls or in online Zoom sessions, because neither of those options existed at that time. Activists in the 1970s were not funded to the level of being provided with plane tickets and hotel rooms, with meals, as they are often today. People often carpooled to meetings and were welcomed into people's homes for a place to stay. And when staying in a hotel, several people shared the same room. One can make the comparison by saying that in the 1970s it was bottom-up, local organizations providing the material support for representatives to join in national activities. Today, because of NGO and foundation resources being invested in movement projects for reform, the process is often top down, with funding coming through an organizing center and then being disbursed to local representation, all expenses covered. The old adage comes into play, sometimes directly and sometimes subtly, "He who pays the piper calls the tune."

> The first meeting was of a small group of seven people who met in Chicago on July 6th. At the second, ALSC was established: "The meeting was attended by invited persons who [had] worked most actively in the organization and mobilization of people to attend the African Liberation Day demonstration on May 27, 1972. The group was composed of thirteen members of the now dissolved African Liberation Day Coordinating Committee (ALDCC) or their designated representatives, the former national ALDCC staff, local ALDCC coordinators and several other persons active in the Pan-Africanist movement in the United States" (ALSC 1972a).

It has to be part of the record that patriarchy was a major negative force in the movement at this time. Women played key roles at all levels of ALSC, but were never fully empowered.

Important decisions were made at the MXLU meeting. The group adopted the name African Liberation Support Committee (ALSC). They also wrote a statement of governing principles and objectives that was formally adopted at the next meeting in Detroit, as well as electing leadership:

1. To provide financial, material, and moral support to the liberation struggles now being fought on the African continent against the remaining European colonial governments.
2. To inform our brothers and sisters in the U.S., Canada, and the Caribbean of the nature and importance of the liberation struggles and to emphasize our relationship to the overall struggles of African people against racism and imperialism.
3. To inform our brothers and sisters on the African continent about our position on the nature of the struggles in the West-

ern Hemisphere with a view toward cultivating a reciprocal relationship.

4. To work for the removal of the military, economic, and political support of white minority ruled governments in Southern Africa.

5. To provide public support and encouragement for all African governments which aid the Southern African Liberation Movement. (ALSC 1972b)

The following officers were elected: Owusu Sadaukai as chairman, Don Lee (now Haki Madhubuti) as vice-chairman, Hisani Mweusi as secretary, and Nelson Johnson as treasurer. This reflected the organizational unity of three cadre organizations: MXLU (Owusu), SOBU/YOBU (Johnson), and CAP (Lee and Mweusi). Eight other areas of work were set in motion: National Collections (Roger Newell and Dianizulu); Fund Raising for Liberation Struggles (John Warfield); African Liberation Day (Gene Locke and Mwanza); Watch dog Committee (Florence Tate); United African Appeal Month (Floyd Johnson); Research (James Turner); Intensive Education Campaign; Gulf Boycott (Randall Robinson).

During these early meetings, several issues were debated that began to shape the political character of ALSC. A global issue was raised by forces close to Stokely Carmichael (Kwame Ture) concerning Israel. The call was for ALSC to condemn Israel as an enemy to African people, especially for their close economic and military relationships with South Africa (Minty and Munazzamat al-Tahrir al-Filastiniyyah 1990). This was not adopted, because a majority led by Courtland Cox said that ALSC was not yet strong enough to resist an attack from the Zionists, and we had to be clear on the relationship between the Arab states and Africans. There was memory of the attack on SNCC for their stand on Israel and people were hesitant to take such a position before ALSC was fully formed (Teltsch 1967).

Despite the initial caution, this stance was advanced by voices in ALSC in subsequent meetings and demonstrations. A press release issued by the Boston African Liberation Support Committee took a clear stand on October 24, 1973: "The Boston

African Liberation Support Committee feels it is important to speak out on the Middle East situation because it is imperative that all Black people become aware of the true nature of this issue and support those people who are potential allies in our struggle against racism and imperialism, contrary to that analysis being given by the national news media, the local press, and some black organizations. . . . [We] call upon all Black people to protest U.S. aid to Israel and to support the Palestinian people and their Arab allies in their just struggle against Zionism and U.S. imperialism" (Boston ALSC 1973).

Second, there was a concern with identity. Roy Innes of CORE charged that mulattoes were a major danger to Black people and a position should be taken against them. This position, reflecting an old discourse between Garvey and Du Bois, was summarily rejected (Payne 2021, 42–45). A position was adopted that no whites would be permitted to participate in the activities of the support committee. However, local ALSC committees could invite organizations of people of color to join in the demonstrations. The African People's Party (APP), represented by Muhammad Ahmad and Modibo Kadalie, advanced the position that Black people in the United States were a captive nation. This position was rejected by majority vote.

These identity issues were necessary challenges to Black unity, themes resulting from the pervasive racism that ravaged the Black experience and forced Black activists to struggle over the issue of who is Black and what should the relationship between Blacks and whites be in the movement. Skin color was rejected as a criterion and separatism was also rejected. Third-world unity was accepted as a path to world revolution, but ALSC was not yet ready to link the Black liberation movement with the multi-national working class in class struggle.

Organizational issues took on greater importance as the months went on. The nature of membership became an issue. In some local areas, one or more local or national organizations formed an ALSC committee, but then individuals also joined, making ALSC the only organization to which they belonged. This led to a crisis of democracy in the ALSC organizational process: how were votes organized, and did individuals or organizations count? This was particularly critical for several locations: New York, Philadelphia, Atlanta, and Northern California. In these cases, national organizations dominated the committees at the expense of individuals who joined ALSC as their only organization. Individual members felt their democratic standing was being marginalized. This continued to be a critical issue that was left to be sorted out at the local level.

The most devastating issue was the use of threats and intimidation to seize leadership. This took place in Northern California. Hard-core dogmatic Black nationalists actually stormed into a meeting with attack dogs barking and gnashing their teeth in order to seize control. This led to the original local leadership, including those on the left, leaving and appealing directly to the national ALSC leadership to intervene. A separate structure was developed, and the gangster clique was delinked and marginalized. This act of desperation was the beginning of political turmoil.

The issue that became the center of debate was the relationship between the struggle in Africa and the Black liberation movement in the United States. Were they comparable? If not, then what were the similarities and differences? The initial decision was to maintain a singular focus on supporting the struggles in Africa. As ALSC committees developed and ramped up their struggle to support African liberation, it became clear that this was also a struggle against the U.S. capitalist class and the state. African liberation support became closely linked to the fight for Black liberation. This became the main issue dominating the ideological struggle that we will discuss at length.

A major statement was made by the ALSC Chairperson Owusu Sadaukai at the December 1972 meeting in Washington, DC. He spoke as a community organizer trying to anchor ALSC in pragmatic mobilization tactics:

> The question of what we do in the U.S. comes to us from two perspectives: 1. That people have to be worked with in terms of their existing concrete reality. To work with people in a significant way is to work with them on those problems that they see existing in their daily lives. 2. On the other hand, a

correct analysis of racism and imperialism indicated that it must be understood in terms of its effect on the day to day lives of Black people. So, although Africa seems abstract and far away, in reality what is happening there, is as close to us as Harlem is. (Peoples College 1975)

Within ALSC, the Black nationalist form of Pan-Africanism was being met by a rising political tendency grounded in the class character of the Black masses in the United States and Africa.

The Black Left

At this time, the Black liberation movement was developing into two wings, one with a primary focus on autonomous forms of cultural self-determination and the other focused on the working-class struggles of the Black masses. Both focused on racism. The cultural tendency had its main national organizational base in the Congress of African People (CAP):

> The Congress of African People [meeting] in Atlanta, Georgia, was the successor to the annual National Black Power Conferences held between 1966 and 1968. . . . That summit signaled the introduction of the leading black nationalists into the national black political community that was just taking shape. The Atlanta Congress also represented a temporary end to the political exclusion of black nationalists from the dynamics of the national political arena." (Woodard 1999, 162–163)

This was symbolized when the newly elected CAP chairman, Heyward Henry, simultaneously "embraced Minister Louis Farrakhan of the Nation of Islam on his right and Whitney Young of the National Urban League on his left, holding their hands aloft in a gesture of unity" (Woodard 1999, 164). While this was a moment of unity, it was not a sustainable relationship. But for ALSC, CAP cadre became an essential organizational resource that built several local committees.

What had also emerged was a Black left. Organizations had formed based on the interests of workers and poor Black people. These organizations developed a criticism of capitalism, in the course of their search for why Black people were oppressed and exploited beyond the simplistic explanation that it was the result of the evil nature of white people from Europe. There had been Black people in the older multi-national communist organizations, namely the Communist Party USA (CPUSA), Socialist Workers Party (SWP), and Progressive Labor Party (PL), as well as spin-offs like the California Communist League. What was new in the period was a Black left that emerged out of the Black liberation movement, people who started out fighting against racism and developed into class-conscious revolutionaries, reflecting their working-class roots (Elbaum 2002, 114–15).

The first major new Black left national organization was the Black Panther Party for Self-Defense, founded in Oakland, California, in October 1966. This was only months after the Black Power slogan was chanted, for the first time, in Mississippi by SNCC activists Stokely Carmichael (aka Kwame Ture) and Willie Ricks (aka Mukasa Dada).

> The Black Panther Party at one time or another, from its founding in October 1966 to early 1971, had official chapters with the same name or affiliated organizations under other names in at least 61 cities in 26 states and the District of Columbia. This activity was conducted under the supervision of 13 Black Panther Party chapters and five branches, twenty National Committees to Combat Fascism (NCCF), and two community information centers. NCCF's were Panther controlled/multi-racial local committees, sometimes referred to as "organizing bureaus", aimed at maintaining a link between black militants and whites willing to work on the Panthers' behalf. The admission of whites to NCCF membership also gave the Party a broader base for fundraising and propaganda purposes. (New York Public Library n.d.)

The organization that represented an awakened Black working class was the League of Revolutionary Black Workers (LRBW), founded in May 1968 (Hamlin and Gibbs 2013; League of Revolutionary Black Workers 1970; Geschwender 1978; Georgakas and Surkin 1998; Kadalie 2000, 192–221; Ahmad 2008, 237–286). This Detroit-based movement led to a nationally-oriented BWC, founded in December 1970 (Black Workers Congress n.d.; "Draft Proposal: Manifesto of the International Black Workers

Congress" n.d.). What made the LRBW so special is that it was the organic expression of Black workers bursting forth from the struggle on the factory floor, first in the automobile factory and then in many other industrial workplaces. The organizational form was a RUM—a "revolutionary union movement" named for the company that employed the workers. The LRBW led wildcat strikes, organized students, and disseminated propaganda in the community via the media, discussion groups, a bookstore, and a publishing project. The Panthers were on the street while the LRBW drilled down into where people worked

> The LRBW was made up of many components such as DRUM [Dodge Revolutionary Union Movement], FRUM [Ford Revolutionary Union Movement], ELRUM, JRUM, and the others in such workers' organizations. These were supposed to be the most important components which were initially the central focus of the major organizational effort. But the League also had many supportive components like the Inner City Voice, the organ of the organization; Black Star Printing; Black Star Productions; and the International Black Appeal. (Kadalie 2000, 314)

Another Black left organization was Peoples College, founded in 1970. It was an example of a left organization in the context of Black Studies, first at Fisk University, and then with bookstores in Nashville, Atlanta, and Riverside, California. Using Marxism as a framework, Peoples College published the first textbook in Black Studies, which is now on display at the Smithsonian Museum of African American History and Culture (Alkalimat 1986).

Pan-Africanist movement activists began to form vanguard organizations, notably the APP (1971), led by Muhammad Ahmad; All African People's Revolutionary Party (APRP) led by Kwame Ture (1972); and the African People's Socialist Party (APSP) (May 1972) led by Omali Yeshitela. All three of these cadre organizations pointed to a post-capitalist future, usually referred to as socialism. Initially, the APP was based in Philadelphia, the APRP in Washington, DC, and the APSP in Florida.

Material Support for African Liberation

One of the first issues taken up by ALSC was fundraising to support its work, which was mainly to provide material support for the fighting forces on the ground in Africa. At a national meeting in Greensboro, North Carolina, on April 28th, 1973, it was decided who would get financial support from ALSC. Nineteen local committees discussed and voted regarding different organizations. What is clear is that decisions were being made by committees with different exposure to the movements possibly to be funded, based on their members' having met with representatives, read material, and listened to comrades make a case. The following discussion is a summation of what took place at the Greensboro meeting (ALSC 1973a).

After considerable discussion, votes were taken on which groups to support. Seven of the nineteen committee votes did not include any groups to support, but instead either voted to support the final decisions of the body and/or simply voted to give no funds to the Organization of African Unity Liberation Committee on the basis that some of the African governments were neocolonial regimes who could not be trusted. Seven groups got votes (Table 6):

Table 6. Liberation groups receiving votes at Greensboro meeting

Group	Votes
PAIGC	11
FRELIMO	10
ZAPU-ZANU	7
UNITA	6
MPLA	2
PAC	2
OAU-LC	2

The most votes went to PAIGC and FRELIMO, the two organizations that had the most direct impact on activists in ALSC, the former because their leading theoretician Amilcar Cabral made great contributions in theory and made such an important trip to the United States and the latter because Owusu had been their guest and reported on his experience in the liberated territory of Mozambique. Fred Brooks, the ALSC representative based in Dar es Salaam, argued that the only organizations waging armed struggle were PAIGC and FRELIMO. The ZAPU-ZANU alliance was supported out of a desire to promote unity in the movement, to set that unity motion as an example.

UNITA was supported in part because they had appealed to a nationalist sentiment, and partly because they had a representative in the United States who had been networking extensively. UNITA was supported by representatives from New Jersey; Texas; Rochester, NY; Los Angeles; and Ohio. Kwadwo Akpan had spent time in Africa building a relationship with UNITA. Lucious Walker, representing IFCO, had just spent three weeks in Zambia and on that basis argued strongly for UNITA. He was joined by Owusu in this debate, who had had a positive connection with UNITA, and was not impressed by MPLA when he was in Africa. The final decision was noted in the ALSC minutes:

> The National African Liberation Support Committee will divide equally 80% of the money collected between the four groups [at the top of the above list]. The other 20% of the money will be set aside for additional funding in 1973 of groups based on the recommendations of a special subcommittee appointed at the meeting. (ALSC 1973a)

The two omissions were the lack of support provided to MPLA in Angola and to all the groups in South Africa. These decisions are especially striking, because MPLA and ANC ended up forming governments after each country gained its independence. MPLA received two votes, as did the Pan African Congress of South Africa. This will be discussed later, as it directly relates to support from the Soviet Union and global support for MPLA and the ANC.

In the future, more-informed decisions would have to be made, with every committee having the necessary information so that a consensus could be reached. The only unanimous decision was to establish a committee to further investigate various liberation movements for ALD 74. The committee consisted of Kwadwo Akpan (chair), Tanya Russell, John Warfield, Jimmy Reeves, Gene Locke, Abdul Alkalimat, Fred Brooks, Nelson Johnson, Alice Reid, and Ron Walton.

African Liberation Day

The plan for ALD 1973 became the main focus of ALSC. The main slogan set the theme at the national level: "There Is No Peace with Honor! African People Are at War with Imperialism at Home and Abroad!" This was a critical change from 1972, when the slogan was "Breaking the Chains of Oppression Thru Black Unity." Where oppression had been the problem before, now imperialism was identified as the opponent, and the method of struggle, formerly unity, was war. This change of theme carried the ideological struggle forward, as ALSC was adapting to the politics of the leading African Liberation Movement organizations, representatives of which were in the United States and had made contact with many ALSC activists.

ALSC was developing as a national network of forces, forming statewide organizing networks for one or more demonstrations. Key cities were the foci in each state. A major decision targeted ALD 73 for local demonstrations instead of one major national one. This was designed to strengthen local organizing, to go deep among the masses with the general line of building an anti-imperialist political culture. This process led every local organization, though the programs of action were diverse, to connect what it was doing to the struggles in Africa. The situations were different, but general issues like health, education, and economic security were common across the country. Then, of course, ALSC committees had to react to the general political line of the African organizations and that began to intensify the debate over the relative importance of racism compared to imperialism.

This was summed up by the ALSC National chairman Owusu Sadaukai:

> By expanding the demonstrations to more locations, we were able to increase the number of people who either planned, organized, or otherwise participated in this year's

demonstrations. This is tremendously important as it expands the base of people who now have some understanding and some commitment to the international struggle of our people. (Owusu Sadaukai cited in Benson 2014, 258)

The organizational plan was implemented in every region of the country. Our evidence is from media and official ALSC national minutes, but we are aware that this does not cover all activity, as people were initiating actions based on personal networking that was not within any formal ALSC organizational process. Here is a list of states and countries where actions took place in 1973 (Table 7).

Table 7. Locations of 1973 African Liberation Day actions

USA–East	USA–South	USA–Midwest	USA–West	International
Massachusetts	Tennessee	Illinois	Northern California	Tanzania
New Jersey	Georgia	Indiana	Southern California	Montreal
Connecticut	Maryland	Michigan	Colorado	Toronto
Washington, DC	North Carolina	Ohio	Oregon	Antigua
New York	Louisiana	Minnesota		St. Vincent
Pennsylvania	Texas			
	South Carolina			
	Delaware			

This description of ALD 73 by region is based on media reports, particularly those in *The African World* and *Muhammad Speaks,* and reports recorded in the national minutes of the ALSC Steering Committee (ALSC 1973b; 1973d; Lee 1973; Mosby, 17X, and Kashif 1973).

The East

The main organizational bases for ALSC on the East Coast were in New York and New Jersey. Three demonstrations—New York City, Rochester, and Buffalo—took place in the former. The New York City ALSC had been active in fundraising, raising $800 in a December benefit with Mark Smith and Don Lee, and $2,400 in February with Owusu and the Tanzanian UN Ambassador Salim Salim. Their fundraising activities during the month of May totaled $5,000, based on sales of buttons, posters, and bumper stickers as well as direct solicitations. The demonstration was a march from rich corporate Manhattan headed north to the Black community of Harlem. Statements were read at the South African Mission and the offices of Union Carbide and General Motors. Approximately 2,500 people participated in the demonstration.

The New York City ALSC formed an ALDCC that replicated the 1972 form of organization, creating an autonomous body without clarity about its organizational commitment to following the national decisions of ALSC. These local activists did not shy from exposing organizational weaknesses. Their self-criticisms were reported in the minutes:

> Speakers list too long . . . Distribution of materials at march inadequate. Didn't establish information centers in other parts of the city. . . . Lack of concrete analyses of local community consistent with conditions faced on day-to-day basis. More youth involvement. . . . More direct personal contact. More security needed following fundraising activities. (ALSC 1973d, 13–14)

Both ALSC activists and representatives of the African liberation organizations spoke at the New York City rally, among them Ambassador Hady Toure of Guinea; Sister Bernice Jones, Black Panther Party; Mark Smith, vice-chairman of YOBU; Tony Gonsalves, PAIGC; Joseph Munzara, ZANU; Colonel Vundasi, UNIA; Waldaba Steward, from Brooklyn; Jitu Weusi of The East; Roger Newell, YOBU; and Brother Charles Kinyatta. Basketball star Earl "The Pearl" Monroe also made a statement of support.

Buffalo had 1,000 people in a demonstration that focused on the fight for educational reform. There were several speakers, including James Williams, principal of Woodlawn Junior High School; Augustus Adair, executive director of the Congressional

Black Caucus; Dr. Claude Clapp, deputy superintendent of the Buffalo School Board; Ted Kirkland, former president of the Afro-American Policeman's Association; Musa Harkeen of Buffalo ALSC; and James Pitts of the Buffalo ALSC.

It rained in Rochester, so events started late, but still the march and rally grew to 1,500. Speakers included Brother Sikhanyiso Ndlovu from ZAPU; a representative of the Welfare Rights Organization; and Brother Akinlabi, the Rochester ALSC chairman. Drummers, dancers, and films were also part of the day of activities.

Twelve ALSC committees were formed in New Jersey for this ALD. People came to Newark in 20 buses and grew to a mass of 2,500. Under ALSC guidelines, third-word organizations were encouraged to participate. Speakers included Amiri Baraka of the Committee for a Unified NewArk and representatives from UNITA, the Kwame Nkrumah Institute in London, the Black Student Organization, and the Spirit House Movers. The Newark Board of Education declared an African Liberation Week.

The Boston ALSC led the way in fundraising for its ALD with over $11,000. Representatives from thirty-five groups were recruited onto the local steering committee. They planned for two days of activities, with lots of media, and a march and rally of over 1,000 people. They marched past Polaroid and protested its involvement with the South African evil passbook system.

Several hundred Black people from cities in Connecticut (Hartford, Bridgeport, Stratford, Middletown, and Waterburg) joined in the march and rally in New Haven. The march made stops to protest at Yale University, Shell Oil, Mobil Oil, and Holiday Inn, and the rally that followed drew over 350 people.

There were two demonstrations in Pennsylvania, a statewide one in Philadelphia and then a local one in Pittsburgh. It rained in Philadelphia, but nevertheless 500 people marched and staged a rally. Speakers included Father Paul Washington, honorary chairman of the Philadelphia ALSC; Diallo Atiba, Mwalimu of Children of Africa School in Harrisburg; Dave Richardson, Pennsylvania state representative; Alice Walker, director of the ARD Self-Help Center; Sarafim Santos of the Angolan Student

Association; and Janet Whittaker, Tony Dodson, and Sam Rosemond, all of the Philadelphia ALSC.

The largest demonstration in the East was in Washington, DC, drawing 5,000 people, even though it rained there as well. A major resource was the extensive coverage by the Howard University radio station WHUR. The march stopped at several places to make statements of protest, including the embassies of Portugal and South Africa and the offices of ITT and International Harvester. Speakers included Donald Isaac, the DC ALSC chairman; Bishop Smallwood Williams; Sister Neil Pendleton on behalf of federal government workers; Ken Wilson, a high school representative; Sister Bobbie McMan, a welfare mother and community organizer; Tim Thomas and John McClendon of YOBU; Brother Doug Moore; and Brother Bill Street.

The South

North Carolina, as it had been since the formation of the ALDCC in 1972, was a major center of activity in the South for ALD 73. Organizing leading up to ALD was carried out in thirty communities throughout the state, with rallies in four major cities: Raleigh, Greensboro, Durham, and Chapel Hill. The biggest ALD demonstration saw 3,000 people gather in Raleigh. What helped boost turnout for this demonstration was that from the rural parts of the state, church buses came, making stops along the way to pick up people in small towns.

Speakers at the rally in Raleigh included Owusu Sadaukai, national chairman of ALSC; Nelson Johnson, YOBU national chairman; Howard Lee, mayor of Chapel Hill; Sister Mack, a community organizer, State Representative H. M. Michaux; Atty. Frank Balance; Clarence Lightner, Raleigh City councilman; Sister Christine Strudwick; Rex Harris; Rev. Wilson Lee; Rev. C. W. Ward; and John Mendez, the North Carolina ALSC chairman.

The Columbia, South Carolina demonstration/rally, in which 5,000 people took part, began on the steps of the state capital and then marched to the rally site in the Black community. Notably, the organizers did outreach in the prisons and got 2,000 inmates to demonstrate their support. Speakers included Lawrence Toliver, organizer of families of prisoners; Mto Whitaker, the South Carolina ALSC chairman; Earl Moultrie, coordinator of ALSC in the prisons; Robert R. Woods, South Carolina state legislator; Brother Redfern II, of The Black-On-Nation; and several additional community activists.

Several groups participated in Baltimore: Pan African Nationalist Union, BWC, George Jackson Freedom Movement, and the Baltimore Black Assembly. Over 200 people participated in a rally with local community speakers. Even with rain in Wilmington, Delaware, almost 500 people participated in the march/rally. Speakers included J. Chaka Duffeh from Gambia; Mbongowah Thembi from Cameroon; and Garveyite Baba Hilbert Keys.

The Atlanta ALD demonstration of 200 people began at the grave of Martin Luther King, went through downtown, and ended up in the Atlanta University Center at Clark College. The organizing committee included the Pan African Work Center, BWC, Black Convention, Peoples Committee to Insure Justice, Radio Free Georgia, Atlanta Black Arts Institute, Institute of the Black World, and the All African Peoples Party. Speakers included Congressman Andrew Young and Zimbabwe Professor Rukudzo Murapa, African Heritage Studies Association.

The New Orleans demonstration was held despite rainy weather. The march went from the Black community through the downtown business area to the International Trade Mart, headquarters for the port of New Orleans. A total of 400 people joined in the demonstration. Speakers included Willie Kgositsile, a South African poet and member of the ANC and SACP; and Lionel Makeni, BWC.

The ALSC chapter in Nashville, Tennessee, was organized by People's College. Organizing efforts created committees in three other cities in Tennessee: Jackson, Memphis, and Chattanooga. An independent ALD committee with their own demonstration was created in Knoxville. In Nashville the march began at First Baptist Church and weaved its way through the Black community to Hadley Park, where the rally took place. The size of the demonstration grew to 1,000. Speakers included Abdul Alkalimat,

Chairman of People's College; Edward Bailey, Nashville ALSC; members of the Rank and File Workers Committee; and members of the A. Philip Randolph Institute.

The Texas ALSC activity was based on monthly meetings in the following cities: Houston, Dallas, Austin, San Antonio, Orange, McKinney, and Huntsville. All the committees came together to demonstrate in Houston; people from Denton, Orange, and Galveston also participated. The total size of the demonstration reached 2,000. The march made stops at the international headquarters of Gulf Oil Corporation, the Houston federal building, the First City National Bank, and in the Black community to speak about Black political prisoners.

The ALD 73 speakers in Houston included the following: Ray London, a postal worker; Bill Stoner, Dallas ALSC; Bobby Everett, attorney and member of the Houston School Board; Dwight Allen, African Youth Party; Cedric Joubert, National Black Law Students; DeLoyd Parker, director of SHAPE Center; Pearce Gqobose, Pan Africanist Congress; and Dawolu Gene Locke, Texas ALSC chairman.

The West

There were two demonstrations in California—Oakland in the north and Los Angeles in the south. The northern demonstration included the following organizations: Family, Peoples' Defense Committee, United Services, the AAPRP, Muhammad Ahmad Defense Committee, Pan African Secretariat, Muslims, and the BWC. In the Bay Area the seeds of conflict between nationalists and Marxists were germinating into open conflict, but not with fatalities such as had occurred during the conflict at UCLA in 1969 (Gordon 2010). The Southern California demonstration was based mainly on older movement activists, numbering about 250.

There was no march in Denver, because ALSC could not obtain a permit. Instead, there were three separate rally events—400 people at the federal building, 500 people at Manual High School, and a final rally of 200. About forty people organized by YOBU drove in from Kansas. The speakers for the day included Dan Muse, a lawyer; Rev. Floyd Parker; Steve Evans, a student at

Denver University; Yasseff Karauma, chairman of Denver ALSC; Watlington Webb; Vatrice Goodloe, Ron Washington, and Duane Vann of YOBU; and Matiswa Chriungo.

The largest demonstration in the west was in Portland, where 5,000 people joined in. Speakers in Portland included Ken Ford, of the Black Panther Party, and Jo Harris, of the Movement New Hope.

The Midwest

The organizing committee for ALD 73 in Chicago included the following: UFOMI, the Confederation of African Organizations, Black Workers, Black Socialist Alliance, the African Student Association, and a few churches. A large crowd of 3,000 gathered in Washington Park to hear the following speakers: Brother Ahmed Sekou Toure, nephew of Guinea President Sekou Toure; poets Gwendolyn Brooks, Don Lee, and Eugene Perkins; Lerone Bennett, Ebony Magazine historian; Dick Gregory, comedian; Lu Palmer, journalist; Bobby Wright, psychologist; Stan Willis, lawyer; Russ Meek; and Simpson Mutambanegue, a representative from Zimbabwe.

The Columbus, Ohio, demonstration drew together 2,500 participants, based on state committees in Columbus, Cleveland, Dayton, Youngstown, Campton, and Wilberforce. A number of organizations helped make the rally possible: the Black Police Association; Freedom, Inc.; CORE; Republic of New Africa; SCIA; Organization for Black Unity; Pan African Core; Umoja Sasa School; Institute of African American Affairs at Kent University; and UNIA. The march included a stop to protest at the federal building. The speakers included Esiah Zheurwara, representative from FROLIZI; Gena Thorton, UNIA head; Ron Daniels, Ohio Black Political Assembly; Dan Viapree, a student from the West Indies; and Jim Roseboro, a Columbus city councilman.

The ALSC-led demonstration in Minnesota was in St. Paul, with people coming from Minneapolis as well. The organization in the organizing process involved the following: Malcolm X Pan African Institute; Institute for African Education; Nationa Time Choir; BWC; Minnesota Black Assembly; and a few Black minsters. About 500 people participated in the march held in the Black community. Key activists spoke at the rally: Lucious Walker, executive director of IFCO; Sister Jahina Karon, Minnesota Correctional Institute for Women; Lansine Kaba, professor of history from Guinea; Professor John Warfield, ALSC National finance chairman; and Kojo Odingo, Minnesota ALSC chairman.

The Detroit demonstration drew together 4,000 people, including people from Lansing, Saginaw, and Windsor, Ontario. Some of the organizations involved were the Pan African Congress, the BWC, Project Dare, Pan-African Students, UNIA, and the Marcus Garvey Institute. Three radio stations covered the rally, so the greater community had full access to the speakers. They include the following: Kwadwo Akpan, Michigan ALSC chairman; Kwame Atta, financial chair of the Michigan ALSC; Nadine Brown, newspaper columnist; Maluzolele Muluto, representative of UNITA; Haywood Brown; and Professor Melba Boyd, sister of a brother killed by Detroit's notorious police unit—"STRESS" (Stop the Robberies, Enjoy Safe Streets).

The largest march/demonstration in the Midwest was in Indianapolis, Indiana, with the participants numbering 4,000. It was attended by people from thirteen cities, including South Bend, Bloomington, Crawford, Fort Wayne, Gary, and Richmond, who had served on the statewide organizing committee. The speakers included Fred Hord, Malcolm X Institute of Wabash College; Wali Siddiq, Congress of African People; Ruwa Chiri, chairman of UFOMI; Julia Carson, Indiana state representative; Reggie Jones, ALSC; Richard Hatcher, mayor of Gary; Walter Fauntroy, U.S. congressman; Mari Evans, poet; and Endesha Alimayn, chairperson of the Indiana ALSC.

International

There were two demonstrations in Canada, in Montreal, Quebec, and Toronto, Ontario. The day's events in Montreal, coordinated by Brenda Paris, international secretary of ALSC, saw 400 people participate. There were two speakers during the march, Hidipo Hamutenya of SWAPO and Jacques Roy, a supporter of MPLA, and another two at the rally, Tami Mhlambiso of the African National

Congress of South Africa and Queen Mother Moore, founder of the Universal Association of Ethiopian Women. Short messages of solidarity from the following were shared: Henry Langdon, Union United Church and UNIA; Sister Charmaine Edmead, Black Education Centre; Brother Carl Whittaker (Lumumba), Negro Community Center; Brother Ashton Lewis, Board of Black Educators; Leroy Butcher, Cote des Neiges Black Community Project; Sister M. Dash, Coloured Women's Club; Sister Adeleine, Comite Haitian Action Patriotique; and Brother Sebastian Ebata, Association des Etudiants Camerounais a Montreal. The Toronto rally grew to 1,000, with speeches by Rosie Douglas from Dominica, Brother Tudawa from Zimbabwe, Petros Johannes from Ethiopia, and several other local activists.

The ALD march and rally in Antigua was led by Tim Hector, the Caribbean representative on the International Steering Committee of ALSC. Hector's organization, the Afro-Caribbean Liberation Movement, organized the day's events. The ALD events in St. Vincent were disrupted by the police and could not be held successfully.

The newly formed ALSC office in Tanzania organized an ALD rally, at which the Tanzanian Minister of Defense, the head of the Youth League of the Tanzanian African National Union, and Fred Brooks, of Tanzanian ALSC, spoke.

What is clear from this description of ALD local demonstrations is that a broad and diverse group of Black activists was being pulled into mass action in support of African liberation—our listing of the speakers and organizers demonstrates this. To some extent the broad unity of 1972 was being maintained, and at the same time there was a shift to a sharper anti-imperialist focus.

It is also clear that culture symbolism was important, as most of the parks and public places were being renamed in honor of African leaders. During the events drummers, dancers, and singers were featured prominently, as were poets.

New ALSC Leadership

The growing local base committees of ALSC and the increased ALD mobilization at the local level increased the need for a national organizational structure to maintain stability of focus and coordination. Driven by the experience of two years of national and local activity, new leadership was elected at the June 1973 Frogmore meeting. This led to a change in the composition of the participants in the national meeting: previously two representatives from each state had taken part, and now it was just the new twelve-member International Executive Committee.

Table 8. 1973–1974 African Liberation Support Committee–International Executive Committee

Position	Name	Location	Employment	Organization
Chairman	Gene Locke	Houston, TX	Movement	Lynn Eusan Institute
Secretary	Brenda Paris	Montreal, QC	College Teacher	ALSC
Treasurer	John Warfield	Austin, TX	College Teacher	ALSC
Research & Development	Abdul Alkalimat	Nashville, TN	College Teacher	Peoples College
Production & Distribution	Nelson Johnson	Greensboro, NC	Movement	YOBU
Fund Raising	Akinlabi	Rochester, NY	Movement	Independent Black School
Investigation	Kwadwo Akpan	Detroit, MI	Freelance Photographer	Pan Africanist Congress USA
Southern Region	Owusu Sadaukai	Greensboro, NC	Movement	MXLU
Northeast Region	Amiri Baraka	Newark, NJ	Movement	CAP
Midwest Region	Don Lee	Chicago, IL	Movement	CAP
Western Region				
Caribbean	Tim Hector	Antigua	Movement	Afro-Caribbean Liberation Movement

The largest number of representatives was based in the south, five out of the twelve. They were not in the territory often designated as the Black Belt Nation, but they demonstrated that the most organized base of ALSC was in the south, the region most steeped in Black history and where the majority of Black people still lived. There was no regional representative yet selected for the Western Region, due to conflicts calling into question the stability of representation.

In general, this new executive committee reflected the radicalization of middle-class activists. The pattern of employment reflects a self-determination thrust, either being based in the movement or a creation thereof (e.g., Black Studies) or being self-employed.

One of the major new developments was in the area of research and development. This committee had been relatively inactive, but now emerged as a major resource for the political coordination of local committees in national campaigns. Political education became a major focus for local committees in preparation for campaigns of struggle.

Immediately after ALD 1973, an ALSC delegation, including ALSC Chairman Dawolu Gene Locke, Secretary Brenda Paris, and Owusu Sadaukai, former chairman and current coordinator of the ALSC southern region, made a month-long visit to Africa. The trip had three objectives: to meet with the designated liberation organizations and deliver money to them and to meet with government officials of Tanzania, Zambia, and Guinea. In Tanzania, the ALSC delegation was hosted for one week by TANU.

Locke prepared a written report on the trip:

> Our discussions with liberation movements and government officials in Tanzania and Guinea tended to reaffirm our already stated position of supporting liberation movements in Africa while struggling against monopoly capitalism and racism here in North America (particularly in the U.S.A.). Representatives of FRELIMO, PAIGC, and ZANU were very clear in their appeal to ALSC about the need to confront imperialism within the U.S.A. President Ahmad Sekou Toure stressed to us our responsibility to challenge imperialism in

the U.S.A., as its defeat is key to the struggles for liberation throughout Africa.

In general, the ALSC delegation was received quite well in Tanzania, Zambia, and Guinea; both as African brothers and sisters from North America and as comrades in struggle. Credit must be given to the ALSC office in Dar es Salaam for its hard work in developing contacts and making the trip productive. The two previous trips by Owusu Sadaukai showed their immense value in introducing the work of ALSC in Tanzania. (Locke 1974a)

Ideological and political discussions, often held on an abstract level, became tangible and focused when connected to actual struggles and not simply the musings of intellectuals. Being on the ground in Africa and in dialogue with the liberation organizations brought clarity to the discussions and debates. During the trip, Malik Chaka, of the ALSC office in Dar es Salaam, detailed the role of African workers and their support of the liberation struggles:

NUTA, The National Union of Tanganyika Workers, voted to have money taken from the salaries of all its members to help the Liberation Fund. The dock workers also pledged to increase the pace of work when racist Rhodesia unilaterally closed the border with neighboring Zambia. In this way the African workers have taken the lead. (Chaka 1973)

Dialectics of Theory and Practice

The plan for ALSC has always been based on the dialectical unity of theory and practice. Ideas came from answering questions raised while building the movement and fighting various forms of oppression and exploitation and from political study of revolutionary theory and the experiences of movements, especially the African liberation movements. The main theoretical development in ALSC came from the practice of organizing the Black community with its working-class social composition, and studying the theoretical work of Kwame Nkrumah, Amilcar Cabral, and Malcolm X. Of course, this led to studying the revolutions in Russia,

100

China, Vietnam, and Cuba. These will be discussed in the next chapter.

Following ALD 1973, the political debate that dominated ALSC concerned how to unify on the basis of a political line, a Statement of Principles. At the founding meeting of ALSC, Courtland Cox had been mandated to chair a committee that would develop a document that would expand on the five governing principles adopted at the meeting (see above). Cox did not convene a committee, but he did write a paper and submit it for discussion (Cox 1972). It was taken up in two national ALSC meetings after ALD 1972 in September and November. Here are the key points (underlined in the original document):

1. We are oppressed.
2. Our struggle has to be one of self-reliance and self-determination.
3. Our struggle must be unified and coordinated with other struggles within the African world in order to be effective.
4. We will focus our human, material and natural resources on the Southern African struggle.
5. We desire to open up communication between African people on both sides of the Atlantic.

There was some discussion, but no decision was reached. A second process was initiated, as reported in the November 1972 minutes:

> "A subcommittee was formed to compose a position paper which is to clarify our (ALSC's) ideological position. The paper must include a) the political thrust of ALSC; b) the focus of our work; c) well defined view of imperialism and racism; d) consideration of the united front character of ALSC. The members of the committee are Ron Walters (Chairman), Courtland Cox, Lou Hunt, Fay Bellamy, and Mwanza. Ron will be responsible for convening the subcommittee and getting the paper duplicated and ready for presentation at the next national meeting" (ALSC 1972c).

At the next meeting in Washington, DC, Ron Walters and Owusu Sadaukai both submitted papers. The Walters paper ended with the following:

"We must therefore: 1. Work ceaselessly to support the Liberation Movements in Angola, Mozambique, Guinea-Bissau, Azania, Zimbabwe, Namibia, and elsewhere; 2. Support the total withdrawal of Europeans from Azania and the restoration of that country to African peoples; 3. Support the philosophy of Pan-Africanism and all progressive African governments; 4. Construct viable lines of communication to organizations and individuals and positive projects which reinforce the notion of linkages within and without the continent" (Walters 1972).

At the Frogmore meeting after ALD 1973 a Statement of Principles was developed and then adopted. The ALSC minutes states that "Documents were presented from California, North Carolina, Tennessee and from Owusu. The body voted to accept the document from North Carolina with additions from the Tennessee document" (ALSC 1973d). Given the importance of this document, and the obvious political and ideological differences that characterized the membership of the ALSC, it is worth reviewing the process by which it was adopted. Owusu lays this out:

> Each state was given copies of the working document, and given time to caucus to review the paper and bring back suggestions for changes. Each section of the paper was discussed separately and voted on separately. Whenever there was any disagreement, more than adequate discussion and debate was allowed to take place in an effort to resolve the differences. In some instances, sub-committees were formed, made up of the disagreeing parties to work on wording they could all agree upon. After the agreement on each section was voted on separately, then finally the whole document was voted on. (Sadaukai, n.d.)

On the basis of this document and the process by which it was adopted, ALSC took its place next to the Pan African Congress movement, the UNIA, the Council on African Affairs, and the American Negro Leadership Conference on Africa in making a major contribution by African Americans to the fight by Africans to gain their independence from European racist colonial domination and imperialist exploitation (ALSC 1973c).

The final document adopted reflected the political development of ALSC based on the changing composition of the local committees and the coalescing of the Pan-African, nationalist, and Black left forces in a united front. Not everyone who had been in the ALDCC endorsed the anti-imperialist position that ALSC shared with the African liberation movements. Some new forces from the left were not in ideological agreement with the Pan-African and nationalist forces. So, the development from this point forward in ALSC included resignations and divergences from the right and the left.

This analysis is not about errors. We want to stress that it is crucial to learn lessons from practice, whatever happens. In science, experiments are tried many times until they work, but each try is a source of lessons. This is a positive view of how knowledge is learned, discovered. The Chinese revolution had the slogan "Fight, fail, fight again, fail again, fight on to victory!" This is the only way forward, for to announce an error presumes that one has the correct answer, like grading a paper in a school classroom. No, this is not appropriate for a movement trying to change society, to change the world.

The Statement of Principles

The ALSC Research Committee identified five sections in the Statement of Principles (SOP) that included thirty-five basic concepts (see Appendix 1):

1. World View: Africa and the Western Hemisphere
2. Finally Got the News
3. Towards a United Front
4. Operational Unity
5. Basic Program

World View

The SOP section on *World View* begins with this paragraph:

> Black people throughout the world are realizing that our freedom will only be won through a protracted struggle against two forces—racism and imperialism. The world

imperialist system festers in Africa and Asia and engulfs the Western Hemisphere as well. In the United States we know it as monopoly capitalism, in Africa it is imperialism in its colonial or neo-colonial form. Wherever it appears, its cornerstone is the white ruling class of the United States of America. (ALSC 1973c)

"Finally Got the News"

Finally Got the News is a slogan taken from the LRBW. Auto workers, while marching during a protest at a UAW convention, chanted "We finally got the news about how our dues are being used!" The LRBW produced a movie about their development and used the slogan as its title. ALSC used it to declare they would bring knowledge to the mass movement about how racism and imperialism, as doctrines, were fundamental to the operations of U.S. capital and the U.S. government.

Towards a United Front

In the section *Towards a United Front*, the SOP opened with a quote from Kwame Nkrumah directing freedom fighters to formulate a plan for unity:

> If we do not formulate plans for unity and take active steps to form political union, we will soon be fighting and warring among ourselves with imperialists and colonialists standing behind the screen and pulling vicious wires, to make us cut each others throats for the sake of their diabolical purposes. (ALSC 1973c)

To prevent the foregoing from happening, the SOP advocated for a flexible approach to theory and practice:

> We cannot be dogmatic. Once we have rooted ourselves in certain principles, we must direct our struggle according to the concrete, changing conditions around us. Real unity will come about not by ignoring differences but by airing those differences and struggling to resolve them. It is through the interplay of ideas and the testing of those ideas in practice that a current position will be hammered out. (ALSC 1973c)

Operational Unity

With an understanding that there is a diversity of ideological positions in the movement, ALSC was concerned that unity be based on what would be possible, so that unity would be operational:

> The struggle we are engaged in must be a broad one—it must be capable of encompassing a diversity of ideological positions, class formations, and social groups. And it must be operational, it cannot be so broad that it cannot function. (ALSC 1973c)

Basic Program

The SOP concluded by presenting a *Basic Program* for ALSC:

1. Raise money for liberation groups in Southern Africa and Guinea-Bissau through the United African Appeal.
2. Conduct educational seminars and programs on racism, feudalism, imperialism, colonialism, and neocolonialism and its effect on the continent of Africa, especially Southern Africa and Guinea-Bissau.
3. Develop and distribute literature, films, and other educational materials on racism, feudalism, imperialism, colonialism, and neo-colonialism and its effect on the continent of Africa, especially Southern Africa and Guinea-Bissau.
4. Participate in and aid the Black community and Black workers in the struggles against oppression in the U.S., Canada, and the Caribbean.
5. Engage in efforts to influence and transform U.S. policy as regards its imperialist role in the world.
6. Engage in mass actions against governments, products, and companies that are involved in or are supportive of racist, illegitimate regimes in Southern Africa and Guinea-Bissau.
7. Support and spearhead annual ALD demonstrations in conjunction with the International African Solidarity Day. (ALSC 1973c)

The adoption of the SOP with this basic program continued to be debated, but avoided the danger always pointed out by Martin Luther King of falling prey to the paralysis of analysis, of getting bogged down in endless debates without doing anything. ALSC debated and continued to wage struggle at the same time, as Table 9 presents:

Table 9. African Liberation Support Committee's practical and theoretical struggles, 1973–1974

Date	Practical Struggles (External)	Theoretical Struggles (Internal)
June 28–July 1		National Steering Committee debates and adopts Statement of Principles at Frogmore, South Carolina
Started in July	National Campaign to Repeal the Byrd Amendment	
November 19–23	Week of Solidarity to Defeat Portuguese Imperialism	
November 24–25		National Steering Committee Second Debate on the Statement of Principles, Greensboro, NC
March 21–28	Week of Solidarity with Struggles Against White Settler Governments in Southern Africa	
May 18–19	Local African Liberation Month Activities, including mass demonstrations	

ALSC Campaigns of Struggle

The Byrd Amendment campaign followed the ALSC program, especially points 4, 5, and 6 listed above. Campaigns of struggle are tactics implementing strategy. This is when theory is turned into action, when talking the talk becomes walking the walk. Up until this point the ALSC research committee had been inactive. In the heat of the struggle over the SOP, the new research committee began producing Handbooks of Struggle to explain to local committees how the campaign was designed to implement the general line of the SOP and help them with tactics in various spheres, including education. The first handbook was on the Byrd Amendment (Peoples College 1977, 11–27).

This struggle involved the importation of chrome by the United States from Zimbabwe, a process that impacted workers there. Chrome is critical to an industrial economy, because when in the form of metallurgical-grade chromite it is an essential component of stainless steel (66%) and alloy steel (16%). Remarkably, at this time southern Rhodesia had 60% of the world reserves of metallurgical-grade chromite (United Nations Association of the United States of America and Student & Young Adult Division 1973, 20, 24).

A crisis began when Ian Smith led the white minority government to declare their independence from Britain in 1965 via a Unilateral Declaration of Independence (UDI), as discussed in chapter 1. This UDI was in opposition to international law, which was oriented toward real anticolonial freedom for the people. The UN Security Council voted eleven to four, with four abstentions, on December 16, 1966, to impose mandatory sanctions on any UN member that imported goods from Rhodesia:

> …the United States supported and voted for this resolution. On May 29, 1968 the Security Council, with the United States vigorously approving, unanimously voted to broaden the sanctions by imposing a virtual total embargo on all trade with, investments in or transfer of funds to Rhodesia. (United Nations Association of the United States of America and Student & Young Adult Division 1973, 17)

All this had happened with the approval of President Lyndon Johnson, marking the first time the United States had followed the UN in sanctioning another country. However, things changed after Richard Nixon became president in 1970:

> On November 17, 1971 President Nixon signed the Military

Procurement Act, which under Section 503, known as the Byrd Amendment, authorized the importation into the United States of any "strategic and critical" metal-bearing ore from a free world country as long as the importation of the same ore from a communist country was not prohibited by law. The wording was deliberately formulated to allow U.S. corporations access to the mineral wealth of Rhodesia, an action that placed Washington in open violation of United Nations (UN) sanctions. The White House decision to defy the global community was based on geopolitical strategy and economic interest but was further reinforced by Nixon's apathy toward the cause of black liberation in southern Africa. (Michel 2018, 1)

This move was in direct support of companies such as Union Carbide and to prevent an increase in importation of chrome from the Soviet Union. There was great controversy in Congress about why this Byrd Amendment was being pushed, but not in the eyes of Congressman Diggs, who sponsored the repeal bill in the House. At a press conference he stated:

In the 1960's the efforts of the American Negro Leadership Conference on Africa, and the African Liberation Day observances of May 1972 and 1973 highlight the continuing efforts by African-Americans to support the African liberation movement in its final phases. In the 1970's the struggle for African liberation in southern Africa represents the last major campaign in this heroic historical process. The Black campaign against the Byrd amendment reflects the continuing Afro-American commitment to total African liberation. (Diggs 1974)

With this campaign, ALSC was confronting U.S. imperialism head-on. By 1973, as a result of the local ALD demonstrations, ALSC had over fifty local committees in formation. These committees lobbied, held protests, and organized a petition drive. A national lobbying effort made contact with about thirty key senators:

On November 26, the National ALSC held a press conference in Washington D.C. on Capitol Hill. Participating ALSC members included Gene Locke, Owusu Sadaukai, Dr. Ronald

Walters (Howard University) & Cheo Hekima—representing Imamu Baraka. Statements of support were given from various national organizations such as the National Black Assembly, Commission for Racial Justice, IFCO and others. After reading the ALSC Press Statement, the approximately 10,000 signatures were presented to Congressman Parron Mitchel and Senator Edward Kennedy. (ALSC, n.d.)

Even before this press conference on the Byrd Amendment, ALSC had carried out its second major campaign, a "Week of Solidarity to Defeat Portuguese Imperialism," from November 19 to 23, 1973. The research committee produced and distributed a second handbook of struggle to all committees (Peoples College 1977, 56–66). Portugal was a poor country and merely fronted for the major imperialist powers. Portugal's area was 35,553 square miles and its population was 8,851,000; in stark contrast, the Portuguese colonies taken together spanned 799,556 square miles and had a population of 12,232,000. Portugal, being underdeveloped, with a 40% illiteracy rate and 43% of its population employed in agriculture, was heavily dependent on its colonies and support from imperialist countries like the United States.

Nixon bankrolled Portugal. From 1946 to 1972 total military aid to Portugal was $334 million, yet Nixon signed the Azores Pact Agreement in December 1971, which promised the country $436 million. The draconian plan to control a colonized population in locked-down places called "strategic villages," designed at Michigan State University and implemented in Vietnam by the United States, was also implemented in Mozambique by the Portuguese. Furthermore, neither the United States nor Portugal had signed the resolution outlawing chemical warfare the UN had approved. The United States used chemical warfare in Vietnam in 1962, and Portugal began using it in its African colonies in 1970. From 1969 to 1972 the United States exported $1,279,790 worth of defoliants, herbicides, and napalm to Portugal for use in Africa.

ALSC had educated thousands of people about the nature of world imperialism in Africa and the role of the United States in this process. The ALSC committees were grasping that the enemy was imperialism, and it was this global system that was the perpetrator of racism against Black people. As the majority of

African nations were aligning with the line of attack of the African liberation organizations, there was a growing realization that our battle was against the same forces exploiting Black people in the United States, and that opened up a new struggle over both theory and practice.

Key statements in the SOP came under closer scrutiny:

> The Time is ripe to develop a United Black people's struggle, a struggle to emerge the Black liberation movement with the process of World Revolution. The question is HOW? . . . Our unity must involve all Black social groups and class formations and we propose that Black workers take the lead. (ALSC 1973c)

To carry this out, the ALSC research committee led by Abdul Alkalimat sent out the SOP to a long list of publications:

Newspapers

- *The Chicago Defender*
- *The New York Amsterdam News*
- *St Louis Argus*
- *Baltimore Afro-American*
- *Atlanta Daily World*
- *Los Angeles Sentinel*
- *Boston Bay State Banner*
- *The Call*
- *Revolution*
- *Guardian*
- *People's Tribune*
- *Challenge*
- *Dailey World*
- *New Solidarity*
- *Militant*
- *El Clariadad*
- *People's World*
- *Black Newark*
- *Muhammad Speaks*
- *Granma*
- *Southern Patriot*

- *Akwansane Notes*
- *News and Letters*
- *Wildcat*
- *Red Tide*
- *Fight Back*
- *The Revolutionary Worker (NJ-NY)*
- *People's Canada Daily News*
- *Workers Daily*
- *New York Times*
- *Wall Street Journal*
- *Liberation News Service*
- *Hsinhua Daily News Service*
- *Palante*

Magazines/Journals
- *Radical America*
- *Socialist Revolution*
- *Monthly Review*
- *Peking Review*
- *New Times*
- *International Affairs*
- *African Agenda*
- *Freedomways*
- *Southern Exposure*
- *Tricontinental News Service*
- *AFL-CIO Federationist*
- *Albania Today*
- *Political Affairs*
- *African Communist*
- *World Marxist Review*
- *Foreign Affairs*

The only publication to reprint the entire SOP was the *Guardian* newspaper in the United States, which did so on September 19, 1973. Florence Tate was a voice in protest as she did not want ALSC to align itself with the "white left." She provides some background:

The following contribution to the [*Guardian* column] Radical Forum is taken from the Statement of Principles formulated at a recent conference of the African Liberation Support Committee. . . . The statement was submitted to the *Guardian* by a member of the ALSC executive committee "for a full review by all progressive forces." (*The Guardian*, September 19, 1973)

Then Tate comments:

Now white radicals in this country, the most treacherous of all white leftists in the world, are being asked to review and make critical comments on ALSC's principles and program. Doesn't that tell us something. . . . [?] (Tate 1972)

Tate was speaking for a certain contingent among the nationalists, who were making the accusation that the Marxist tendency was subverting the Black struggle by seeking approval from the white left, proof that if one was a Marxist then one was an agent of white people. In this case, the *Guardian* was the main movement newspaper covering all movements of social progress. Of course, the opposing view was intended to demonstrate the power of the autonomous self-determination motion of Black activism.

Another initiative was the National Anti-Imperialist Conference in Solidarity with African Liberation (NAIMSAL) that the Communist Party held in Chicago on October 19–21, 1973. The CPUSA had followed the development of ALD 1972 and 1973, as well as that of ALSC, and had recognized that African liberation was a fertile battlefront for mobilizing the Black masses and working with Black activists, as evidenced by the following conference announcement:

TENS OF THOUSANDS of people have marched in the May 26 African Liberation Day demonstrations. African Liberation Day Committees around the country have played a major role in mobilizing some sentiment in the Black community. . . . These efforts have been immeasurably important, but more, much more, must be done to inform, organize and mobilize the people of the United States in order to stop the enemies of freedom—whether freedom for the peoples of Africa or freedom for us in the United States. (National Anti-Imperialist Conference in Solidarity With African Liberation 1973)

NAIMSAL saw the discussion of issues and the passing of resolutions that were consistent with and in fact duplicated the positions of ALSC. One example is the workshop on "The Domestic Fight against Monopoly and Racism as Related to African Liberation." This was co-chaired by Johnny Tillman, executive director of the National Welfare Rights Organization, and Jarvis Tyner, national chairman of the Young Workers Liberation League (CPUSA). Here are three key resolutions passed by that workshop:

1. Resolve that this conference oppose the Byrd Amendment and call for its immediate repeal;
2. That the conference go on record as calling for the repeal of the Azores Agreement which gives 436 million dollars to Portugal;
3. That the conference resolves to support the Diggs Bill which would deny government contracts to those corporations that do business with the Republic of South Africa. (Rogers 1973)

The question has to be asked: Why the duplication? Or, why did the CPUSA not simply join in the work of ALSC and help build the movement that was already in motion? Many of the people listed as sponsors had been previously associated with the ALD demonstrations. The answer lies in ideology, not politics: the CPUSA had strategic differences with versions of Pan-Africanism that prevented it from working toward agreed-upon political objectives. Ideas got in their way, and in the way of serving the people.

They were acting on a thesis advanced by Henry Winston, the Afro-American national chairman of the CPUSA (Winston 1987). Winston held the view that, regardless of the apparent unity between the different political forces, the main danger was the Black nationalists, who represented a form of neo-Pan-Africanism. He saw this as a continuation of a Garvey line of development in opposition to the Du Bois approach:

> For DuBois, Pan-Africanism was at all times an anti-racist, anti-imperialist concept. But the Pan-Africanism of Innis, Baraka, Foreman, Boggs, Carmichael, and others,

while invoking the name of DuBois, takes its inspiration from George Padmore, C.L.R. James and Marcus Garvey. (Winston 1987, 45)

So, with this sweeping generalization, Winston negates the possibility of a revolutionary trend with Black nationalism as its backbone as compared to a narrow Black capitalist-oriented Black nationalism, i.e., the difference between Foreman and Boggs versus Innis. We would argue that the historical development of the movement demonstrates that, while nationalism was a pervasive part of the spontaneous uprising of the Black masses, the fact is that everywhere in the world, as movements faced up to capitalist exploitation, a class perspective developed that led to a conscious revolutionary path.

This polarity need not have arisen as it did. As someone who was in the leadership of a local organization, People's College, and on the executive committee of ALSC, as well as someone personally familiar with CPUSA activists in Chicago with a history of involvement in the Black liberation movement, I attended the first planning meeting of NAIMSAL. My argument was that we needed a political unity that brought in all who wanted to mobilize the masses in support of African liberation, while at the same time we could continue to discuss and debate about the revolutionary line of march.

This was the same position I took as I joined the U.S. delegation to the 10th World Festival of Youth and Students held in Berlin in 1973 (National Union of Students 1973). The majority of the participants from the United States were part of the CPUSA network, but I upheld the anti-imperialist position of the ALSC. We met with delegations of the African liberation movements and had frank discussions about the level of support they had in the United States. The litmus test was not what ideas you had in your head, but what kind of action you were taking to oppose imperialism and support national liberation in Africa. We could argue and learn from each other as long as our actions supported the African liberation movements and opposed imperialism. There was no need to rush to judgement.

As mentioned, a key aspect of ALSC is how it kept making

efforts to build unity and kept a discussion going to clarify agreements and disagreements. One such activity was a joint plenary session involving ALSC and AHSA leadership at the national conference of the African Heritage Studies Association (AHSA) held on April 6, 1974, at the Statler Hilton Hotel in New York City. Representing ALSC was Dawolu Gene Locke, Amiri Baraka, and Owusu Sadaukai, and representing AHSA was James Turner, Ron Walters, Lynn Dozier, and Leonard Jefferies. The session was chaired by me (Abdul Alkalimat); I opened with these words:

> This is an historically significant meeting since it brings together two large mass formations within our movement: one from the struggle in the academy fighting against the ideological tools of racism and imperialism, the other linking the guerrillas of Southern Africa and the Republic of Guinea Bissau with the Black worker, welfare recipient, and tenant in the U.S.A. in anti-racist, anti-imperialist mass struggles. This symposium speaks to the necessity of the intellectual and the political activist coming together. (Peoples College 1977, 227)

There were two main points of agreement: the role of Black intellectuals as exponents of theory, to clarify all the dimensions of the oppression and exploitation experienced by Black people in Africa and the African Diaspora; and the role of the Black liberation movement, which is to mobilize the masses of Black people toward a practical line of march that applies that theory toward freedom and justice. This was a major attempt to reunite Black Studies with the Black liberation movement.

Another action to accomplish this was a conference on the Caribbean at Fisk University, November 8–9, 1973. In addition to U.S. speakers, participants from the following countries spoke: Guyana, Barbados, Antigua, Haiti, Jamaica, and Puerto Rico. In the minutes of the ALSC Southern Regional Meeting on November 24th is this summary:

> A recently held conference 'Crisis, Conflict, and Change: The Caribbean in the 1970s' sponsored by the Afro-American Studies Program at Fisk University, provided the first public platform for ALSC to address itself to the question of the

Caribbean. ALSC involvement in the conference was key as several members of the Executive Committee discussed the ALSC position on the Caribbean. Executive committee members participating were Tim Hector, Caribbean Regional Chairperson, Owusu Sadaukai, Southern Regional Chairperson. Dawolu Gene Locke, International Chairperson of ALSC, and Abdul Alkalimat, Chairperson of the Research and Development Committee. (Official ALSC Minutes; archive of Abdul Alkalimat)

The ALSC Research Committee was hard at work. To help the local committees have a better understanding of their immediate situations, in December 1973 a research guide was developed that focused on class structure, the history of struggle, and the institutions of power. On January 4, 1974, a resolution and a study guide, "Oil and the Crisis of Imperialism," developed by the research committee, was adopted by the executive committee. This targeted the major oil companies as bulwarks of imperialism and aligned ALSC with the righteous struggle of the Palestinian people (Peoples College 1977, 106–120, 121–136).

Internal discussion in ALSC heated up and required a second major formal debate over the SOP. This time the class issues were moving more and more to center stage. The plan was to have a full meeting in February 1974 in Greensboro in order to deal, once and for all, with the issues surrounding the SOP. Several people in leading positions raised key objections to the SOP (listed below) that had to be addressed:

1. De-emphasis on Africa and emphasis on local U.S. problems
2. Marxist or left-wing language
3. Definitions of problems Black people face
4. Definition of "Black workers take the lead"
5. Why we're anti (like anti-imperialism) rather than what we are for
6. Concept of a united front

These issues reflect the contradictions faced when moving from a general Black perspective to an anti-imperialist perspective, a change that brings forward an understanding of fighting a system of exploitation. The struggle became one of clarification and re-unification. Some differences became so pronounced that they led to splits.

The Greensboro meeting was the result of local committees carrying out study programs and discussions that led to higher levels of theoretical development. Sometimes this led to consolidation of beliefs and sometimes people changed and took up new ideas. People had a sense that what they thought and did was important, so in preparing for the Greensboro meeting local committees prepared written statements either for or against the SOP; statements in favor did, however, propose revisions of the SOP.

Two of the main statements against the SOP came from Illinois and Ohio. The main concern of the Chicago chapter of ALSC, led by Don Lee (aka Haki Madhubuti), had to do with identity:

> We are an Afrikan People. More specifically, we are Afrikans in America. Our ties with other Afrikans around the world are cultural, historical, and political. . . . Our enemies are white people. We feel this should be a clearly articulated fact in any position developed by ALSC. . . . We must stop attributing our problems to only the white ruling class of the United States. The reality is that everywhere in the world whites dominate and oppress Afrikans and other people of color and this is a racial oppression not a class oppression. (Document presented to the 1974 ALSC meeting, Greensboro, NC; archive of Abdul Alkalimat)

They anticipated criticism of their position:

> We understand that with this assessment we may be stereotypically termed "Narrow Nationalist" but we accept that in our attempt to do justice to our feelings and bring clarity to our position.

Their position was presented in two pages, and made its final major point about Black workers:

> ALSC should stop pushing the misconception that workers have a historic role to come to the forefront to spearhead the liberation movement. The first problem is that the interests of white workers and black workers are different because of the fact that white workers have in many cases become

pro-capitalistic and more racist as a result of more liberal policies on the part of management and union concessions and benefits. Black workers on the other hand, suffer the discrimination and unfair practices they experience primarily because they are black and not because they are workers. Their identification with the liberation struggle must be a result of their understanding of their historic role as oppressed Afrikans not as oppressed workers. This idea does not prevent them from participating in operational unity as a group of workers but the cohesion of that unity is based on our Afrikan identity not on our job assignment in this country. (Document presented to the 1974 ALSC meeting, Greensboro, NC; archive of Abdul Alkalimat)

The Ohio committee staked out essentially the same position through their definition of a global African reality:

A correct historical analysis of black people in the world affirms that we are an African People, meaning we are descendants of people who have their origins on the African continent, an inheritance that despite our present geographic location does not alter the reality of who we are. African people the world over are one people with a common history, a common identity, suffering under the same political, economic, and social oppression and domination by a common European enemy. (Document presented to the 1974 ALSC meeting, Greensboro, NC; archive of Abdul Alkalimat)

This Illinois and Ohio thinking seems to fit the criticism of neo-Pan-Africanism articulated by Winston. However, this was a minority view in ALSC, so Winston was able to evade his responsibility to unite and contest the main thrust of the anti-imperialism of ALSC and its SOP by making the false claim that he was defending the revolutionary line of march when he lumped all non-CPUSA-connected Pan-Africanists as racialist collaborators with capital. (More on this in the next chapter.)

Critical support for the ALSC SOP was offered by committees in Georgia, Texas, Louisiana, Minnesota, and Michigan. The main point of unity was that ALSC had an anti-imperialist, antiracist analysis and program. There were calls for more clarification and expansion of the analysis. The New Orleans committee wanted more on imperialism within the United States, in Africa, and in places like Canada and the Caribbean. The Austin committee wanted to make sure the language was accessible to the masses of Black people, and that there was a "clear correlation between national, international, and local struggles."

The two most critical issues had to do with the concept of a united front and the role of Black workers. Three committees raised the issue of the ALSC form of organization: Louisiana, Michigan, and Minnesota. The New Orleans committee ended their document with this question: "Finally, is ALSC a mass organization being built in a united front manner or is ALSC the United Front? For here is a distinction should be made on what factors bring about a united front, which would be independent of ALSC's will."

This important concern is a direct reflection of the transition from ALD 1972, which was clearly the effort to build a united coalition of individuals and groups, to ALD 1973 and beyond, when more and more individuals joined ALSC committees as their only organization, although a few national organizations continued to play prominent roles, including CAP, YOBU, and the BWC. This was an inevitable contradiction within such an organizational process.

The Detroit committee took this a step further by proposing the organizational name be changed to fit the emerging mass organization:

> Therefore, we call for a political union of all African people in support of African liberation in the Americas and on the African continent. This union must oppose exploitation by advocating the equal distribution of wealth among those who produce it. It must oppose imperialism by advocating the right of African people to determine our own destiny without external force. . . . This union of African people must focus upon African people; it must organize among African people; it must be controlled only by African people and it must struggle around the questions that affect African people on the continent, in the Caribbean, and in North America. (Document presented to the 1974 ALSC meeting, Greensboro, NC; archive of Abdul Alkalimat)

Sounding much like the Chicago call for an independent Black political party in their paper, the Detroit proposal called for an African Political Union. The National Black Political Convention, which was moving in that direction, had held its meeting in Gary, Indiana, on March 10–12, 1972, just before ALD. Many of the Black activists and institutional leaders active in the Gary political process also joined in the mobilization for ALD. However, the broad nature of people interested in electoral politics was not carried over entirely into the anti-imperialist struggle in support of African liberation. The main point is that this proposal was also a reflection of the progress being made toward a greater unity that would lead to a common mass formation.

The other critical issue was about the slogan "Black workers take the lead." A key person in the Washington meeting of ALSC had sarcastically commented that there were more junior high school students, so we might as well say they should take the lead. Some thought that comment funny, but most took the class issue as being more important, whether for or against the slogan.

This led to the major statement in support of the SOP by two executive committee members, Abdul Alkalimat (the author of this book) and Nelson Johnson, which brings up an interesting anecdote about the technological challenge to political unity. The document was written and printed in Nashville and then brought to North Carolina. We used an IBM Selectric typewriter, with a large 10-pitch font, and finished with comb binding. After reviewing the document, the comrades in North Carolina insisted that one change on one page was necessary to maintain our unity. We reached an agreement, but then needed the right typewriter to revise the page, get it printed, and find a comb binding machine. It was the day before the ALSC meeting, but we were able to revise, print, and bind all one hundred copies. Whew!

The meeting for this discussion was tense, but committees had prepared and presented their statements engaging in lively discussion. When I (Abdul Alkalimat) was called to make the presentation, a box was opened and printed booklets of sixty pages were distributed to all seventy participants, creating quite a contrast with the two- to five-page documents that had been distributed previously. In fact, Baraka was so impressed that he complained that it looked too official! This document was a comprehensive defense of the SOP, anticipating and answering the major criticisms, not as an official ALSC-approved document, but reflecting the personal views of the two authors (Alkalimat and Johnson 1974).

The document begins by describing the ideological struggle as a two-line struggle, between race theory and the theory of class struggle:

> These two lines reflect the basic tendencies of the total Black liberation struggle at this time, and therefore the fundamental issue is larger than ALSC. These two lines reflect a long historical struggle that goes back over two hundred years, and involves all areas of life. There are manifestations of these lines in economics, politics, education, Africa, the world revolution, etc. Therefore we must understand each tendency and struggle to unite all who can be united. This paper is written from a position of full support of the statement of Principles. We present this paper to all ALSC members for a full review in order to consolidate our united front around clearly understood principles. (Alkalimat and Johnson 1974, 150)

After summing up the four main sections of the SOP, this paper argued a defense of the SOP against the six criticisms mentioned above, followed by a theoretical basis for the defense. Within the united front there were differences in ideology among the executive committee members as well as throughout the country in the local committees. This paper was a defense from the left within ALSC but was not a position adopted by ALSC. The official document was the SOP. On the basis of whatever ideology they upheld, each participant was asked to support the SOP or not.

The question of class was at the center of this discussion/ debate. The slogan was aimed at the working class, but not intended to minimize the need to unite all who could be united. The first point was to define the class nature of Black people:

> The vast majority of Black people are wage (or salaried) working people with a proletarian (or petty bourgeois) class position. And with certain petty bourgeois positions, like

teachers and social workers, there is a decided proletarian character to ones work and political organization into unions. (Alkalimat and Johnson 1974, 17)

Then we made the point that the slogan "Black workers take the lead" was more of a strategic slogan than an immediate tactical one, something to work toward:

Of course, we are not so naïve as to think that this can happen overnight. Our concern is first that we consolidate ALSC and unify around a statement of principles that puts the Black working class at the center of our movement. Then, on this basis we can project programs that will link up our current participants with workers engaged in a struggle inside of the very corporations that are oppressing and exploiting the peoples of Africa. Recent examples of this type of motion include the League of Revolutionary Black workers in the auto plants of Detroit, Polaroid Revolutionary Workers Movement, International Longshoreman's Association, and Oil, Chemical and Atomic Workers. (Alkalimat and Johnson 1974, 18)

We then affirmed that we remain committed to uniting all who can be united to support the fight for African liberation and our fight in the United States as well:

It must be made clear that this in no way is an exclusive view of putting the working class against the other class elements. Rather what we are discussing is how do we organize a center for our united front. All of the class formations and social groups in the Black community are needed to unite in a principled manner in order that our united front can be as strong as possible. Only in this way will we be successful. (Alkalimat and Johnson 1974, 19)

The paper's next step is to present an empirical analysis of the class structure of Black American society:

Black workers are concentrated in specific occupations. Over 75% of Black males have jobs classified by the U.S. Census as crafts, operatives, unskilled labor, and service. On the other hand, over 82% of Black females are in jobs classified as clerical, operative, service, and domestic. The largest category of males is operatives, for females its service.

(Alkalimat and Johnson 1974, 42)

The discussion developed as a two-line struggle between the race theory and the class theory, a struggle to determine the future of ALSC and other organized contexts of the Black liberation movement as well. The result was that the leading race theory advocates resigned: Don Lee (Haki Madhubuti) from Chicago and the ALSC Executive Committee, Jitu Weusi from Brooklyn (chair of the New York ALSC committee), and Mwanza from Ohio (chair of the ALSC committee). Mwanza put their argument forward in his letter of resignation, which was published in *Black News*, organ of The East headed by Jitu Weusi:

> It has been a nightmare watching the Marxist takeover of ALSC. . . . We went to the national meeting in Greensboro with high hopes. We were naïve in thinking that the Marxist rhetoric that had come from the negro communist in Nashville represented a minority point of view. We thought that the national body would reject this 1860 white Marxist bullshit and return to the revolutionary spirit of Garvey, Malcolm and Lumumba. We can no longer play tricks on ourselves and pretend that ALSC has simply been infiltrated by a handful of European-controlled negroes, ALSC is now clearly a white Marxist-dominated United Front. Once this became clear to people in Ohio and other people throughout the Midwest, our unswerving commitment to ALSC ceased. (Mwanza 1974)

The national debate was so heated that neither the Frogmore nor the Greensboro meeting was going to settle the issues for long. These resignations from the ALSC leadership were decisive in transforming the Black liberation movement. This became sharper and more public heading into ALD 1974.

Kwame Nkrumah, Ghana, Leader of the modern Pan-African Movement / This and all images courtesy of the author unless otherwise indicated

Amilcar Cabral, Guinea-Bissau, Major theoretician for African liberation / Public domain, obtained from Wikimedia.org, photographer unknown

Owusu Sadaukai, International Chairperson of ALSC

Nelson Johnson, YOBU National Chairperson, speaking at ALD Rally in Raleigh North
Carolina

ALD 1973 march led by Amiri and Amina Baraka, leadership of the Congress of African People

ALD 1973 march in Indianapolis, Indiana

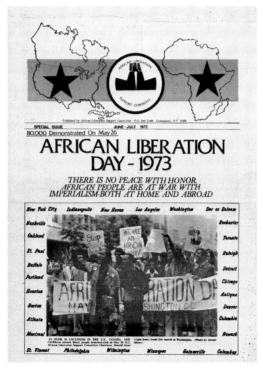

ALSC international report on ALD 1973

ALSC executive committee meeting in Jubilee Hall, Fisk University during 1973-1974, left to right, Owusu Sadaukai (Howard Fuller), John Warfield, Brenda Paris, Dawolu Gene Locke, Akinlabi (of Rochester, NY), Amiri Baraka, Abdul Alkalimat

ALSC and the African Heritage Studies Association in New York City, April 6, 1974, left to right, Owusu Sadaukai, Abdul Alkalimat, James Turner, Amiri Baraka, Leonard Jefferies, Gene Locke, Ron Walters, and Lynn Dozier

The 60-page Handbook of Struggle prepared by the
ALSC Research and Development Committee

TOWARD THE IDEOLOGICAL UNITY OF THE

AFRICAN LIBERATION SUPPORT COMMITTEE

A Response to Criticisms of the

A.L.S.C.
Statement of Principles

ADOPTED AT FROGMORE,
SOUTH CAROLINA
JUNE – JULY, 1973

Major position paper by Abdul Alkalimat and Nelson Johnson in support of the ALSC Statement of Principles, 60 pages

ALD 1973 march in Raleigh, North Carolina

ALD 1973 Rally in Denver Colorado, Vatrice Goodloe of YOBU speaking, seated to her left Ron "Slim" Washington of YOBU Kansas

1973 ALD forum in Chicago. Speaking is Lerone Bennett, Historian at Ebony Magazine, seated Standish Willis (lawyer), Gwendolyn Brooks (poet), Lu Palmer (journalist), Ahmed Sekou Toure (nephew of Guinea president Sekou Toure) and Useni Eugene Perkins (poet)

ALD 1973 march in Washington DC, led by YOBU leader Tim Thomas and Donald Isaac, ALSC Washington DC Chairperson

1972 ALD Demonstration in Antigua, West Indies

1972 ALD Demonstration in Oakland California

a delegation of the TANU Youth League at an ALSC forum in
Dar es Salaam

Chapter 3
1974: Class Struggle

ALSC became the major progressive Black social movement organization of the mid-1970s. It led a mass movement that supported the African liberation struggle, and it was the key organizational network for the deepening radicalization of Black militant activism. While it started out with a broad multiclass united front action to carry out ALD 1972, it then took to the streets in local communities in 1973 and spread throughout the country as a network of militant activists. Heading into 1974 it was at the center of the rise of Marxism as a force in the Black liberation movement, transforming many Black nationalists and Pan-Africanists into working-class and socialist-oriented revolutionaries.

The development building toward ALD 1974 helps answer key questions: Where does anti-imperialist struggle lead, especially after the end of direct colonialism? What happens to a mass movement when faced with the racist forces of capitalist state power? The answers to these questions help us to understand the external political environment for ALSC as well as the internal development of activists within ALSC. This is the focus of Chapter 3.

Toward the End of Colonialism

The direction the movement took in the United States in part was a reaction to what was happening in Africa. The African liberation movements were transforming, and correspondingly ALSC was transforming as well. First, the revolution in Portugal took place, which led to the releasing of the bonds of colonial rule, and then the changes in the white settler colonies followed in the next decade.

As stated earlier, Portugal was a poor country, reliant on its colonies and support from its NATO imperialist allies. ALSC conducted its International Week of Solidarity to Defeat Portuguese Imperialism in November 1973. Beginning in April 1974, Portuguese imperialism imploded from within and revolutionary changes were unleashed. The colonial wars had been a drain on the economy and conscription into the military weighed heavily on young men, with many, including students, leaving the country to avoid military service in the colonies.

Military officers planned a coup against the fascist government by organizing the Armed Forces Movement, a secret organization of low-ranking military officers. They set up secret signals via songs to be played on the radio that would announce the time to act. When that happened, the masses joined the soldiers in revolt, notably placing carnations in the barrels of the guns, by which the coup got its name as the Carnation Revolution:

> Portugal's new regime pledged to end the colonial wars, and began negotiations with the African independence movements. By the end of 1974, Portuguese troops were withdrawn from Portuguese Guinea and the latter was a UN member state. This was followed by the independence of Cape Verde, Mozambique, Sao Tome and Principe and Angola in 1975. The Carnation Revolution also led to Portugal's withdrawal from East Timor in south-east Asia. These events prompted a mass exodus of Portuguese citizens from Portugal's African territories (mostly from Angola and Mozambique), creating over a million Portuguese refugees – the *retornados*. ("Carnation Revolution" 2021)

The formal beginning of the dismantling of the colonial apparatus in Africa was marked by the new Portuguese government's signing of an agreement with PAIGC on August 26, 1974, that recognized the new Republic of Guinea and committed to pulling out all colonial troops. The next move was in Angola when the Alvor Agreement was signed by the MPLA, FNLA, and UNITA on January 15, 1975, and the Portuguese government began to set up a coalition government. By June 1975, a final agreement had been signed with FRELIMO, according to which their president would become the new president of Mozambique. But with the end of the struggle against direct colonial rule by a European power, a new form of struggle opened up, that between different African forces within each country.

This posed a serious problem for the Black liberation movement in the United States, because a mass spontaneous nationalism had identified with the freedom struggle in Africa against the European imperialist invaders and made a valuable contribution on that basis. However, now the situation was developing according to contradictions between Africans themselves. The slogan had been "White man's hands, off Black man's lands." Now, with the contradiction among African themselves, it switched to the prophetic statement by Bob Marley at the liberation of Zimbabwe: "So soon we'll find out/who is the real revolutionaries." Nkrumah takes this up in his book *Class Struggle in Africa*:

> The exposure and the defeat of the African bourgeoisie, therefore, provides the key to the successful accomplishment of the worker-peasant struggle to achieve total liberation and socialism, and to advance the cause of the entire world socialist revolution. (Nkrumah 1970, 63)

The most challenging struggle took place in Angola. After the coalition government option disintegrated into open conflict, it became increasingly clear that MPLA was the legitimate expression of Angolan self-determination and that UNITA and FNLA were connected to the imperialist interests of the United States and South Africa. South Africa invaded to move against MPLA's taking power. Cuba responded with a substantive gesture of international solidarity:

> On Nov. 7, the first 82 soldiers, dressed in civilian clothes and

carrying light artillery, set off on a Cubana Airlines flight to Luanda. Over the coming weeks and months, Cuban troops would pour into Angola by air and by sea. By the end of the year, they would number nearly 10,000. More than a decade later, before the end of apartheid, there would be as many as 36,000 troops throughout the country. (Pepe 2020)

The Cuban government named this campaign after Carlota, an Afro-Cuban woman who led a slave rebellion in Cuba in 1843. MPLA and the Cubans stopped the South African military and drove them out of the country. UNITA and FNLA for their part became agents of neocolonialism, collaborators required by the imperialist powers to continue their control of the economy.

The white settler regimes came to an end in ways that raised different issues. The Portuguese colonies got free in the 1970s, while the peoples under white settler regimes made their moves in the next decades: Zimbabwe, 1978–1980; Namibia, 1988; and South Africa, 1990–1994.

Ian Smith, the leader of the white settler minority government in Zimbabwe, had come to an understanding with the United Kingdom prior to promulgating the UDI. However, this led to international sanctions against his government that hamstrung the country's economic development. In response, he struck a deal in 1978 with a Methodist minister, Bishop Abel Muzorewa, who had been trained in the United States. Muzorewa opposed armed struggle and did not condone the militancy of ZANU and ZAPU. After a quick election in 1979, Bishop Muzorewa became prime minister, though he clearly did not have moral or political authority over the people. The UK government called a meeting in London at Lancaster House with Muzorewa, Mugabe, and Nkomo that produced an agreement ending the liberation war. A new election led to Mugabe's being elected head of government.

After the election, ZAPU was absorbed into a ZANU-led formation of the Patriotic Front. They had to continue fighting for the next decade against the attacks from South Africa. ZANU and ZAPU were part of the global struggle within the socialist camp, to be discussed in the next chapter.

The main organization leading the struggle in Namibia was SWAPO and its armed wing, PLAN (Peoples Liberation Army of Namibia). Because SWAPO's core ideological position was Marxist, it closely allied itself with the Soviet Union, Cuba, and Angola. This placed them in opposition to South Africa (which had global recognition of its control over what was then called South West Africa) and the United States, South Africa's ally. An agreement was reached in 1988 that would grant independence to Namibia as long as the Cuban troops withdrew from the region and MPLA ceased military support of PLAN. It took one year for this agreement to be fully implemented and all South African troops to be withdrawn. Namibia adopted a new constitution in 1990.

South Africa was the last white settler–dominated country to change. The regime lifted the ban on the ANC in 1990 and freed Nelson Mandela and other political prisoners unconditionally after twenty-seven years of confinement. A Convention for a Democratic South Africa (CODESA) process was set up to negotiate the process of independence during 1991–1992, involving 228 delegates from 19 different political parties, white and Black. Inkatha, a Zulu-based organization, joined with white apartheid forces to challenge the negotiations. Violent acts began to undermine the progress of the negotiations, including the assassination of Chris Hani, the leader of uMkhonto we Sizwe (Spear of the Nation), the armed wing of the ANC, on April 10, 1993.

Because of what they perceived as a threat to this globally important country, Europe and the United States backed both white and Black political leaders in an attempt to calm things down and maintain the status quo. Mandela changed policy, ending the demand for the nationalization of the economy and the repatriation of the land stolen from the Africans. He won the election in 1994 and, to avoid conflict, went to Zululand and offered the Zulu leader Mangosuthu Buthelezi the position of Minister of Home Affairs of South Africa, a position he held from 1994 to 2004.

The new government had the ANC as the top leading policy makers, with bureaucratic administrators from the former white-settler apartheid regime led by Frederik Willem de Klerk. An alliance of the ANC, the Congress of South African Trade Unions

(COSATU), and the Communist Party of South Africa (CPSA) took power, but imperialism still had its grip on the main aspects of the economy and the military.

In all six countries we have been discussing, as the organizations moved beyond being national liberation movements, each began to take on the character of a political party working to build socialism, although some tendencies were still championing a capitalist path. They all began with their countries in a capitalist structure tied into a colonial economic system. Another key lesson is that cadres developed to fight a national liberation war are different than the cadre needed to administer a government and raise the cultural level of the working class and peasantry. Therefore, the strength of these movements' top leadership reflected a weakness of their organizational capacity to build a democratic political culture. Much like the history of socialist countries, the early leadership tended to take the legitimacy of their leadership in the independence struggle and extend it into presidential terms that lasted from five to thirty-eight years.

Table 10. Southern African presidents following independence

Country	Beginning/End	Years	President
Angola	1979–2017	38	Jose Eduardo dos Santos
Mozambique	1975–1986	11	Samora Machel
	1986–2005	19	Joaquim Chissano
Zimbabwe	1980–2017	37	Robert Mugabe
Namibia	1990–2005	15	Sam Nujoma
South Africa	1994–1999	5	Nelson Mandela
	1999–2008	9	Thambo Mbeki
	2009–2018	9	Jacob Zuma

This created a static bureaucracy instead of what was needed, a dynamic democratic culture. The professional and educated middle class was small and unable to assume transgenerational administrative control of the state. Furthermore, the national liberation organizations were facing mass illiteracy and a demobilized mass of people. This objectively prevents each successive generation from providing leadership to the country. Eventually, there is always a handoff from the revolutionary generation, and that's when the crisis emerges, because the next generation has not been prepared to take power.

In Africa, three main changes happened that influenced the movement in the United States:

1. Contradiction of political power: Direct European (white) colonialism ended and was replaced by different African (Black) forces contending for power.
2. Contradiction of political organization: African liberation organizations were transformed from broad-based movements into political parties.
3. Contradiction of ideology: African liberation organizations had members with low levels of literacy, but the new parties began to take up Marxism-Leninism as their official ideology.

New Communist Movement Party Building

During the same general time-frame of this organizational change in the African liberation movements, cadre-based parties were developing out of the mass movements of the 1960s in the United States. Because they were based on Marxism and were relying heavily on Lenin's *What Is To Be Done?* as an organizational manual, collectively they became a New Communist Movement (NCM) (Elbaum 2002, 148–151).

There were two main sources for the NCM: the old CPUSA and the mass organizations of the 1960s, especially those established by students. The main mass organization for white students was the Students for a Democratic Society (SDS). This was comparable to SNCC for Black students. Their origin was in being united around a document written in 1960 called the Port Huron Statement, named after where it was written in Michigan. By 1969 it was estimated that SDS had grown to 300 chapters with 30,000 members, of whom a portion were high school students.

The three main national party organizations of the NCM

were the Communist Labor Party (CLP), the Revolutionary Communist Party (RCP), and the Communist Party Marxist-Leninist (CP[M-L]).

The CLP originated in a caucus that came out of the old CPUSA, first in the form of the Provisional Organizing Committee (POC). Nelson Peery and some of his colleagues in Los Angeles then left the POC to form the California Communist League, dropping the state designation when it began to organize on a national level. This included the Marxist Leninist Workers Association, a student organization that had split from SDS in 1969 and united with some Latino activists. The major development leading into the CLP was the recruitment of a large number of Black workers from the League of Revolutionary Black Workers, which was based in Detroit.

The RCP, which emerged out of SDS in Northern California, was known first as the Bay Area Revolutionary Union, then as the Revolutionary Union, and finally as the Revolutionary Communist Party. The SDS connection with veteran communists was linked to the initial connection between Bob Avakian and Leibel Bergman (Avakian 2005, 188–191). Others from the old CPUSA joined in, notably the red diaper baby Mickey Jarvis, who became vice chairman of the RCP ("Mickey Jarvis - KeyWiki" 2021).

The October League (OL), the organization that led to the CP(M-L) came out of the SDS fraction called the Revolutionary Youth Movement II, initially led by Mike Klonsky. They united with the Georgia Communist League, which was led by Lynn Wells. Their CPUSA connection was with Harry Haywood, who had been a member of the CPUSA Central Committee and political bureau. Haywood had been the general secretary of the League of Struggle for Negro Rights.

The NCM engaged in several attempts to unite in the process of party building. On a theoretical level, the focus was on what was called the burning issues facing the movement. The most intense convergence was a series of four forums in 1973 organized by the *Guardian* newspaper in New York City, the topics of which were party building, the African American national question, women, and building a workers movement. The party building forum drew

Chapter 3

1,200, by far the largest audience.

Irwin Silber spoke for the *Guardian* and placed the debate in the context of what he called an American revolutionary tradition:

> There is an American revolutionary tradition—and I don't mean the revolution whose 200th anniversary Richard Nixon is preparing to turn into a monument of national jingoism. That was a bourgeois revolution and in its time it was progressive. But I am speaking of the revolutionary tradition of Nat Turner, Harriet Tubman and John Brown who dared to struggle on behalf of the most oppressed; of Tecumseh and Sitting Bull who struggled against the wildfire of American genocidal expansionism; of the Molly Maguires and the Haymarket martyrs, of the IWW and the striking Ludlow miners who picked up guns to fight off John D. Rockefeller's coal company police; of 10,000 blacks lynched—"legally" and illegally—who were murdered for showing a spark of resistance. One could go on and on, for the revolutionary traditions of this country are real and it is to these that a new communist party must address itself in helping the American working class learn its own history. (Silber 1973)

Mike Klonsky, speaking for the October League, called for building the party from within the mass anti-imperialist struggles by uniting the emerging communist formations:

> Well, the main thing at this time is not to abandon the mass struggle to build the anti-imperialist united front and to develop those close ties with the masses, to integrate ourselves in mass struggle. Secondly, in relations with other groups, we've got to combat the notion that any one of our groups is the vanguard or that they only represent the "true" communist forces at this time. We've got to unite the communist forces and we've got to combat everything that stands in the way of unity, whether it be on the level of divisive rumor-spreading and gossip which the police and revisionists use to their advantage—to the approach of always putting differences first or looking for differences as the main thing. We have to see that within every Communist party there is sharp struggle. We've got to build unity and we've got to fight for unity. (Klonsky 1973)

Mike Hamlin, representing the BWC, addressed the question of

143

why it was a Black organization in the communist movement.

Cadre in the BWC, if asked the question, do you understand that the only solution to the problems of blacks in the U.S. is a proletarian revolution led by a multi-national communist party, to every man and woman would answer yes. If asked why are you then not a multi-national form, they would tell you that no communist party exists in this country and it must be built out of the struggles of the people and when it comes into being if it is to be genuine it must have some blacks in it who are highly developed theoretically and strongly rooted in the black working masses. . . . We would like to be able to bring thousands of black workers and revolutionaries into the new communist party when it is formed rather than enter into it as a small group, isolated from the black community. . . . We see our main task in this period as building stable leadership at all levels of the black struggle by building and strengthening mass anti-imperialist and working class organizations. Only by this means can we bring the black people's struggle (at present at a low ebb) forward step by step and finally together with the whole worker's movement, and together lead the mass revolutionary high tide which will certainly come. (Hamlin 1973)

Don Wright spoke for the Revolutionary Union, the organization that led to the RCP. His emphasis was on the African American national question:

Of the three tasks—party building, building the unity of the working class and proletarian leadership in the united front struggles, and building the united front—we say that these are not just the tasks of the movement but of the society as a whole. We see that at this time the principal contradiction, the key link that will move the rest is the national question, the question of the unity of the working class, and its leadership.

We believe that there is a black nation of a new type, an overwhelmingly proletarian nation, historically constituted with a class structure and class struggle going on within it. It is a social phenomenon that the black proletariat is more class conscious, more determined in struggle and it has to do with the dual oppression of black people. Which is not to say that every black worker is more advanced than every white worker, but due to the history of oppression, it is true overall.

> It is important to understand that in order to build a lasting multi-national proletarian party you must raise the proletarian banner in the black nation and defeat bourgeois nationalism. We see the need at this time for multi-national and national forms. With the upsurge in the consciousness of white workers, favorable conditions exist to build both national and multi-national forms with a clear class line. It is not just multi-national organizations that can put forward a clear class line. (Wright 1973)

These quotes merely suggest points of unity and creative approaches to the application of Marxist theories to the U.S. context. In this party building forum, different takes on the African American national question were expressed, followed by a full forum on that issue as well. Other differences between these organizations and within each of them resulted in the unity effort's devolving into a series of antagonistic polemics.

The usual focus is on how the left has been unable to unite, and therefore has failed to sustain movements for social progress. A more useful approach is to examine each social motion in its context in order to learn lessons—both positive and negative—applicable to our current situation. This is a scientific approach and is summed up by a well-known slogan: *Fight, fail, fight again, fail again, fight on to victory!* The logic is based on learning from experience, because to condemn experience is to choose blindness over vision.

Party Building Out of ALSC

Black people have been a historical foundation of the capitalist system, as enslaved persons, as sharecroppers, and as wage workers. President Richard Nixon was the first American politician to promote the illusion that they could become capitalists, so "Black Capitalism" became a major policy:

> While a generation of white Americans had gained wealth through discriminatory government-sponsored credit subsidies for student and mortgage loans, Mr. Nixon pointed blacks to the free market and wished them luck. Black

capitalism was so politically appealing, every administration since Mr. Nixon's has adopted it in some form. Black capitalism morphed into Ronald Reagan's "enterprise zone" policy, Bill Clinton's "new market tax credits," and Barack Obama's "promise zones." (Baradaran 2019)

This Black capitalism policy appealed to many Black nationalists with their small-business aspirations, even drawing some into the Republican Party. In the struggle for day-to-day survival, the creation of small businesses in the Black community in some cases is a positive development. There continues to be a need for drugstores, grocery stores, gas stations, and other services for the functioning of the community. However, as a strategic goal the achievement of Black capitalism would not end the suffering and exploitation of Black people, nor would it end the monopoly basis of U.S. imperialism.

This recognition of the systemic nature of capitalism forced a rethinking of the history of Black resistance that had seen Black radicals many times before turned to Marxism and the path taken by world revolutionary forces. Most important were the development of the New Communist Movement and the continued transgenerational support of Black Marxists like James Boggs, Harry Haywood, and Abner Berry. Cadre development organizations in ALSC, particularly CAP and MXLU/YOBU, moved in the direction of pre-party formations and the study of Marxist theories.

Congress of African PeopleCAP developed as a national organization, initially under the ideological and organizational leadership of Maulana Karenga and his Kawaida theory. Baraka became a follower and was designated by Karenga as an Imamu of Kawaida, a spiritual leader. Baraka embraced this, but, given his connection to community struggles in Newark, the straightjacket of this organization and ideology was not enough to power a movement forward. Baraka began a move to the left by repositioning himself as a developer of what he called Revolutionary Kawaida:

> The shifting of the ideological emphasis from the rote memorization of Kawaida doctrine points to the more complex

discussion of the interrelated concepts of Nationalism (domestic focus), Pan-Africanism (global African focus), and Socialism (global oppressed peoples focus) meant that the organization was going to move in a direction more closely aligned to other African and Third World liberation movements. (Simanga 2015, 90)

Though Baraka by this time had become the head of CAP, he soon was separating himself from Karenga. Nineteen seventy-four was the decisive year for Baraka's move from nationalism to Marxism. This was done with amazing speed, because the year did not start out that way. In a letter to the ALSC chair dated February 28, 1974, Baraka took exception to the Alkalimat-Johnson defense of the ALSC SOP, which he labeled "a stomp down defense of a dogmatic soviet position" though he ended up anchoring his argument in Lenin and Yuri Popov in a November 1974 *Black World* article, "Toward Ideological Clarity." Even the mainstream *New York Times* paid attention to his ideological shift and quickly tried to attack lest he influence too many (Sullivan 1974).

His change was accomplished in three key speeches that separated him from the nationalists with whom he had been united. His April 1, 1974 speech at a CAP meeting was a bolt of lightning that sent shock waves through the organization:

This was the first time in a public speech that Baraka elevated the theoretical concepts of Marxism above those of African American and African theorists. The speech was given at a public program during the last evening of a two-day conference of CAP chapters, those in the process of organizing CAP chapters, and many who were supporters of CAP in the Midwest. (Simanga 2015, 107)

The meeting, in Chicago, was hosted by the CAP leader there, Haki Madhubuti. Tension filled the room. A split was being felt and anticipated, and:

…the next day, both Haki Madhubuti and Jitu Weusi, a well-known educator and activist who headed The East, a significant nationalist organization in Brooklyn that was also the CAP chapter there, resigned and withdrew their organizations from CAP. This was the first major split in the organization involving Kawaida influenced nationalists who were also nationally known and respected activists in the nationalist community. (Simanga 2015, 108)

Later in April, Baraka spoke in Little Rock, Arkansas, at a national meeting of the Black Political Assembly, which had been formed in Gary, Indiana. He continued his ideological shift by calling for a socialist revolution in a national policy speech to the delegates. This was very upsetting to people who were leading advocates of the assembly, notably Ron Walters and Ron Daniels.

His next major speech in 1974 was at the ALSC national conference discussed below. During this time, CAP members espoused contradictory beliefs and rituals. As an Imamu, Baraka was officiating at official Kawaida marriage ceremonies, and his birthday was an organizational holiday to honor his spiritual leadership. On the other hand, the study of Marxism ran counter to these religious practices: he was supposed to be a comrade, equal to others based on his practical and theoretical leadership. In fact, some analysts thought every CAP document was written by Baraka, but in key cases these documents had been collectively written by committees.

CAP was experiencing an ideological shift toward Marxism, was being secularized away from a religion, and organizationally there was movement toward equality. This was particularly clear with regard to the role of women. There was a pronounced sexism in the Kawaida doctrine, and even as early as the Revolutionary Kawaida stage things had to change. Amina Baraka and her sister comrades became a force against male supremacy, thus transforming CAP in another fundamental way.

The ideological journey of CAP led to its renaming itself the Revolutionary Communist League (RCL) in 1976. This will be discussed in the next chapter.

Malcolm X Liberation University / Youth Organization for Black Unity

A similar move to the left in the direction of Marxism-Leninism and party building was undertaken by MXLU and YOBU forces, who were based in North Carolina but had contacts throughout the country.

One aspect of this development was the study of political economy. Clarence Munford, an African American from Cleveland who had earned his first degrees at Case Western Reserve University and then his PhD in 1962 from Karl Marx University in Leipzig (in what was then East Germany), was a Marxist political economist teaching at the University of Guelph in Guelph, Ontario. Munford offered a class on *Capital* by Marx for Black activists from the United States that was held one weekend per month. This class was attended by some workers from Detroit and a delegation from MXLU/YOBU.

They began to develop close ties with other organizations, mainly the Lynn Euson Institute in Texas and Peoples College in Tennessee. One anecdote of the leftward movement of these relationships involves an event in Nashville, Tennessee, narrated by the following document:

> Joint Statement of Peoples College and Youth Organization for Black Unity / Malcolm X Liberation University June 10, 1973
>
> At the invitation of Peoples College of Nashville, Tennessee, representatives of the Youth Organization for Black Unity/ Malcolm X University met with representatives of Peoples College from June 8–10, 1973, in Nashville.
>
> The two organizations had fraternal and productive discussions on the histories of the two organizations, on their respective views on the current stage of the movement, on the present crisis of capitalism and its particular implications for Black people in the U.S., and on joint projects and future working relationships.
>
> These talks have prompted us to jointly agree on the following points:
>
> 1. That socialist revolution by the United States working class is the only means for the total freedom of Black people.
> 2. That the only vehicle capable of achieving socialist revolution as defined is a multi-national Leninist party.
> 3. That we are presently committed to the creation of strong Black pre-party formations rooted in the Black working class

and capable of advancing working class leadership on the Black Liberation Movement as a whole.

4. That because of the urgent need for theoretical clarity, we agree to intensify our study, discussion, and exchange of views on the following topics: The National Question, Party-Building, and the Political Economy of the United States.

5. That the present split within the socialist camp is not the principle question that inhibits the further and ever-broadening unity of Black revolutionary forces in the United States.

6. That we will intensify and rededicate our work in support of the liberation struggle on the African continent and build the African Liberation Support Committee as a broad anti-imperialist front capable of deepening revolutionary consciousness in the Black community.

7. That we will continue our work in the Save Black Schools Project in fighting for the right for an education for Black youth in the United States and to heighten the revolutionary consciousness of Black students. Implicit in this is the struggle to make Black institutions of higher learning actually serve the needs of the masses of Black people.

8. That we commit ourselves to the building of a journal of the "Black left" as a part of our overall belief in the necessity to:

   A. Summarize the experiences of Black people in general and the Black Liberation Movement in particular.

   D. Help bring clarity in theory and program to the ever-intensifying Black Liberation Movement.

   C. Promote unity among the existing and emerging progressive forces in the Black community.

A new anti-imperialist organization based on the study of Marxism was being formed, so student work had to change. A progressive student delegation was formed to make a trip to Cuba to study the revolutionary process there and network with their Federation of University Students. The trip was made during August 1974 and summed up in the pamphlet *Viva Cuba: Down with US Imperialism!*:

> The Progressive Student Delegation, as far as we know, was the first exclusively Black student delegation to visit Cuba. It was made up of anti-imperialist Black students from the

northeastern, southern, midwestern, and western regions of the United States. We represent the National Save and Change Black Schools Project, the Youth Organization for Black Unity, the Black Student Collective at Harvard University, the Harambe Organization in New Jersey, and the Peoples College in Tennessee. (Progressive Student Delegation 1974, 6)

This trip was preparation for transforming the student organizing by YOBU into a new formation, the February First Movement. This was to be an anti-imperialist organization of youth named after the date of the first sit-in movement of 1960. I (Abdul Al-kalimat) gave the keynote address on December 27, 1974, at its founding convention at Princeton University. Years of anchoring theory in practice shaped the agenda for the meeting, and was a focus of the keynote:

An anti-imperialist student movement must be based on scientific consciousness of current patterns of oppression and exploitation and a grasp of the historical role students have played in revolutionary struggle. This means that you must study, not just books though that is absolutely essential, but with newspapers, the mass media in general, and most important of all—make direct investigation among the masses of students, workers, and throughout the Black community. Learn how to listen to people, learn how to learn from the peoples experience. And be objective, be systematic, and be thorough.

One more point on study. Our main task is to combine the advanced learners with the average learners by having a clear understanding of what one's objectives are, what problems need solving. Remember that the same books can be read by people on different theoretical levels and much be gained by it, and remember that theory is good only as a guide to action. The task is not merely to understand the world but to change it. (Alkalimat 1974b, 23)

The activists leading the move to Marxism came out of struggles in North Carolina, Kansas, and Tennessee. This led to the formation of the Revolutionary Workers League (RWL) in 1974; here is an account of it by Ron Washington, a former YOBU cadre in

Kansas:

> We were able to build the RWL, based upon the extensive and nationwide chapters of YOBU, unity with Abdul Alkalimat's People's College folk, Owusu Sadaukai's Malcolm X University forces and a few other revolutionary Marxist forces that we had built unity within the African Liberation Support Committee (ALSC). In addition, RWL sent the first all black Marxist delegation to China in 1974 to build unity with the then leading party of the worldwide anti-revisionist communist movement, the Communist Party of China. The trip helped to cement unity between the old and new forces that came to make up RWL. (Washington 2009, 4)

These party-building motions were at the heart of ALSC organizing from 1973 into 1974. The focus was on building a mass base for anti-imperialist united front struggle, and in that context to develop cadres for the next period when a higher level of struggle was anticipated. This was the basis for planning the ALD activities for 1974 that declared the entire month of May African Liberation Month.

African Liberation Month (May 1974)

The ALSC Research and Development Committee distributed a sixty-page handbook of struggle for the month's activities that included a schedule: May 1–18 for local educational forums, May 18–19 for local demonstrations and rallies, May 23–24 for a national ALSC conference in Washington, DC, and May 25 for a national demonstration in the same city. African Liberation Month— May 1974 was a combination of what had taken place in both 1972 and 1973 on a local and a national level.

This level of organization was needed to coordinate the network of ALSC having grown to fifty chapters:

- Los Angeles, CA
- Oakland, CA
- Washington, DC
- New Haven, CT
- Waterbury, CT

- Denver, CO
- Atlanta, GA
- Macon, GA
- Chicago, IL
- South Bend, IN
- Lawrence, KS
- New Orleans, LA
- Spearsville, LA
- Baltimore, MD
- Boston, MA
- Springfield, MA
- Detroit, MI
- Minneapolis, MN
- St. Louis, MO
- Newark, NJ
- Buffalo, NY
- New York, NY
- Rochester, NY
- Durham, NC
- Greensboro, NC
- Raleigh, NC
- Omaha, NE
- Dayton, OH
- Columbus, OH
- Cincinnati, OH
- Youngstown, OH
- Oklahoma City, OK
- Portland, OR
- Philadelphia, PA
- Pittsburgh, PA
- Providence, RI
- Columbia, SC
- Austin, TX
- Dallas, TX
- Houston, TX
- McKinney, TX
- San Antonio, TX

- Nashville, TN
- Yakima, WA
- Montreal, QC
- Toronto, ON
- St John's, Antigua
- Roseau, Dominica
- St. George's, Grenada
- Dar-es-Salaam, Tanzania

First there was a new slogan: *"Imperialism No! Nixon Must Go! Black People Must be Free!"* This made it clear that the fight to free Africa was linked to the fight against the capitalist state of the United States. Nixon was directly linked to imperialism. Calling for Black people to be free extended the linkage by referring to all of Africa and the African Diaspora. This was a step toward a revolutionary internationalism.

The ALSC handbook for African Liberation Month spelled out the strategic and tactical design for the ALSC committees to follow based on their local conditions. This is a critical aspect of how ALSC carried out the crucial task of maintaining the relationship between theory and practice. There were cadres who were part of organizations that stressed study and organizational discipline, but they were in the minority. As a volunteer organization building a social movement, people would weave in and out, attending meetings and missing meetings. People represented different levels of development and experience that had to be coordinated into any plan of action. African Liberation Month was a complex plan that needed a handbook.

The focus remained on building a united front, and in fact ALSC was itself becoming more of a mass organization. The handbook spelled this out:

> Even though African Liberation Month and the local demonstrations are spearheaded by ALSC, it is critically important to involve the broadest possible number of people in the process. In line with our Statement of Principles, local demonstrations try "to unite all social groups and class formations within the Black community in a common struggle. . . . Every effort should be made to involve groups

154

and individuals in the planning and implementation of local demonstrations. Try to involve groups outside of ALSC to some extent in planning. People are generally more willing to work on something when they see that they are a real part of it. (Alkalimat 1974a, 8)

Within the broad focus on the strategic goal of defeating imperialism, there were four primary issues: oil and the crisis of imperialism, police repression and political prisoners, the impeachment of Nixon, and support for African liberation. The handbook presented detailed information on each of these issues, clarifying that the fight against imperialism was the critical way to support the freedom struggle in Africa and the United States. The handbook also provided instructions concerning how to plan forums and rallies, outreach to the media, and activities to document the experience.

In addition to the handbook, a special issue of *The African World* (July 1974) carried a comprehensive summation of the African Liberation Month 1974 activities. During the conference, four workshops, each led by a panel of speakers, on the topics of labor and the unemployed, politics, youth and education, and women in the struggle took place. These demonstrated that advanced cadres were developing in these areas, cadres that were central to work in the local areas. One outstanding example of this was the workshop on women in the struggle:

> The panelists, all women, sought (1) to explore the historical nature of the status and roles of women and (2) to define the position of women in the current Black liberation struggle. . . . Participating were: Sis Njeri Jangha of the AAPRP, Bibi Amina Baraka of the Congress of African People (CAP), Sis Joyce Johnson, Chairperson of Greensboro ALSC, and Queen Mother Moore of the African Peoples Party (APP). The session was chaired by Sis. Charisie Hedgepeth of the Durham ALSC Chapter. (YOBU 1974, 5)

At the heart of the conference were two four-hour plenary sessions, both with three speakers, who each had forty-five minutes to speak, followed by ninety minutes of questions from the audience. This was not an occasion for a speaker to be shorted on time. This was an innovative plan that allowed for the full statement of ideological positions and sufficient time for clarifying differences.

This was a democratic approach to ideological struggle, during which people were challenged, people learned more about each other, and people had a chance to experience positions without personal attacks confusing and distracting them. This was a Black version of what the *Guardian* had organized, as discussed above, and was equally important for the revolutionary movement.

Plenary Session1

a. Muhammad Ahmad, Saladin Muhammad, Abner Berry – African People's Party
b. Kwame Ture – All-African People's Revolutionary Party
c. Abdul Alkalimat – People's College – ALSC

Plenary Session 2

a. Kwadwo Akpan – Pan Africanist Congress USA – ALSC
b. Amiri Baraka – Congress of African People – ALSC
c. Owusu Sadaukai (formerly MXLU, union organizer) – ALSC

These six speakers were aligned with national networks of activists along a wide spectrum of ideological orientation. *The African World* (YOBU 1974) summed up the diversity this way:

> The six major presentations at the conference showed a generally serious attitude on the part of the participants toward ideological struggle. The positions that were laid out fell into three categories. The first was the "Free Africa first" line. This position was outlined by Akpan and Carmichael. . . . The second general position presented in the conference was the "National Liberation must precede proletarian revolution" line. This position was outlined explicitly in the collective presentation of AAPP and was implicit throughout the presentation of Imamu Baraka. . . . The third major position presented was the "Proletarian revolution is the precondition for Black liberation" line. . . . This position was taken by Abdul Alkalimat. Owusu Sadaukai's presentation, though not so explicitly, supported this position. (YOBU 1974, 15)

The sessions were held at Howard University, in Washington, DC, in Crampton Auditorium, which was filled to capacity—SRO. Following are excerpts from *The African World* summations of each talk.

Kwadwo Akpan

Kwadwo Akpan of the Pan-African Congress opened his presentation with a statement of the positive nature of the conference. "The decision to hold this conference has been proved to be even more correct, as a result of the kind of discussions that have gone on for the past two days, than we had originally thought when it was proposed some months ago."

Akpan then moved to the body of his presentation. "In our view the principal problem facing Black people in the world today is imperialism and its contingent manifestation problems, racism and capitalism."

Turning to the U.S., Akpan said, "The Pan-African Congress USA views the oppression of African people in this country as a continuing phenomenon of institutionalized American racism based historically on economic exploitation."

Akpan then stated, "Given the historic condition of African people and the economic, political and social structure of the U.S., the elimination of such oppression and exploitation solely in the framework of this country is impractical, unrealistic and indeed impossible."

He further asserted, "From an economic standpoint, our people have ceased to be a productive asset to the economy and are in fact, becoming an increasing liability to the U.S. government. . . . Similarly, from a political standpoint African people in the United States are mere pawns in a game that they do not control and for the most part, do not even understand."

Akpan then described the history leading to the emergence of Black mayors presiding over decaying urban areas in the North. He went on to say that in the South, Black people are being rapidly forced into urban, industrialized areas. He concluded, "Contrary to the propaganda about the progress and new political influence of our people, statistics indicate that in the past one hundred years the political influence of our people has declined . . . "

Akpan went on to say that therefore, Africa is the key to the solution to our problems. "I we have secured in Africa the kind of influence that will give the white ruling class cause to think again, cause to wonder how its actions here will affect the resources that it is getting from Africa, cause enough to change its ugly ways, not because it wants to, but because it has to in order to maintain any level of survival."

"Clearly then," he continued, "the position of African people in the U.S. is precarious at best.

"Thus, the PAC, USA regards Pan-Africanism to be the most practical solution to the plight of all African people. Understanding this, therefore, the correct strategy for African people in the western hemisphere, and in the U.S. in particular, is to provide massive support and assistance to those efforts designed to secure and develop an African power base for our people."

After adding that the task of Pan-Africanists is to create an African identity among Black people in this country, Akpan asserted, "We are in America but not of America in the sense that white people are, regardless of what class we are talking about.

"It is absolutely essential that we destroy the ugly, insane notion among our people that America is our country. . . . Our people must begin to view themselves as overseas Africans. . . . We must come to view our presence in America as merely a temporary interval in our continued existence as Africans."

Stokely Carmichael (aka Kwame Ture)

Stokely Carmichael of the All-African People's Revolutionary Party (AAPRP) opened his speech with thanks to the leadership of ALSC for the invitation to speak, saying "we want to thank you for the struggles you have been waging on behalf of our people all over the world."

Carmichael then proceeded to the heart of his analysis, saying "It is Africa that is going to bury imperialism . . . not just because Africa is the home of the Black man, but because of the crucial position that it plays in world struggle. Once Africa's wealth and labor is channeled for the benefit of Africa, African will make a leap and bring the rest of the world along with it."

He stated, "We (AAPRP) are Nkrumahists, that's our ideology, our objective is Pan-Africanism. We define Pan-Africanism as the total liberation and unification of Africa under scientific socialism. We understand that when this objective is achieved, the Black man will be free all over the world and Africa will play a powerful force in world socialist revolution."

He continued, "The question before us is not a question of class struggle. Any serious revolutionary knows that class struggle is the motivating struggle, is the major struggle, that is not a question."

Thus, having stated his position that class struggle is the "motivating struggle," Carmichael continued, "The question before us now is what is the role of nationalism and what phase has the African revolution now entered. The only question before the Black community is the question of nationalism! I tell you that is the only question!"

Of America, he went on to say, "A backward interpretation of our history will make you think this land really belongs to us because we worked and sweated and worked and sweated. That is the most backward capitalist thinking one has ever found."

Continuing, he said, "That we are Africans is undeniable. No one can deny that. Matter is primary, everybody knows that. The question is whether our interests lie with Africa or lie with America."

Concerning the destruction of imperialism, Carmichael said, "Africa is supporting world imperialism proper now. If you liberate Africa, it helps bring down world imperialism much quicker and gives you a stronger base from which to work to attack imperialism."

He stated his view of the fate of America. "Nobody denies that socialism will come to America, of course it must come. Black workers will take the lead. But for real socialist transformation to come to America, the white working class is the crucial element. But it is necessary for the white people, for those brothers and sisters who adhere to that policy to be working in the white working-class community trying to heighten the consciousness of the white working class. The white working class is oppressed, but they are not aware of their oppression."

Carmichael returned to a point central to his call to liberate Africa first, "Unless the Black man has a power behind him to speak on his behalf and to protect him, he will never be respected." He stated that neither the Black or white communities in the U.S. have organized mass, revolutionary forces, and added, "Thus what is needed is building and developing the Black vanguard. While doing that, we must constantly try to raise the level of the white working class. We must do that."

"But," Carmichael intoned, "our primary objective must be the building of Africa. Our primary objective must be the consolidation of socialism in Africa!"

Carmichael concluded, "We understand the nationalist struggle is not the final struggle, but it is a prerequisite to serious anti-imperialist struggle."

All African Peoples'Party

The presentation of the All African People's party (AAPP) was given by three people as a "collective analysis" because, in the words of APP chairman, Muhammad Ahmad, "too long have we engaged in personality polemics." The other two spokesmen were Saladin Muhammad, Secretary-General of AAPP and brother Sufu (formerly Winston Berry).

Muhammad Ahmad

In giving AAPP's opening statement, Ahmad covered a variety of topics, elaborating on few. He criticized those who shed "croco-dile tears for Malcolm," noting that he knew Malcolm closely and now does not even have a large picture of Malcolm in his room.

He mentioned briefly the "colony of New Africa," which was a clue to the AAPP analysis to come.

Saladin Muhammad

Saladin Muhammad laid out the basic theoretical positions of AAPP. He set the framework saying, "If we deal with imperialism and racism as an oppressed nation, then the answers we get (on how to deal with it), will be different than if we deal with it as an oppressed minority."

To those "brothers and sisters who struggle to deal with the contradictions in the schools, the contradictions in the plants, the whole social and economic contradiction in this country," Saladin posed a number of rhetorical questions.

"When we talk about better housing, do we talk about better U.S. housing or better housing as a nation?"

"Are we Black workers a part of the oppressor nation, or are we a colonized nation in which the oppressor attempts to reap super profits?"

"Are we fighting to legitimate ourselves as African-Americans?"

"What does the means of production mean to a colonized nation?"

Saladin continued, "It is a race-class problem. And when scientific nationalists begin to deal with the economic contradiction, many times the left will co-opt that because we have brothers and sisters who don't understand historical materialism trying to deal with dialectical materialism. We will not understand the social laws that govern the actions of our people unless we understand historically what our people went through."

Saladin went on to say "We are not claiming that there are not class contradictions within the U.S." He explained, "The less the oppressor nation receives from the African colonies, the harder they will have to come down on the so-called white proletariat. When he comes down on the white workers, then we will precipitate the class struggle that is taking place, not in our nation, but in the oppressor nation."

Thus, he added, "We should organize brothers and sisters to struggle around national interests, not some class interests. . . . African people need a cultural revolution.

Saladin concluded, "The only demand that is being made (by many others) is to change the American structure so that we can be part of it. As Pan-African nationalists, we don't want to be a part of it."

Brother Sufu (formerly Winston Berry)

Brother Sufu, a veteran of struggle, over 70 years in age, started his presentation with an account of a number of Black rebellions through the years. He cited, for example, the 1935 uprising in Harlem "which resulted the next day in the hiring of many Black workers." He cited many others. Then he concluded "These rebellions showed the contradiction between the colonized and the colonizers as the predominant contradiction of the time."

He added "You have seen many strikes, you've even seen strikes by Black workers, but none of them have raised one point relating to national liberation. Therefore, when we look at it historically, we see the struggle between the colonized and the colonizer as the predominant contradiction of the time."

Sufu continued, "There is a class struggle, but this class struggle between white workers and the capitalists is dormant, asleep, and we can't wait until it wakes up before we struggle for our demands."

Brother Sufu concluded his presentation saying, "If we have our national consciousness high enough, it will be possible for us to develop that national struggle to such a point that we will precipitate between white capitalists and the working class to wake up and do something. But they aren't going to wake up until we take the lead and carry our fight to an end.

Amiri Baraka

Imamu Amiri Baraka began his presentation by quoting Lenin's definition of imperialism. "Imperialism is capitalism in that stage of development in which the dominance of monopoly and finance capital has established itself, in which the export of capital has acquired pronounced importance, in which the division of the world among the international trusts has begun, in which the division of the globe among the major capitalist powers has been completed. Imperialism, as interpreted above, undoubtedly represents a special stage in the development of capitalism."

Baraka then defined racism, separating it from other forms of ethnocentricity, in that, "Ethnocentricity merely defines the world almost exclusively through the eyes of one people. Chauvinism, on the other hand, tends to solidify that one-sided method of defining a broader view. Chauvinism represents that one people are superior to another; racism must be backed up by an actual show of that superiority. In other words, the racist must have 'the power to enforce that superiority in the objective world usually by military force.' Therefore, ethnocentricity and chauvinism can exist even in African people towards others, even towards Europeans, but racism cannot cease to exist until Black people actually subdue the European in their homes and there, in Europe, direct the economy in the interest of great capitalists living in Africa."

In the next section of his presentation, Baraka began outlining what he saw as the general tasks of our struggle. He stated, "If the principal problem is the struggle against imperialist domination with the realization that this must include the conscious and deliberate struggle against racism, whether it takes the form of economic exploitation, political repression, police brutality, or cultural aggression, then the question arises, how can we struggle in the most effective way? First, it seems evident that imperialism has oppressed us nationally, racially, and culturally in order to make profits, but also as a result of the reproduction of racist systems and institutions, philosophy, and way of life that perpetuates itself with no specific profit motive, although that is its base."

He then went on to say that "therefore, as a people, we are Africans in North America, a subordinate nation which is what national minority means, a dependent or subject nation as Lenin provided."

Baraka then moved on to defend what he saw as the independent national character of the liberation struggle from those lines that he perceived as trying to deny this and to submerge the liberation struggle in the general struggle for working class revolution and socialism.

In this regard he stated, "The fact of racism in America is real, not theoretical, just as the fact of our racial distinction is real.

When we project our struggle as simply a class struggle or render ourselves invisible within the phraseology of a struggle simply between the working masses and the ruling class with no further revelation of the essential reality of the existence of any potential transnational interracial working class; to say as some multinational formations do, that they represent the entire working class, is not to go to the depths of analysis and investigations of American society. Racism renders talk about the entire working class, at this time, as idealist conjecture."

Baraka continued, "Dialectically our struggle takes on a nationalist character if only because it is a struggle, at one point, against racial oppression. But there is a class nature to our struggle itself, since we understand the economic reasons behind that oppression, though by the time of imperialism the white ruling class and the white masses of Europe and America were convinced that people of color around the world should be exploited because we were colored and therefor inferior.

"But in our class relationship to the ruling class the complication, again, is the racial character of capitalist oppression. The greater portion of that monopoly capitalist ruling class is white though that is finally secondary to the fact that they are a ruling class."

Based on his analysis, Baraka, in the last section of his presentation, spoke of the organizational needs of the Black liberation struggle.

He stated that our struggle "demands the mobilization and organization of the nationalist forces within the framework of, and by the action of a strong, well organized, well-structured political organization."

Baraka goes on to talk about Lenin's concept of a vanguard party and applies this to what he sees to be the needs of our struggle today. "The one thing that Lenin was firm about regardless of conditions varying from country to country, was the need for a vanguard party whose members all recognize the necessary difference between themselves and the revolutionary masses, and who have a firm ideology, programmatic summation, and discipline before they go to the masses, interact with them and give them leadership."

"If the chief revolutionary social force is the peasant, as in China, then base the party on the peasantry. If it is the Black masses, as in the United States, then build the revolutionary party on the basis of a Black revolutionary social force."

Baraka closed his presentation saying, "Building strong disciplined organizations based on the correct ideology, based on nationalism, Pan-Africanism and socialism, an analysis of the concrete conditions, we are able to actively pursue concrete programs to mobilize, organize and politicize the masses and move them objectively to transform the entire society. And in so doing we help alter objective and subjective conditions throughout the world. . . . "

Abdul Alkalimat

Abdul Alkalimat of People's College in Nashville, Tenn., presented an analysis of what he felt to be the correct strategy and tactics for the Black liberation struggle from a Marxist perspective.

Initially, he outlined four basic questions he would speak to.

1. What is our problem – its historical development and current structure?
2. Who are our friends and who are our enemies?
3. What are the correct solutions to our problems – the maximum and minimum programs for change?
4. What are the differences and similarities between our struggle in the United States and the struggle on the African continent?

Turning to the first question of how Black people are exploited and oppressed, he mentioned two views. First was the view that racial oppression was the problem, all Black people are the same, and race is the lever that turns history and the single most important fact of life. Second was the view that class exploitation was the only problem of capitalist society and class struggle will automatically eliminate all other problems.

Alkalimat asserted, "Both of these views are incorrect." He stated that the correct view would "point to the total character of exploitation and oppression, wearing blinders to neither class nor race."

Alkalimat then declared, "We fit directly into the class analysis under capitalism. The principal contradiction is the class contradiction and Black people fit essentially into the exploited class of workers. In this contradiction, national oppression and class exploitation are joined."

Continuing, he said, "There are three secondary contradictions, that while not the principal contradiction, are very important and reflect the dialectical struggle of national oppression and class exploitation. First, the contradiction between all Black people and monopoly capitalism and it is precisely this contradiction that we struggle to overcome by waging a Black liberation struggle and moving toward the goal of national liberation.

"Secondly, there is the contradiction between white and Black workers – the contradiction that the ruling class uses to keep the working divided. And third, the class contradiction inside the Black community, the contradiction that keeps the Black liberation struggle from developing."

Alkalimat then talked of the ruling class strategy for continued domination, noting that it uses the double strategy of dividing workers and reenforcing a "lacky servant class in the Black community."

Alkalimat asserted, capitalists have "projected petty bourgeois opportunists, who have violated the militant tradition of King, and race theorists who distort Malcolm's motion toward revolution and instead turn toward cultism."

Alkalimat summed this portion of his presentation with a quote from Mao Tse-tung which said, "The struggle of the Black people in the United States is bound to merge with the American workers movement and this will eventually end the criminal rule of the U. S. monopoly capitalist class."

In answer to his second question, Alkalimat stated, "Our enemies are the entire capitalist class, particularly the leading elements of the monopoly capitalists and the high petty bourgeois servants of the monopolies." He included in this group, trade union bureaucrats like George Meany and Leonard Woodcock, the foundations run by the likes of Ford and Rockefeller, as well as government agents like Nixon and Kissinger. He said, "These are our enemies, clearly and always." He said friends are "the masses of Black people, the white working class and the peasants and workers of third world peoples inside the country." He said these groupings were friends "because their objective interest lies with socialist revolution."

He went on to state that he felt that the national liberation struggle should not be separated from the class struggle and declared "The only revolutionary nationalists today are those who are guided by the science of the working class and are simultaneously fighting to destroy the capitalist system."

He further declared, "If there can be no unity at a particular time with a specific section of the white working class, then the masses of Black people will continue to fight and will eventually overcome the disunity of the working class."

In answer to his third question, Alkalimat stated that the maximum goal must be socialist revolution because "there can be no solution under capitalism."

"Defense, democracy and development," were the key aspects of the minimum program he outlined. "We must defend Black workers from the attacks of the monopolies and by so doing, defend the interests of the total Black community. . . . We must fight for democracy inside the trade unions and by so doing, raise the banner of democracy for all people. . . . We must develop tools of struggle, organizations which mold the Black working class into a fighting, class conscious sector of the proletariat, and organizations which mold Black people into a vital revolutionary force. . . ."

Alkalimat stated that the struggle in Africa and the struggle in the U.S. are similar in that both situations are subject to the same general laws of social development and both are part of the world socialist revolution.

He cited important differences as first the fact that "the United States is an advanced capitalist country and Black people are a part of this advanced industrial or clerical working class, while Africa is dominated by a peasant majority. Secondly, whether we like it or not, Black people have, in fact, been struggling within this country while Africa, by virtue of its colonial history, is characterized by state-to-state relations and state-to-state struggle."

Alkalimat concluded his presentation by asserting the need to study the science of revolution, to build coalitions for struggle locally, to strive to become thorough anti-imperialist fighters, while keeping Africa in the center of our concern and supporting the anti-imperialist struggles of oppressed people everywhere.

Owusu Sadaukai

Owusu Sadaukai began his presentation by admitting that he personally was presently engaged in intense internal struggle.

He said, "I come before you as a person who quite honestly and frankly is struggling with a lot of things. I've been struggling with some of the things that I have said to those of you who are here over the past three to four years; struggling with some of the positions that now that I understand things a little bit better, I think were incorrect."

Sadaukai further explained, "It is my belief that racism is a product of the early development of capitalism. That is to say that racism developed as part of the superstructure developed out of the material base of capitalism.

He continued, "To look at it more concretely, racism is and has been used as a justification to keep Black people out of jobs. The end result of this is and was the continued existence of a surplus labor force which in effect depresses the wages of the entire working class. The ruling class, however, used the fact that we are out of work to say that niggers don't want to work, they're lazy and all they want to do is get on welfare, thereby reenforcing the racist ideas and notions on the part of all sectors of the white community."

Sadaukai then defined imperialism. "Imperialism is the higher extension of capitalism." He quoted Amilcar Cabral's definition of imperialism, "the worldwide expression of the search for profits and the ever increasing accumulation of surplus value by monopoly finance capital centered in two parts of the world – Europe and North America."

Sadaukai then talked about the historically interrelated development of racism and capitalism. In the 15th century, he explained, capitalism was just beginning to emerge as the dominant economic system in Europe, displacing the decaying feudalist system. Sadaukai pointed out that at this point, the burning question among European capitalists was how to accumulate even greater amounts of capital to further entrench the capitalist system.

"This question was answered in part by the invasion of Africa and the establishment of the slave trade," Sadaukai said. "Therefore the plundering and exploitation of Africa and other areas was and still remains an integral component to the maintenance of capitalism and imperialism." Sadaukai insisted that economic interests were the basis of the invasion of Africa and the subjugation of her people. "Racism was simply a ploy used later to justify the economic and human exploitation of African people."

Sadaukai quoted Sekou Toure's article *The Dialectical Approach to Culture*: "We have clearly adopted the analysis of Marx and Engels that the superstructure results from the material base and influences it dialectically." Sadaukai stated that, therefore, "in the end it was, and is, not that they took our language or our drums or our artifacts that is the major factor. It is that they took control or our productive forces and solidified that by destroying, where possible, the existence of our spiritual reality by the consolidation and internalization of racism. Now from that point on, Brothers and sisters, whether we want to deal with it or not, our relationship to white people and our relationship with each other was qualitatively changed. Our existence as African people was fundamentally altered and today we arc still struggling with the effects of that alteration."

Next Sadaukai emphasized that "we must study the classics, Marx, Lenin, Mao, and only an idiot would not understand that you have to study Cabral, Toure, and those Brothers and Sisters who are waging struggle on the African continent. How can you not study Cabral?

Why the working class? Because clearly the overwhelming number of our people are in the working class. They are in the most objective position to seize and control the means of production. There is a difference between taking over a library on a university campus and taking over General Motors. The dialectics of capitalist development produces the seeds of its own negation. It brings large numbers of workers into socialized production which gives rise to a collective, organized struggle against the ruling class."

He went on to say that we should also build a United Front inside the Black community because there are intense contradictions between the ruling class and the entire Black community. He then stated that, "we should support all anti-imperialist struggles throughout the world, starting with Africa, because of our heritage, because of the sentiments of our people, but we must support whoever is objectively struggling against imperialism, and incidentally, there should never be another time when we miss a thing like we did the Vietnam War."

Sadaukai closed with a personal statement. "In the final analysis, all of this will be validated by practice. And in the last 5 years, I have spent too much time in airplanes and running from place to place begging for money for Malcolm X, asking people to support MXLU and ALSC, to do this, to do that, all of which had its positive value.

"But the problem is that by doing that in a constant ongoing basis, you begin to lose sight of the real reality, the gut level problems of our people. So I promise you that for the next 12 to 18 months, you can find me in Durham, North Carolina, dealing with the problems of Black People, trying, in fact, to organize the Black Working Class and organize the Black community so that I can learn, because too many of us who claim to be revolutionaries and speechmakers, haven't visited Black People lately."

Future of the Conference Ideological Struggle

The conference was full of questions and answers, and stimulated much discussion, leading to a new stage of study and struggle driving the Black liberation movement. This was not the end of ideological struggle. The conference was leading to a new stage. The editorial statement in *The African World* pointed the way by

stating key questions that remain with us today (YOBU 1974, 15):
Questions to be answered:

1. How exactly does Black liberation fit into proletarian revolution in the United States?
2. How do we guard against fascism consolidating a base among white workers that could be used to crush any anti-capitalist activity?
3. If the struggle of the white working class is dormant, do we have any responsibility to wake it, or do we simply wait for it to awaken?
4. What role do all Black organizations play? Do they make us any less vulnerable to fascism, or do they aid in isolating us from the white working class?
5. How can all-Black organizations effectively lead struggles in integrated work places?

The 6th Pan African Congress

The very next month, the Sixth Pan African Congress was convened in Tanzania, at which African Americans were prominent. There were about 600 people in attendance, of which 175 were elected delegates. There was a problem with delegate planning: of the 200 African Americans in attendance, 88 had been elected as delegates, yet only 10 could be seated on the official delegate floor, while the rest were positioned in the balcony with the observers and media. At first there was one delegation of North America, but then it broke into two, the United States and Canada.

The United States was well represented in the leadership of the congress. Courtland Cox, from the leadership of the Center for Black Education in Washington, DC, was the secretary general of the congress, the head of the secretariat, and the main organizer. James Turner, professor at Cornell University, served as head of the North American delegation. And two people were major speakers in plenary sessions: Owusu Sadaukai and Amiri Baraka. All four of these activists had served in ALSC leadership roles.

Walter Rodney, although not able to attend, sent a paper to be delivered before the congress that set high goals (Tanzanian

Publishing House 1976, 33–34):

> Whatever may emerge from the Sixth Pan African Congress, it is necessary that some participants should be identified with a platform which recognizes that:

1. The principal enemies of the African people are the capitalist class in the USA, Western Europe and Japan.
2. African liberation and unity will be realized only through struggle against the African allies of international capital.
3. African freedom and development require disengagement from international monopoly capital.
4. Exploitation of Africa can be terminated only through the construction of a Socialist society, and technology must be related to this goal.
5. Contemporary state boundaries must be removed to make way for genuine politico-economic unity of the continent.
6. The Liberation Movements of Southern Africa are revolutionary and anti-imperialist and must therefore be defended against petty bourgeois state hegemony.
7. The unity of Africa requires the unity of progressive groups, organizations and institutions rather than merely being the preserve of states.
8. Pan-Africanism must be an internationalist, anti-imperialist and Socialist weapon.

These points were at the heart of the ideological struggle that took place at the congress. This debate demonstrated that the ALSC debate was not particular to the United States, but a manifestation of a global ideological trend. The editorial board of the Tanzanian Publishing House summed up the ideological positions this way:

> One position was that analysis of the African situation must be based on the class struggle, and thence firm opposition to imperialism, colonialism, and neo-colonialism. Others saw colour and the special problems confronted by victims of racism as the key. Still others synthesized the two approaches, realizing that racism is the twisted offspring of world capitalism, which itself is the real enemy of all exploited

peoples. (comments on back cover, Tanzanian Publishing House 1976)

The ALSC line struggle reemerged in the congress, and things often got loud and emotional. The nationalist line was advanced by Oba T'Shaka from Northern California, Edward Vaughn of Detroit, Kalamu ya Salaam from New Orleans, and Haki Madhubuti from Chicago. The socialist-oriented ALSC leadership was represented by Owusu Sadaukai, Gene Locke, Jeanette Walton from Philadelphia, Curtis Porter from Pittsburgh, and Bill Sales from New York. This debate played out among the delegates and even in meetings with African leaders.

Another important point raised by Rodney was a key point of struggle in the congress. Was this a meeting of governments, movements, or both? The case of Grenada was a burning issue, because that country had achieved independence in February 1974. Prime Minister Eric Gairy was opposed by the New Jewell Movement led by Maurice Bishop. Gairy was scheduled to speak and all hell was about to break out, including a decision of the U.S. delegation to stage a walkout. Courtland Cox rushed to calm things, arguing that this would be a terrible embarrassment to the host Tanzanian government. The decision was made to remain in the hall, but it turned out to be a farce, because Gairy made a fool of himself spouting such nonsense that people laughed at him. Nevertheless, whether the representatives in the Pan-African movement should be states or movements remains a difficult question even today.

In the end, the Sixth Pan African Congress made considerable progress in giving ideological direction to the global movement, as stated in its final declaration:

> Revolutionary Pan Africanism inscribes itself within the context of the class struggle. Not to be conscious of this would be to expose ourselves to confusion, which imperialism would not fail to exploit.

We must never forget that the imperialism we are fighting, the imperialism which nearly exterminated us in Africa and is still daily committing crimes of genocide here, was not generated through the internal historical process which took place in Africa. Imperialism was generated by capitalism and it therefore concerns the entire world. If it is to be effective, the liquidation of imperialism, that is, the liberation of the people, must be general. The universality of imperialism implies the universality of the anti-imperialist struggle. . . .

The strategy of Revolutionary Pan Africanism is basically defined in terms of the anti-imperialist, anti-colonialist, anti-neocolonialist, anti-capitalist and anti-racist struggle that it considers to be a means of promoting democracy and developing a new society: (a) The people must form the basis of this generalized struggle and the aspirations of the masses and working classes must constitute the moving force behind it; (b) It must be defined in terms of the class struggle at the national and international level, as the rational basis for explaining and finding solution to social injustices, exploitation, oppression, and racism. (Tanzanian Publishing House 1976, 89, 90)

Houston ALSC Meeting – August 1974

The next ALSC meeting, held in August, was a chance to assess after a summer of intense struggle and advancement of the left in the United States and in Africa as well:

> ALSC's International Steering Committee met in Houston, Texas over the weekend of August 17–18, 1974. In attendance were 85 delegates representing 27 local chapters in the U.S. and Canada. The meeting took a bold step in moving ALSC more concretely into the world-wide anti-imperialist movement. The programmatic thrust of ALSC in the struggle against racism and imperialism was clarified; important structural changes were made in the organizations operations, and election of leadership was held for 1974–75. (Houston ALSC 1974, 1)

The final responses to narrow nationalist resignations were made at this time, as these resignations were attacks against ALSC. *Muhammad Speaks*, newspaper of the Nation of Islam, issued its third attack on ALSC in its June 14, 1974 issue. They claimed that ALSC was a tool of the white left, specifically the *Guardian* newspaper, and that its leadership were pawns of this white left conspiracy. The basic errors here are that the *Guardian* was not an organization carrying out any such plan, nor was the Black left under the white left, but rather was an expression of the self-determination of Black revolutionary activists. The YOBU editorial committee of *The African World* delineated the unity without uniformity of the ALSC:

> Just as the Marxist-Leninist members of ALSC have a right to their own views, so do ALSC members who consider themselves Kawaida advocates, revolutionary nationalists, Pan-Africanists, and anti-imperialists. The only position binding an ALSC member is the ALSC Statement of Principles—a position hailed as a positive advance in the Black Liberation Struggle by leaders of African Liberation movements and other progressive forces on the continent. (YOBU 1974, 6)

Dawolu Gene Locke made a major response to three critical attacks on ALSC—by Mwanza, a former ALSC chairperson of Ohio; by The East publication *Black News*; and by *Muhammad Speaks*. Locke argued that there are three ways that these criticisms were similar:

> Common to all these attacks is the unprincipled way in which the criticisms were made; the personal slander and attack, presenting speculation as fact, and drawing conclusions with little or no information on which to base them. . . . A second feature common to these right wing assaults on ALSC is an incorrect analysis of imperialism and world revolution and their relation to class struggle and Black people in the USA. . . . A third common feature of the criticisms is their reflection of a petty-bourgeoisie in a time of the escalation of the mass struggle. This ideology is bourgeois nationalism: the ideology which places in the forefront the supposed interest of the oppressed nation or nationality as a while without regard to class divisions; but, in reality, pushed the special interests of the native or national bourgeoisie or petty bourgeoisie. (Locke 1974b, 5, 6)

A third major counterattack ran in *The Black Scholar*. Mark Smith, one of the main organizers of ALD 1972 and former vice chair of YOBU, responded to a nationalist attack by Haki Madhubuti.

Madhubuti was alarmed that a Marxist tendency had developed in ALSC and CAP, both of which he participated in at a leadership level. His line was that this was a plot by the white left, leading Black people into a suicidal world revolution:

> One thing is for sure, they are both pushing for the "world socialist revolution" and both feel that at some point in the future, Black people in the West must align themselves with the white workers to make the revolution. But the saddest part of their new thrust is that they see Black people as the vanguard for the "world revolution". (Madhubuti 1974, 46)

He goes on to argue the primacy of racism delinked from its manifestation under capitalism, thus making it impossible for Black-white unity:

> It is important to understand that the ideology of white supremacy precedes the economic structure of capitalism and imperialism, the latter of which are falsely stated as the cause of racism. To believe that the white boy mis-used and manipulated us for centuries up until today for purely economic reasons is racist and void of any historical value. (Madhubuti 1974, 46)

Smith takes on this argument and demonstrates that this is not only a misreading of the left in ALSC, especially the agreed-upon SOP, it is also a misreading of Marxism as only a European theory, with the suggestion that the Sino-Soviet split was racial in nature (M. Smith 1975). (More on this in chapter 4.)

The Houston meeting thus took place at an intense time for ALSC, both theoretically and practically. Oppositional nationalist forces had withdrawn, and forces farther to the left were moving in. ALSC had become the most dynamic context for the radicalization of the Black liberation movement for anti-imperialist action. Indeed, the call was for Black activists to focus on class struggle for Black liberation in the United States and Africa.

One of the key debates both before and during the meeting was whether to disband ALSC. This issue came to the fore because in some cases the limited number of cadres in a given organization were so focused on the African liberation support work that other work was being neglected. Partly this was a crisis in the practical application of the SOP, how to link anti-imperialism in a global context to the particularities of local work. The task was for cadres to sink deep roots into the working class, and that was going to take time and patience to gain trust. Students becoming workers was going to be a big task as well. The key question for the organizations involved in ALSC was how to keep doing African liberation support work at the same time.

Several local committees took positions to support the decision to continue to build ALSC as a vehicle for doing mass anti-imperialist movement building.

The road forward was then planned after discussing several proposals:

After extensive debate on each proposal a subcommittee was formed to draft a summary resolution for three key areas: theoretical positions and questions, program for ALSC, and the structure for ALSC. These resolutions were adopted by unanimous vote and will serve as the basic framework for ALSC for the coming year. (Houston ALSC 1974, 2)

In addition, a new leadership team was elected, composing what would now be called a National Secretariat.

Table 11. African Liberation Support Committee National Secretariat, August 1974

Position	Person	Location
International Representative	Dawolu Gene Locke	Houston, TX
Information Director	Carl Turpin	Washington, DC
Administrative Secretary	Jeledi Endesha	South Bend, IN
At Large	Joyce Johnson	Greensboro, NC
At Large	Owusu Sadaukai	Durham, NC
At Large	Imamu Baraka	Newark, NJ
At Large	Jeanette Walton	Philadelphia, PA
At Large	Ethel Shepton	Boston, MA

The main crisis of the meeting revolved around the relationship between theory and practice. The ALSC approach to that point had been that theoretical struggle would lead to an intensification of campaigns of struggle as discussed in chapter 2. However, the Houston meeting reversed that and pointed to more theoretical work. This made the political study program for the cadre organizations in ALSC the same as for ALSC as a mass organization. The adopted committee report stated this plainly:

This resolution calls for full discussion, study, debate of the questions below with the context of ALSC. . . . If conditions permit a national forum should be called by the national secretariat.

1. What does "Black workers take the lead" mean?
2. What should be the correct policy in developing relationships, alliances and coalitions with white and other oppressed nationalities?
3. Is there a single working class within the U.S. or are there two distinct working classes (whites and oppressed nationalities)?
4. What is the nature of the contradiction between the Black Bourgeoisie (comprador and national) and what should be the proletarian policy toward them?
5. Is a two stage revolution necessary in the U.S. from national liberation to socialist revolution or are they merged into a single stage?
6. What is the United Front? What is its basis? Is there any validity for a Black United Front in the U.S.?
7. What should be the nature of ALSC's political line? Should it be narrow or broad enough to encompass a wide spectrum of thought?
8. What is male chauvinism? How has it manifested itself in ALSC? How can we eradicate it?
9. Are white workers as counter revolutionary as the bourgeoisie? What is the revolutionary potential of white workers (historically and presently)? What is the nature of the contradiction between white workers and monopoly capitalists?
10. What is a colony? Do Blacks in the U.S. represent an internal colony? What are the similarities and differences between

the character of oppression of Blacks in the USA and the character of oppression of Blacks in Guinea-Bissau?
11. What is an anti-imperialist and anti-racist stance?
12. What is anti-imperialist and anti-racist work in the U.S.?

These questions pointed the discussion in ALSC toward unifying the left on an ideological basis, but there was another option. The research committee had developed a questionnaire that directed each ALSC committee to research the nature of their local community, moving them from abstract discussion to the concrete socioeconomic and political realities the community faced. By anchoring ideology in material reality, seeking unity would be more of an open unity-building process. There is a difference between arguing over abstract definitions versus discussing the social and economic forces in a community where you can describe the social structure and political actions that operate there.

The left in ALSC had the option of moving out into the masses of Black people to win them over to struggle. The key was to determine what was principle, action leading to higher consciousness, or seeking higher levels of thinking as a precondition to action. This is the difference between cadre development and building a mass movement. The logical development of a mass movement is the relationship between cadre and mass, the cadre leads with theory and the mass with action. The summation and analysis of action provide the theoretical basis for the development of activists in the mass movement. This is the role of cadre.

The practice of the local chapters was not being organized on a national level to make sure ALSC was maintaining its unity based in practical struggle. The decision of the Houston meeting set them loose without uniting in the effort to strike common blows against the system:

> Local ALSC committees are encouraged to use independence and initiative in active militant struggle against antagonistic contradictions facing Black people in local areas. Local ALSC committees are encouraged to join with all possible genuine revolutionary forces to build anti-racist anti-imperialist solidarity and struggle. This should take the form of tactical coalitions, preserving the Black form of ALSC while raising

high its anti-racist, anti-imperialist line. (Houston ALSC 1974, 4)

This move, which served the party-building process of the Black left organizations making up ALSC, was both a source of strength and of weakness. This is the subject of chapter 4.

Chapter 4

1975: World Revolution

It is necessary to place ALSC in the context of world and national events in order to establish it as part of the logic of development that sums up the times. What ALSC undertook was not an isolated organizational process, it was a reflection of global and national trends that impacted the Black liberation movement. So, the lessons that can be learned from all three levels of struggle need to be grasped to understand the past and help activists today to intervene in the future historical process, at a global level, a national level, and within the Black left in particular.

This chapter is about how the revolutionary high tide of the mid-1970s led to cadre-based party-building organizations. Parties were formed, but then a global focus took over and practice yielded primacy to abstract theoretical issues. The battle of ideas, the political line, became the logic of development for the left, on a global level, a national level, and within the Black left in particular. The best of the 1960s generation turned to the left and then turned on themselves. What was achieved was a great outpouring of intellectual work, but what was missed was the opportunity to sink deep roots among the masses of people, build organizations, and maintain sustainability. While we have the luxury of 20/20 hindsight, we don't want to run roughshod over what advances were made then.

ALSC is a good case study for the development of anti-imperialist struggle in the United States in the second half of the twentieth century. It demonstrated the dialectical struggle Marxist and nationalist forces faced in working together, both when they were successful in doing so and when they were not. It represented the greatest working relationship between forces in the New Communist Movement with Marxist forces organically emerging out of the Black liberation movement. At the most abstract level, it is a historical case study of the organizational dialectics of cadres working to develop a social movement.

These questions are relevant today, even though the current period is very different from the time of ALSC. One of the major differences is that then there were two contrasting global systems in place, with countries being either capitalist or socialist, even though both systems were in crisis. Furthermore, at that time Africa was under direct colonialism, and now it is suffering under the neocolonial domination of the International Monetary Fund and the World Bank and the imperialist countries associated with those entities—the United States, France, the United Kingdom, Germany, Belgium, and Japan.

Unity and Disunity in World Revolution

ALSC developed within the Black liberation movement, in the general context of the processes of world revolution, national liberation in Africa, and socialism. The center of gravity of world revolution in the twentieth century was the Soviet Union (USSR), the first country to break with capitalism and feudalism and create socialism in 1917. The leading theoreticians of the Russian revolution, Lenin, Stalin, and Trotsky, laid the basis for both the unity and disunity of world revolutionary forces. A textbook commissioned by Stalin that presented lessons from the Soviet experience, *History of the Communist Party of the Soviet Union (Bolsheviks): Short Course*, was used to organize communist parties all over the world. ("History of the Communist Party of the Soviet Union (Bolsheviks): Short Course" 1939)

On most questions the work of Lenin stood above all others.

Chapter 4

His pamphlet, *What Is To Be Done?* (1902), about the dialectical struggle of theory and practice out of which the Russian Bolshevik Party was formed, became a text for global study as well:

> Its main theme was to have been the three questions raised in the article "Where To Begin"—the character and main content of our political agitation; our organisational tasks; and the plan for building, simultaneously and from various sides, a militant, all-Russia organization. (Lenin 1975, 3)

Lenin's focus was on the task of revolutionary cadres working within the mass movement, particularly among workers and their trade unions.

The great global challenge for both capitalism and socialism was the development of a perverse extension of capitalism into its fascist form in Germany, Italy, Spain, and Japan. The urgent task was to unite the many to defeat the few. The Communist International (1919–1943) was the organizational form that united all communist parties on a global level. Known as the Comintern, this organization, led by Gregori Dimitrov from 1934 to 1943, developed a comprehensive theory of the United Front to confront and defeat fascism:

> What is and ought to be the basic content of the united front at the present stage? The defense of the immediate economic and political interests of the working class, the defense of the working class against fascism, must form the *starting point* and *main content* of the united front in all capitalist countries.
>
> We must not confine ourselves to bare appeals to struggle for the proletarian dictatorship. We must find and advance those slogans and forms of struggle which arise from the vital needs of the masses, from the level of their fighting capacity at the present stage of development.
>
> We must point out to the masses what they must do *today* to defend themselves against capitalist spoliation and fascist barbarity.
>
> We must strive to establish the widest united front with the aid of joint action by workers' organizations of different trends for the defense of the vital interests of the laboring

masses. This means:

- *First*, joint struggle really to shift the burden of the consequences of the crisis onto the shoulders of the ruling classes, the shoulders of the capitalists and landlords—in a word, onto the shoulders of the rich.

- *Second*, joint struggle against all forms of the fascist offensive, in defense of the gains and the rights of the working people, against the abolition of bourgeois-democratic liberties.

- *Third*, joint struggle against the approaching danger of an imperialist war, a struggle that will make the preparation of such a war more difficult. . . .

Communists, of course, cannot and must not for a moment abandon their own *independent work* of Communist education, organization and mobilization of the masses. (Dimitrov 1935)

This led to a successful coalition headed by Franklin D. Roosevelt (United States), Winston Churchill (United Kingdom), and Joseph Stalin (Soviet Union), capitalists and communists working together to defeat fascism. But it also resulted in a disaster in the United States, as the leader of the CPUSA, Earl Browder, led the move to disband that party and reverse global thinking on the independent role of communists in a united front. William Z. Foster writes about Browder's revisionism:

It had gone to its last extreme in the liquidation of the Party. Browder had not only revised the principles and policies of the Party, he had also dissolved the Party itself. He did this under the pretext that the C.P.A. [Communist Political Association] was a better instrument to work with. This was an abandonment and betrayal of the most fundamental concepts of Marxism-Leninism. It was a surrender to the Social-Democratic and bourgeois demand that the C.P. be abolished, an attempt to deprive the working class of its indispensable leading political party. In its convention of May, 1944, the Communist Party of the United States made the greatest political mistake in all its history. (Foster 1968, 431)

The world revolution took a historic turn when the Chinese Communist Party led a revolutionary seizure of power in China in 1949. With this major event the world was put on notice that socialist revolution and the theory of Marxism-Leninism could become a force in the anticolonial national liberation movements. The Chinese party had operated under the umbrella of the international democratic centralism established by the Comintern. They then delinked from the Comintern representatives sent to China, because their decisions had led to setbacks. Mao rose to power in the party during the famous Long March (1934–1935).

Mao became the first theoretician to successfully apply Marxism-Leninism to a non-European country, and as such sent a message to all freedom-loving activists in Africa. He advanced a theory of New Democracy (1940).

> Although such a revolution in a colonial and semi-colonial country is still fundamentally bourgeois-democratic in its social character during its first stage or first step, and although its objective mission is to clear the path for the development of capitalism, it is no longer a revolution of the old type led by the bourgeoisie with the aim of establishing a capitalist society and a state under bourgeois dictatorship. It belongs to the new type of revolution led by the proletariat with the aim, in the first stage, of establishing a new-democratic society and a state under the joint dictatorship of all the revolutionary classes. Thus, this revolution actually serves the purpose of clearing a still wider path for the development of socialism. In the course of its progress, there may be a number of further sub-stages, because of changes on the enemy's side and within the ranks of our allies, but the fundamental character of the revolution remains unchanged. (Mao 1965, 344)

Differences had been growing between the parties in China and the Soviet Union, and finally in 1963 a clear break was publicly acknowledged in letters exchanged between the parties. The Chinese summed up their take on what the parties needed to agree upon in *A Proposal Concerning the General Line of the International Communist Movement*:

> Workers of all countries, unite; workers of the world, unite with the oppressed peoples and oppressed nations; oppose

imperialism and reaction in all countries; strive for world peace, national liberation, people's democracy and socialism; consolidate and expand the socialist camp; bring the proletarian world revolution step by step to complete victory; and establish a new world without imperialism, without capitalism and without the exploitation of man by man. This, in our view, is the general line of the international communist movement at the present stage. (Zhongguo gong chan dang and Zhong yang wei yuan hui 1963, 4)

This came to be called the Sino-Soviet Split; in turn, it generated splits in revolutionary movements all over the world. Though many issues had caused the rupture, the two most salient were:

1. The Chinese argued that the principal contradiction in the world was imperialism versus the anti-colonial national liberation movements. This challenged the notion that the main task was to support actually existing socialism, focusing on the USSR;
2. The Soviet ideologists advanced the notion that their form of socialism had created a state of the whole people, and the Chinese critically charged that even under socialism classes and class struggle continued to exist.

These two points help us to understand how both countries experienced the resurgence of capitalism, and how the Sino-Soviet split reflected global trends. This impacted the liberation movements in Angola, Zimbabwe, and South Africa. While supporting African liberation was the major motivation of the Soviet Union and China, it seems that equally important was backing organizations upon which they could rely as allies:

The policy of a Communist power, and this goes for both the Soviet Union and for China, has always two aspects—the aspect of normal power politics, of national interest, of the *raison d'état*, on the one hand, and the aspect of Communist ideology, of the sense of mission, of the world-wide ideological aim, on the other. (Richard Lowenthal, quoted in Hamrell and Widstrand 1964, 131)

Unfortunately, this often meant that the global polarity of the Sino-Soviet Split resulted in the destructive search for hegemony in fratricidal civil wars being carried out within the liberation movements.

In Angola, the Chinese were supporting UNITA, while the Soviet Union supported MPLA. However, neither country provided the amount and type of weaponry needed to defeat the forces of South Africa, which were backed by the United States. The support from Cuba was the deciding factor. Cuba was closer to the Soviet Union than China, but her action was on her own initiative. That nation, under the leadership of Fidel Castro, was committed to Africa as part of its internationalism and its fidelity to the African Diaspora. Even the OAU, first committed to a unity government that included all liberation organizations, finally stood with MPLA as the legitimate government of Angola, after condemning UNITA's military assault on MPLA. As mentioned above, UNITA was eventually exposed as being in alliance with South Africa and the United States.

A different situation developed in Zimbabwe. There, China supported ZANU and the Soviet Union supported ZAPU. In particular, China provided ZANU with a blueprint for their military campaign:

> Mao Tse-Tung's strategy of protracted war or guerilla war is broadly divided into three phases. The first phase is that of strategic defensive, the second, of strategic offensive and finally, the third of mobile warfare. Mao also stresses the importance of foreign support during a protracted war. (Pandya 1988, 18)

It was the *chimurenga* (a Shona word meaning "revolutionary struggle") led by ZANU that was decisive in Zimbabwe, both prior to the unity formation of FROLIZI and after it. This is how the white settler regime viewed the situation:

> ZANU and ZAPU have been under some pressure from the OAU and several leading African politicians to merge their efforts. In spite of the split between the USSR and PRC, Moscow and Peking have not appeared averse to such a union. In fact, the first 'military' training undergone by Rhodesian African terrorists was in the People's Republic of China in early 1963. Since that year, ZAPU (formerly known

as the People's Caretaker Council), has received financial and material aid from the Soviet bloc. The other organization, ZANU, has had some continuing support from the Soviet bloc but, more recently, has become increasingly dependent on the PRC. In response to the pressure for unity, on 1 October 1971 the Front for the Liberation of Zimbabwe (FROLIZI) was formed. The constitution and manifesto of FROLIZI are heavily larded with communist verbiage. FROLIZI is headed by James R.P. Chikerema and its effectiveness as a fusion liberation group is still doubtful. In any case, ZANU and ZAPU continue to operate apparently as separate units. Some observers suggest that FROLIZI really represents a coalition of dissidents from ZAPU and ZANU organized behind Chikerema for his own challenge for leadership of the entire Zimbabwe liberation movement. (Professor Walter Darnell Jacobs of the University of Maryland, quoted in Rhodesian Ministry of Foreign Affairs 1975)

So, the reverse happened compared to Angola. In Angola, the Soviet support went to the MPLA, which took control of the new state, while Chinese support for ZANU led to that group's supremacy in Zimbabwe.

In South Africa, the Soviet Union supported the ANC while China supported the PAC. The CPSA had formed in 1921 as a member of the Comintern, hence its origin linked it to the Soviet Union. The line of Soviet support continued with the journal *The African Communist*, to serve as the organ of the South African Communist Party. From this followed the Soviet Union's involvement with and support for the ANC and COSACTU. As mentioned above, the key document around which the alliance united was the Freedom Charter. The breakaway PAC essentially rejected this and turned back to the Native Thesis National Question as developed by the Comintern, which focused on the national liberation of the African masses.

This created a great schism in the global anti-apartheid movement. ANC supporters were dominant in most parts of the world and they would not grant any speaking time to supporters of the PAC in forums advocating African liberation. So the Sino-Soviet split was an active disrupting force in Africa, but it did not stop the motion forward past the period of direct colonial rule.

Unity and Disunity in the U.S. New Communist Movement

Sustainable unity has never been the norm for revolutionary movements in the United States. From the very beginning, the unity of socialists and communists has consistently been unfinished business, often erupting in splits and new organizational formations. The Sino-Soviet split created a global divergence that fed into the multiple conflicts between the CPUSA and the student movement and the Black liberation movement of the 1960s. New possibilities were being glimpsed after the Chinese revolution of 1949, the Cuban revolution in 1959, and the great advance of Vietnam in 1975. The CPUSA could not retain its hegemony in this new era of revolutionary movement catalyzed by the Sino-Soviet split.

As mentioned above, there were three main organizational centers of the New Communist Movement: the CLP (1974), the RCP (1975), and the CP(M-L) (1977). There were many smaller collectives that danced into unity and disunity with these three major tendencies (Elbaum 2002). The unity–disunity dialectic developed around three main issues: China, party building, and the African American national question.

The Cultural Revolution in China (1966–1976) was a class struggle within the party that spread throughout the socialist society of that country. This was an internal contradiction in China that reflected the issues of the Sino-Soviet split. The main issue was about which class was in power, and how to carry out the class struggle in a socialist society. A polarity developed between what came to be called the "Gang of Four" (Chiang Ching, Chang Chun-chiao, Wang Hung-wen, and Yao Wen-yuan) and forces aligned with Teng Hsiao Ping and Hua Kuo-feng. Some argued that Mao was part of the Gang of Four, making it a "Gang of Five" (Lotta 1978).

Mao died in 1976. Inside the RCP, the polarity of Avakian versus the Jarvis-Bergman factions mirrored the Chinese struggle and hardened as cadres took sides on the Chinese polarity. The Avakian forces sided with the Gang of Four, while the Jarvis-Bergman forces regarded them as making an ultra-left error. The

RCP almost split in half over this struggle in 1977 (Revolutionary Communist Party, USA 1978; Revolutionary Workers Headquarters 1978).

Mao had raised the slogan "Grasp revolution, promote production" as a way of stating the need for the unity of theory and practice. This has been the goal of all revolutionary movements, but is the hardest balance to maintain. The main thrust of the RCP had been in organizing in workplaces and among the unemployed to great success. The Avakian forces remained in control of the RCP, but began to place their main emphasis on "grasping revolution." They ended up championing Bob Avakian Thought as a new stage of Marxist theory (calling for BA Everywhere!), but without the practice that could validate their viewpoint.

For their part, the Jarvis-Bergman forces reorganized themselves into the Revolutionary Workers Headquarters and focused on continuing to sink communist roots in the working class. They ended up uniting with the Proletarian Unity League to form the Freedom Road Socialist Organization in 1985, which itself then split in 1999. In this trend activism dominated over theory.

The October League transformed into the CP(M-L) in 1977. This was preceded by a split based on a faction led by Martin Nicolaus, who opposed the Gang of Four. The CP(M-L) leadership initially agreed with the Gang of Four, but then flipped to supporting Hua Kuo-feng. In August of 1977, China gave a sort of official recognition from the post-Mao regime when Hua Kuo-feng, the new Chinese leader, received CP(M-L) chairman Mike Klonsky. Again, China was a key factor in both the unity and disunity of a U.S. revolutionary organization (Avakian 2005, 363–67; Nicolaus 1977).

The unity-disunity dialectic of party building was typical of organizations in the emerging communist movement. The process had begun in local collectives that formed themselves into pre-party networks, sometimes around shared theoretical statements and sometimes around shared practical work in the working-class or mass organizations. With the aim of creating a revolutionary party to represent the working class, different networks came to different conclusions. Along the way, differences developed, and a whole library of polemics created a cacophony of theoretical discord.

A major initiative to address the unity-disunity dialectic was organized by the *Guardian* newspaper, as described above. This newspaper was an institution on the left, with a history that went back to its founding in 1948. The newspaper staff was at one time close to the OL/CP(M-L) process, but that fell apart with the Martin Nicolaus affair.

The Revolutionary Union, on its way to becoming the RCP (1975), organized the National Liaison Committee (1972–1974) as their attempt at a movement-wide party-building process. At some point they included the BWC, The Puerto Rican Revolutionary Workers Organization, the I Wok Kuen, and some *Guardian* members.

Out of a conference of North American Marxist-Leninists held in Chicago in 1973, the Communist League (CL) led a party-building process called the National Continuations Committee. This involved the Motor City Labor League, the League for Proletarian Revolution, the August Twenty-Ninth Movement, the BWC, and the Puerto Rican Revolutionary Workers Movement. After several splits, called "purges," the CLP was formed in 1974.

Splits continued to plague the process; hence, while there were exemplary battles fought, no party gained a dominant position either among revolutionary cadres or in the mass movements. What did happen is that most cadres in the parties that were formed became relatively isolated into small networks. Many were so traumatized by the intense polemics and extreme behavior that they dropped out of both cadre-level communist and mass movement activity.

The issue that most impacted people in ALSC and the Black liberation movement as a whole was the African American National Question. Black people have been at the foundation of capitalist exploitation, and in response have been at the heart of every challenge to the capitalist system. So, the focus has been on understanding of whom these people are and what kind of politics will advance their struggle and contribute to the overall revolutionary process in the United States.

The revolutionary starting point at the theoretical level on the national question has been the one put forward by Joseph Stalin as part of the doctrine of the Communist Party of the Soviet Union: "A nation is a historically evolved, stable community of language, territory, economic life, and psychological make-up manifested in a community of culture" (Stalin 1971, 53). The thinking of Lenin and Stalin led to the foundational resolutions adopted in 1928 and 1930 by the Sixth Congress of the Comintern on African Americans (Adi 2013,47-66). This analysis argued that African Americans constituted a nation in the Black Belt South and a national minority in all other areas of the country. The critical aspect of the nation thesis is the strategic demand for self-determination. The revolutionary demand everywhere was for democratic rights, but, for those people in the Black Belt nation, what had to be upheld was their right to a state form, up to and including the right of seccession. The Political Secretariat of the Comintern expanded on the 1928 thesis in 1930:

> The struggle of the Communists for the equal rights of the Negroes applies to all Negroes, in the North as well as in the South. The struggle for this slogan embraces all or almost all of the important special interests of the Negroes in the North, but not in the South, where the main Communist slogan must be: *The right of self-determination of the Negroes in the Black Belt.* These two slogans, however, are most closely connected. The Negroes in the North are very much interested in winning the right of self-determination for the Negro population of the Black Belt and can thereby hope for strong support for the establishment of true equality of the Negroes in the North. (Young 1975, 23)

The CPUSA adopted the line of the Comintern and it guided their work fighting for Black liberation. In fact, the concept of liberation was based on Black people being a nation and not simply one component of the working class facing special forms of oppression. All of the major theorists of the party upheld this line (Allen 1984; Ford and Berry 1938; Foster 1947; Haywood 1976). However, after World War II and the capitulation of Browder, the CP dropped the Black Belt nation thesis (Foster 1952, 432). After some struggle, they purged Haywood over his dissent:

> The CPUSA's decision to change its position on the African-American national question was a central factor in Haywood's expulsion. Though the CPUSA had not been as active in the South since the dissolution of the Sharecroppers Union, in 1959 the CPUSA officially dropped its demand for self-determination for African Americans there. (The demand had been dropped earlier when Browder liquidated the party in 1944.) The CPUSA instead held that as American capitalism developed, so too would Black-White unity.

> In 1957 he [Haywood] wrote "For a Revolutionary Position on the Negro Question" (later published by Liberator Press) but was unsuccessful at changing the direction of the Party. In 1959, Haywood, although no longer a functioning party member, attempted to intervene one last time. He wrote "On the Negro Question", which was distributed at the Seventeenth National Convention by and in the name of African Blood Brotherhood founder Cyril Briggs. ("Harry Haywood" 2020)

The antirevisionist New Communist Movement, greatly influenced by the Black liberation movement, revived Stalin's definition of a nation, and most cadres began their theoretical work on the question by starting with the 1928–1930 Comintern policy that African Americans constituted a national question.

The Communist League, the membership of which included veteran activists with backgrounds in the CPUSA, made following the Comintern's position on African Americans a major part of its theoretical foundation. They published *The Negro National Colonial Question* in 1972, in which they state, "This collective effort represents the fundamental position of the Central Committee of the Communist League. It is a reaffirmation of the position of the Communist International and the position of V.I. Lenin and J.V. Stalin the greatest of all thinkers on the question of oppressed peoples and nations" (Peery 1978).

The CL made great efforts to deracialize the concept of the Negro nation, asserting that everyone in the Black Belt, Blacks and whites, were all part of the Negro nation:

Within the general territory which makes up the Negro Nation, a majority of the population is made up of Negro men and women. In the territorial core of the Negro Nation—that is, the Black Belt, there is a continuous stretch of overwhelming Negro majority. . . . History and economic development has absolutely linked the destinies of the surrounding area with the Black Belt. Therefore we see that a large minority of the people of the Negro Nation are Anglo-American. (Peery 1978)

In this document, they also argue that this was a colonial question, ending with the slogan "Independence for the Negro Nation!" However, later the CL would change their line completely. Peery presented a new analysis of the African American experience in 1992—from the field to the factory to the street:

The formation of the African American people is unique. Their consolidation was not based on common land or religion. There is no internal dynamic to hold them together. The force that formed the African Americans into a people has always been the legal and extra-legal pressure of the whites.

There could only be two tactics in the fight. One was to separate into a political entity and, as a group, seek equality with white America. Their physical dispersal throughout the country prevented this. The other tactic was to fight for integration through desegregation and equality. The natural and consistently expressed drive of the African Americans has been to become equal members of American society. There has been bitter struggle over tactics, but there has never been serious struggle over goals. (Peery 1992, 9)

The OL also adopted the Comintern position. They passed a resolution on the Afro-American Struggle at their Second Congress (1973), stating the following:

Today it is our recognition of the Afro-American question as a National Question that distinguishes us from those opportunists who, under the mantle of Marxism, have sided with the millionaires in their onslaught against Black people and who parot [parrot] the imperialist phrase that "industrialization has done away with national differences."

It is based on this recognition that we in the October League must take on our revolutionary responsibilities to UPHOLD THE RIGHT OF SELF-DETERMINATION UP TO AND INCLUDING SECESSION OF THE AFRO-AMERICAN PEOPLE IN THE BLACK BELT SOUTH. This slogan is one aimed at the U.S. workers, particularly the white workers, and its aim is to break them from the chauvinist policies which chain them to the bourgeoisie. (October League 1973, 8–9)

This line was developed further by leading OL activists, including Carl Davidson and Harry Haywood (C. Davidson 1976; Haywood 1978).

The Revolutionary Union (RU) also started with the Comintern, but their initial analysis in *Red Papers 5* involved a qualitative change:

In sum: the whole history of the Black people's oppression and resistance in the heart of the south, while, of course, interrelated with the experience of whites in the region, is completely distinct and forms their historical basis as a separate nation. In fact, the heart of the south, like the rest of the country today, is inhabited by at least two nations: the Black nation and the dominant white-European nation formed out of several nationalities.

But today the Black nation is overwhelmingly working class: the Black workers, south and north, are members of the single U.S. working class. Those who try to ignore or distort this in order to cling to analysis that correctly—or partially—reflected reality in 1880 or 1930, but not reality in the 1970's, violate the Marxist-Leninist method which Stalin himself repeatedly emphasizes in dealing with the national question: "The solution of the national question is possible only in connection with the historical conditions taken in their development. . . . To repeat: the concrete historical conditions as the starting point, and the dialectical presentation of the question as the only correct way of presenting it—such is the key to solving the national question" (Stalin, Vol. 2, pp. 325, 331). (Revolutionary Communist Party 1972)

They extended their analysis in response to Black cadres within RU and in formations like the BWC. In *Red Papers 6* they raised the issue of Bundism. The Bund was an organization of Jewish workers and students who united with and then left the Bolshevik Party several times on the basis of claiming to represent the Jewish people and not being in full agreement with party decisions representing the interests of all workers. They wanted to retain special rights as though they belonged to a federation, not a party with democratic centralism. *Red Papers 6* claimed that organizing Black party members or a Black community organization could fall into being a Bundist tendency:

> The difference boils down to the fact that BWC and PRRWO are treating the struggle of Black people and other oppressed nationalities for liberation as something separate from and above the struggle of the working class to emancipate itself and all other oppressed people. As the polemics show, this has come down to several points: the BWC-PRRWO attitude that Black and other third world communists should have a "special place" in the new Party when it is formed, in their position that Black workers are automatically advanced (reflected in the slogan "Black Workers Take the Lead") and white workers are too racist and politically backward to provide leadership; and most recently in the argument that self-determination for Black people in the "Black Belt" South and "land to the tiller" is at the very heart of the Black liberation struggle, that Blacks should re-constitute themselves in the old plantation area in order to achieve these aims—and anybody who says different is a racist and revisionist. (Revolutionary Communist Party 1974)

After the split from the RCP, the Revolutionary Workers Headquarters argued against this point regarding cadre policy:

> This was wrong on two accounts. First off, it broke the chain of knowledge and said that inside a Marxist-Leninist organization experience is no longer a question. Secondly, it didn't deal with the reality that for Black Marxists to fully release their initiative, to give full play to their experience, revolutionary drive, and will to lead the people, all traces of the ideology and practice of white supremacy must be combatted. There must be an atmosphere created in which Black Marxists can be confident in leading the Black people, that their directions and goals are truly in the interest of Black

people and that this is not another case of whites telling Blacks what to do.

> Being a Black Marxist representing what is seen as a mostly white organization inside the BLM is a rough spot to be in. We must create the room to work out this contradiction. (Revolutionary Workers Headquarters 1981, 73)

The positions of the CLP, CP(M-L), and RCP were the dominant ones in the New Communist Movement that followed from the Comintern Resolutions of 1928 and 1930. The other major tendency was to argue against the nation thesis and to focus on racism.

The Racism Research Project published an important essay by Harry Chang, *Critique of the Black Nation Thesis* (1975). He starts with the definition by Stalin, and argues that people have been mistaken in understanding it to mean that the four characteristics define the nation rather than creating the conditions for a possible nation. He argues that the African American people have never acted as a nation and thus have not been a unique entity, due to contradictions regarding a common territory and a common economic life. Chang argues that it is racism that is the ultimate evil that needs to be understood and combatted, not used to isolate the struggle of Black people as an aspect of a separate nation:

> Perhaps the most disturbing aspect of the current revival of the Black Nation Thesis is that it is probably an attempt to make "multi-national" virtue out of racial vice. The unsavory state of the racially divided organizational workings of the U.S. Left is crying out for a theoretical justification. The lack of a Marxist analysis of racism has long been the Achilles heel through which a chauvinistic approach to the anti-racism struggle has managed to seep into the Left. The inroad of racism into the Left has usually taken the same theoretical route: sunder [split apart] the dialectic of racial categories, then set the stage for conceiving the anti-racism struggle as the exclusive province of Blacks. This way, Blacks are supposed to be attempting to achieve what the implied "White Nation" is supposed to have achieved long ago. Black Liberation as a "national minority" struggle is merely the most outspoken version of this formulation, a formulation

which makes Blacks the gladiators and Whites the spectators in the latter-day Roman arena. (Chang 1975, 31)

The Philadelphia Workers' Organizing Committee (PWOC) dove directly into a racism thesis without taking the time to deal with the nation thesis at all. PWOC took aim at how racism divides the working class and pushed a section of white workers into the bourgeois camp so that they (the workers) targeted Black workers and not the class who actually exploits them (Griffin 1980).

A third and very influential analysis of the racism thesis was made by Harold Baron, former Director of Research for the Chicago Urban League. His essay, *The Demand for Black Labor: Historical Notes on the Political Economy of Racism*, had a big impact on the thinking of Black radical activists. He makes reference to what he sees as strides toward class-based nation building in the activities of Booker T. Washington, and efforts in Kansas, Oklahoma, and Indiana, but observes that these were not successful, and ends with this statement: "Militant forms of black nationalism would not re-emerge until a black proletariat developed in the urban centers" (Baron 1971, 19).

Unity and Disunity in the Black Left in ALSC

The dynamic developments in the national movements around the globe were matched by similar developments in the Black liberation movement of ALSC. After the Houston meeting, a new media unit replaced the research committee. Carl Turpin began editing the ALSC newsletter, *Finally Got the News*, which replaced *The African World* as the main ALSC organ. The name is significant in that it was taken from a slogan created by the League of Revolutionary Black Workers in Detroit during a protest at a UAW convention ("We finally got the news about how our dues are being used!").

In an October 1974 report to ALSC, Turpin stated the purpose of the newsletter:

1. Provide a forum for discussion of ideological differences inside ALSC. (The starting point should be the ideological questions from the International Steering Committee meeting on August 17–18.)

2. Sum up various activities of ALSC locals.
3. Include various articles on the anti-imperialist and anti-racist struggles in the U.S., Africa, and other third world countries. (Turpin 1974, 2)

Four issues came out: October, 1974; December, 1974; January, 1975; and April, 1975. In the first issue, *Finally Got the News* called for a summation of practice:

> We issue this call for all ALSC locals and participants in the Black Liberation Movement to sum up their local struggles and send those summations to the newsletter. (*Finally Got the News*, October 1974)

In each newsletter, local activities were reported in a column titled "ALSC in Action." For example, the Atlanta local committee was active in fighting to stop the importation of coal from South Africa; the Boston local committee took up supporting Eritrea; the Baltimore local committee focused on police repression; Newark took up a housing struggle; the Philadelphia local committee began supporting the Palestinian Liberation Organization; and the New Orleans local committee supported a bus drivers' strike. The ALSC local committees were staying active in fighting for social justice, both in Africa and in the United States. However, there was no longer the coordination that had guided the committees to realize a common program of action in 1972–1974, and consequently a unified national movement was not sustained.

In addition, after the Houston meeting, party building had preoccupied the left forces that were now dominant in ALSC. For these organizations, there were three questions, the first of which was whether the task was to form a Black party or form a pre-party organization that was national in scope in preparation for becoming part of a multi-national party. In either case, the second question was whether to guide cadres working in ALSC to build the anti-imperialist movement or to build the party. Finally, there was the question of how to integrate the theory and practice of world revolution with the conditions of carrying out our revolutionary work in the United States. The experiences of six organizations testify to how the Black left developed and how the development of ALSC in turn was shaped.

Three existing parties were based on Black membership: the AAPRP, the APSP, and the APP. All had participated early on in ALSC. The AAPRP was led by Kwame Ture, as his attempt to implement the proposal for such a party by Kwame Nkrumah (Nkrumah 1973, 486–487). Ture set up study circles designed to prepare cadres for the party. He offered some extremely valuable advice to the movement: beware of the surveillance and subversion caused by the CIA, and be vigilant in resisting the influence of Zionists in the United States and their opposition to the Palestinian struggle. AAPRP for the most part lacked a program to build an anti-imperialist movement; in addition, paranoia replaced political practice in many cases. The one major activity each year was to sponsor an African Liberation Day event, usually in Washington, DC. This was the basis for their participation in the first three years of ALD mobilizations.

The tendency created by AAPRP as part of the emerging Black left can be summed up by their self-definition as ideologically committed followers of the thought and practice of Kwame Nkrumah. Of course, this was supplemented by the theoretical contribution of Kwame Ture. The weakness of this position is that it usually abstracted Nkrumah's thinking out of its Ghanaian context in particular and Africa in general. This is not unlike the way that Mao Tse-tung's thought was often abstracted out of China or Marxism out of Europe. Of course, there is always the search for universal knowledge, but then only on the basis of the practice referenced as the original source of the knowledge. Practice is always the basis for testing the validity of ideas (theory).

The APSP, the membership of which consisted solely of people of African identity and ancestry, emerged in Florida and then spread out to other parts of the country. This organization was closely aligned with the theoretical contributions of Omali Yeshitela, the chairman of the organization. Their current website explains their origin and mission:

> In May of 1972, at a time when the Black Liberation Movement had been destroyed as a movement and in a climate of political terror and brutal repression, Chairman

Omali Yeshitela founded the African People's Socialist Party (APSP). The APSP was formed by the merging of three organizations. The dominant organization was JOMO because of its political experience, longer history and its base in the working class base and character. The other two organizations were the Black Rights Fighters from Ft. Myers, Florida and the Black Study Group of Gainesville, Florida. The aims and objectives of the APSP-USA are to lead the struggle of the African working class and oppressed masses against U.S. capitalist-colonialist domination and all the manifestations of oppression and exploitation that result from this relationship. The Party recognizes that the particular character of the oppression of African people within U.S. borders is domestic or internal colonialism. Leading the struggle to end the system of domestic colonialism and smash the U.S. capitalist-colonialist state is the immediate task of the African People's Socialist Party-USA and the African working class in the U.S. (African People's Socialist Party 2021)

There were attempts by the AAPRP and the APSP to unite, but they did not succeed due to organizational incompatibilities and leadership conflicts. Both were anchored in ideological dogma advanced by their respective charismatic leaders, and neither was willing to embrace the other as an equal, so unity was not possible. Because they were active in different geographical areas, conflict between them was minimized.

The APP, one of the successors to the Revolutionary Action Movement, was a national revolutionary organization based in Philadelphia and with a presence in a number of other large cities. They grew by merging with more local formations, such as the Black Guard in Philadelphia. The APP's foundation in revolutionary theory and practice was due in no small part to their relationship with Abner Berry, a veteran comrade formerly in the leadership of the CPUSA.

These three parties were central to the general movement tendency called revolutionary nationalism. Their most significant contribution was the development of cadres that remained active in mass struggles and in subsequent organization affiliations, but as parties they did not make a strong effort to organize a working-class base.

So, what about the Black working class? The main reform organization of Black workers was the Coalition of Black Trade Unionists, a mass organization that encompassed a diverse set of labor activists associated with the CPUSA and other left organizations that included some nationalists. The main revolutionary tendency of Black workers was more connected to what came out of the LRBW, including the BWC, the Revolutionary Workers Congress, and a small section of the Black Panther Party. One exception was the North Carolina-based Black Workers for Justice (BWFJ), formed in 1981. The proletarian tendency that emerged out of the APP reorganized itself around workplace organizing and formed the Black Workers League. They hooked up with the Amilcar Cabral-Paul Robeson Collective to create the BWFJ in 1981. The Cabral-Robeson organization joined Freedom Road in 1988, but the local activists remained cadre in BWFJ. The strength of this unity move was that BWFJ has become a major force in North Carolina trade union organizing and mass anti-imperialist movement activity. For years they published a newspaper, *Justice Speaks*, and made theoretical contributions as a Black left force in the South. They built UE Local 150, a statewide trade union organization in North Carolina, an example of what they call a social justice union connected to both workplace and community struggles. Their weakness in recent years has been minimizing the theoretical development of cadre.

Three Black left organizations developed in direct relationship to their involvement in ALSC: the RWL, the RCL, and the BWC. All three were national in form, while committed to working to build a multi-national communist party that would reflect the entire multi-national working class Though narrow nationalists opposed these formations, as did some white Marxist formations, this was the most important context for the development of Black revolutionary activists.

After the Houston meeting and the report on political education, a new crisis emerged in ALSC. This was a direct result of the party-building agenda of the three main left forces providing the cadre organizers who had been key staff for building

ALSC local committees. Tension was building because there were independent left forces that were attracted to ALSC after the narrow nationalists withdrew because of the anti-imperialist line of the SOP. Their concern was how to build ALSC, not primarily party building. Two key questions became central to the internal struggle in ALSC following the Houston meeting:

1. Should ALSC be maintained as an organization?
2. If so, what should its purpose be?

This became the central discussion at a national ALSC meeting in Washington, DC, attended by around two hundred people. The meeting was thrown into crisis when a RWL spokesperson was recognized to speak. RWL, formed by leading members of ALSC, as an organization was not a recognized part of ALSC at that time, because no such organization had been. In fact, they were dominant and held firm control of the meeting. The RWL position was to liquidate ALSC. This was explosive, and caused many to be confused about why an RWL member would even have come to speak at the meeting. At the Houston meeting the RWL members had earlier argued for the continuation of ALSC, and then at this meeting voiced a completely opposite position put forward as the RWL official position.

After a brief recess, a proposal was made to create an ALSC Continuations Committee, based on the assumption that the ALSC Secretariat was being closed down. This was a surprise to many, but the members of the secretariat ended up being invited to participate on the Continuations Committee, if one so desired and could be at the meetings.

The crisis in 1974 was the disaffection of key nationalist forces, mainly in New York, Illinois, Ohio, California, and Louisiana, who opposed deepening ALSC as an anti-imperialist organization. By 1975, ALSC had become a united front of the Black left, not exclusively, but mainly. However, a new crisis arose, as the left across the country was fracturing along ideological lines, and the three national parties most involved in ALSC could not avoid being engulfed. These three national organizations, CAP, RWL, and BWC, were present at the meeting on November 1, 1975, of the ALSC Continuations Committee. This was a very difficult time, and it is very important to review what was happening (League of Revolutionary Struggle 1980, 103–106).

The leading Black left organization in ALSC was the RWL, and in fact Owusu Sadaukai, Gene Locke, Nelson Johnson, Mark Smith, and Abdul Alkalimat had been in the leadership of both groups. What developed inside RWL was a dual process of ideological struggle and unity moves toward building a party that took people away from ALSC. Conflicts in this process polarized comrades who took different paths. As mentioned above, this is a situation in which one party says, I quit, but the other says, no, you are being purged. As will be shown, what is key in the long run is that people who differ at one stage continue on in programs that serve the people and advance the movement. The process of social transformation is a long-distance run, and what often appears critical to young activists at a given moment sometimes pales in significance as time goes on.

In terms of the unity-building process, the options at the national level included merging with multi-national formations like the OL and the RU. Both were rejected and the struggles resulted in key RWL leaders leaving. RWL then merged into what was called the Revolutionary Wing:

> Comrades, we put forth that there are three areas in which we can draw an absolute line between the two wings. These are: (1) theory as the leading factor in all our work; (2) correct attitude towards criticism, self-criticism, repudiation and transformation; and, (3) Marxist-Leninist line on how and what kind of party we're trying to build. The revolutionary wing, composed of all genuine Marxist-Leninists and led by comrades from the August Twenty Ninth Movement (ATM), the Puerto Rican Revolutionary Workers Organization (PPRWO), and the Revolutionary Workers League (M-L) holds basically correct lines on these questions and the opportunist wing, currently led by O.L. and WVO and tailed by WC, IWK, CAP, MLOC and others are fundamentally incorrect on these lines. (Revolutionary Workers League 1976)

This revolutionary wing did not fly, but turned its talons on itself. During the period of unity of RWL with PRRWO, out of intense dogmatic ideological sessions the line was developed that party building was the main and only task for revolutionary forces, and that meant an end to all mass organizing except efforts to win the most militant activists to the party. This led to collective violence against comrades as punishment for failing to advance the line of whoever was in leadership. Friends turned on each other and trust was destroyed (Fuller and Page 2014a, 158–159).

On the other hand, some RWL forces in Greensboro, including Nelson Johnson, had broken away to form the Bolshevik Organizing Committee. This group rethought their relationship with the Workers Viewpoint Organization (WVO) and by the fall of 1976 they joined. WVO, formed in 1976, grew out of the Asian Study Group formed in 1973. So, the unity with the Greensboro activists greatly contributed to the composition of WVO, Black and Asian. By October of 1979, WVO had transitioned into the Communist Workers Party (CWP). They suffered a beatdown when they organized a "Death to the Klan" rally the following month, and the KKK sent death squads that murdered five members of the CWP (Bermanzohn and Bermanzohn 1980, 106–33).

Several years after the Greensboro Massacre, the CWP again made a transformative retreat from being communist to espousing social democracy. They formed the New Democratic Movement and the Greensboro Justice Fund, the latter of which continues its work today.

The second most active Black left organization in ALSC was the RCL, led by Amiri Baraka, which grew out of CAP:

> RCL (CAP formally changed its name to the Revolutionary Communist League (M-L-M) in 1976) was never formally a part of the "Wing" and opposed its sectarianism and the lines of the "Wing" forces on a number of key questions. (League of Revolutionary Struggle 1980, 117)

On the other hand, the RCL was pulled into delinking theory from practice by turning party building into study of ideological documents and debating at forums. But the main base was in Newark, and that kept a certain amount of practice ongoing, although key

CAP projects like the African Free School had been disbanded.

Out of this party-building process, the next organizational transformation involved the League of Revolutionary Struggle (LRS) three years later:

> In 1979, the RCL (M-L-M) and the LRS (M-L) agreed to merge forces into on organization. This was the result of a series of meetings, discussions, and working together for more than a year that finally led to the unification of these organizations. It is interesting to note that out of all of the new communist organizations, the LRS was composed mostly of people of color because it had been born out of the merger of two organizations, I Wor Kuen (IWK) and the August 29th Movement (ATM). IWK was a predominantly Asian American organization and ATM was mainly a Chicano organization. They both had experience similar to CAP in their respective communities, emerging as revolutionary leadership in the Asian American and Chicano movements. (Simanga 2015, 153)

Ten years later the LRS retreated from Marxism-Leninism and faded into social democracy.

The Black left organization most based in the industrial proletariat was the BWC, which, as mentioned above, was an organizational development by forces in Detroit coming out of the LRBW. The BWC was founded in December of 1970. In addition to having members from the LRBW, the BWC drew activists from the United Black Brothers in Newark; union caucuses in Baltimore, Milwaukee, Chicago, Cleveland, and Gary, Indiana; and former members of SNCC and the Black Panther Party.

By 1975 the BWC had gotten so deep into political line struggle without making unity a priority that they split into four different groups: the WC(M-L), the Revolutionary Workers Congress, the Marxist-Leninist Organizing Committee, and the Revolutionary Bloc. And even then, the splitting continued.

So, what do these dialectics of disunity of the Black left have to do with the internal life of ALSC? They became the dominant aspect of the political life of ALSC. Each ALSC chapter took on an identity and a process that reflected how these Black left forces operated in committee meetings.

Dialectics of ALSC Local Chapters

A particularly instructive case is the New York ALSC chapter. This summation is based on meeting minutes and interviews with ALSC activists Bill Sales, Pat Wagner, Sam Anderson, and Elombe Brath (B. Sales 1976; Wagner 1976; Anderson 1976; Brath 1976). New York is a global city with strong and broad connections to Africa and the African Diaspora. The Black community of Harlem has been home to immigration from throughout the African Diaspora, and historically has been a cauldron of Pan-Africanism. This is connected to the United Nations and its resident delegations from every country. During the 1970s a major influence was the Ethiopian Student Union of North America and its Marxist study programs.

The New York chapter was initially dominated by nationalist forces, chaired by Jitu Weusi of The East and CAP, from 1972 to 1974. Another major figure giving early leadership was Elombe Brath, leading the Patrice Lumumba Coalition based in Harlem. ALSC brought these older forces together with student activists tied to YOBU, who were based at Columbia University. Each of these two forces had a publication, *Black News* of The East, and *The African World* of YOBU.

Mobilization for ALD 1972 and 1973 were mainly nationalist events with limited involvement of the New York Black left. Things began to change when the SOP was adopted and distributed widely in 1973. Another major event that impacted activists in New York was a forum on "Imperialism and Black People" held on April 6, 1974. This brought two major organizations together: ALSC (Dawolu Gene Locke, Owusu Sadaukai, Imamu Amiri Baraka, and Abdul Alkalimat) and the African Heritage Studies Association (James Turner, Ron Walters, Leonard Jeffries, and Lynn Dozier).

Ideological struggle developed between Marxists and nationalists over whether the main enemy was imperialism or white people, thus beginning what came to be known as the two-line struggle. The debates in May 1974 led to a polarization in the broader Black liberation movement, although one positive outcome was that people began to study Marxism in numbers not seen since the high tide of the CPUSA in the 1940s and 1950s. In practical terms, there was a struggle over money when Weusi demanded reimbursement for a $600 loan for button production, even to the point of wanting to take the money from the account holding the funds raised for the African liberation organizations. This was resolved but ended his involvement, as he simply never returned to an ALSC meeting.

The end of the struggle against narrow nationalism led to a polarizing debate on the left. The strength of ALSC from 1972 to 1974 had been its linking of theory and practice. People had grasped what Mao advanced with the slogan "Grasp revolution, promote production" to connect study of theory with advancing the practice of mass struggle. This was the function of the Handbooks of Struggle developed by the ALSC Research Committee based in Nashville. However, though these documents had been sent to the leadership of ALSC committees, in the case of New York they were not shared with the chapter members.

At the ALSC Houston meeting in August 1974, the political education committee was chaired by Amiri Baraka, who was moving toward Marxism. (This resulted in CAP becoming the Revolutionary Communist League in 1976.) He led the development of the 12 questions for study, moving ALSC from a mass anti-imperialist organization united around the SOP to a higher level of ideological unity.

The New York chapter, now mainly a coalition of left groups, took up the study program, initially choosing to focus on four key questions:

1. What is the meaning of the slogan "Black Workers Take the Lead"?
2. In the U.S. is there one working class or two, one white and one Black?
3. What class contradictions exist among Black people? Does a Black capitalist class exist?
4. Do Black people constitute an internal colony in the U.S.?

The discussions devolved into ideological polemics, a struggle between empirical investigation and polarity of language and ideological dogma. From September 1974 to March 1975, these four questions occupied every monthly meeting. A handful of people from the RWL, the CAP, and the African Information Service dominated every meeting, silencing the few independent people attracted to the meeting out of desire to assist the fight for liberation in Africa. The meetings started out with forty to fifty people in September, but by March had about twenty people in attendance. The 1975 ALD march in New York was in Harlem, causing a debate over the multi-national composition of the participants (WVO Chinese activists and SWP white activists).

Two events led to the demise of ALSC. The national meeting of August 1975 became a full-force public confrontation between all the major organization of the Black left. RWL surfaced publicly for the first time, pulled into conflict with the CAP and the RWC. Each of these national organizations had leadership of one or more ALSC chapters, so the polemic was both national and local.

The main event that ended ALSC was a forum in November 1975 on the struggle in Angola held at Harlem Hospital. Forty people attended to hear the polemics of support for MPLA (Bill Sales) versus those of support for the coalition government in opposition to both US imperialism and Soviet Social Imperialism (Viola Plummer and Paul Nakawa). This disagreement became so intense that at the next meeting the chapter voted to purge Bill Sales and Sam Anderson, because they deviated from the line being advanced by forces uniting around RWL.

It is important to note that RWL had been moving into idealist dogma divorced from practical work, replacing a mass line rooted in practice with book worship. Key leadership had left and/or been purged. There was also the ominous threat of violence, as someone commented after the purge vote, "We got to deal with them." Nothing happened then, but the desperate need to smash the opposition violently rather than win people over though discussion and persuasion was held by some. Revolution was being negated by self-proclaimed revolutionaries.

Another important ALSC chapter was in Philadelphia. This summation is based on interviews with Josephine Hood, Jennette

Walton, and Judy Claude (Hood 1976; Walton 1976; Claude 1976). Philadelphia was loosely organized for the ALD demonstrations in 1972 and 1973, without a formal chapter. After the SOP was adopted, a group of politically progressive Black women got interested and attended the planning session leading into ALD 1974. There were several contradictions that impacted the work of ALSC in Philadelphia.

To begin with, the organizational status of the chapter was in question because of a difference between CAP members and others, representing independents as well as members of the Black Panther Party and SWP. CAP members, operating with instructions from Baraka, the regional coordinator of ALSC, claimed that the group was an official chapter and by implication should be following instructions from Baraka, whereas the others felt they were an autonomous body in a social movement, not a formal organization. When this was resolved and Philadelphia became a formal chapter, there remained a difference between people who came in representing organizations, thinking they were in a united front retaining their right to independence and initiative, versus people who as individuals were in ALSC as their sole organization.

Compounding the crisis was the hesitancy by some of the brothers to accept political leadership from more advanced women. This was connected to the lack of cadre development, that is, a lack of people who studied the issues and followed through with assignments accepted in meetings. Women were more advanced and were doing the work, whereas some of the brothers had a tendency to value gender roles associated with the tradition of subordinating women in more cultural nationalist settings. There was also a class aspect to this. The chapter first tried to charge dues of $3, then reduced it to $2 per month, but the working-class members paid more than the middle-class people, again raising the question of who was a committed cadre of ALSC.

Another critical issue was the crisis of linking theory with practice. The chapter aimed to follow through with the SOP. This was easy and clear in the campaign to oppose the Byrd Amendment, because the workers on the docks and the chapter members could easily see the link between opposing imperialism in this case. Their fighting back by refusing to unload illegal ore was a direct contribution to the fight in Africa. On the other hand, when workers were striking at a plant that made ball bearings, it was not clear. In fact, there were new members who had never confronted the term "imperialism" before and needed very basic political education, but it was never offered.

This led to organizational differences at both the local and national levels. At the local level, a breakaway group attended one meeting claiming the status of the legitimate ALSC chapter, so there was a split. On the other hand, the national secretariat was being run by an RWL faction in an undemocratic manner. Walton was on the national secretariat, but along with three other members was not included in the decision-making. Apparently, the decisions were being made by the RWL majority. A key example of this was a conference on the importation of South African coal to be held in Atlanta. Word came to Philadelphia that ALSC was participating and that Locke and Sadaukai were going to speak, so several ALSC chapters sent representatives. But after arriving, a Houston ALSC activist told people that Gene wasn't coming and that they should not participate as ALSC. This caused a conflict, with some staying out, but the ALSC chapters from Atlanta and New Orleans (both dominated by BWC) did participate in the conference as ALSC.

These contradictions were showing up throughout the country in various ways, most notably with each chapter being in crisis. This led to a breakdown not only in the ALSC Continuations Committee at the national level (whether as a mass organization or a united front coalition), but also in maintaining the focus on the annual ALD mobilization. The end of ALSC, as it had been, led to at least four developments. ALD was taken over as the main activity of the AAPRP, under the leadership of Kwame Ture. It maintained an anti-imperialist orientation, and built unity with other national liberation forces, especially native peoples in the United States and the Palestinians.

Two sections out of RWL carried on ALSC with WVO and as RWL. The RWL line was that party building was the main and only task, so ALSC should serve that purpose. This was objectively a liquidation of ALSC, because the activists were not ready to join a process to form a communist party. The WVO line was to carry forth the main process of ALSC, guided by new principles of unity, mainly to become multi-national and to oppose both US imperialism and Soviet Social imperialism. WVO sponsored a newspaper that advanced their work in ALSC, *All Africa Is Standing Up*, and organized ALD activities in 1977 and 1978. A fourth separate activity was taken up by forces aligned with the RCP and the Revolutionary Student Brigade, the Organizing Committee for a New ALSC. They organized for ALD 1977.

What is interesting is that the WVO forces and the OC-ALSC forces both waged campaigns against the sale of the Kruggerand, a South African gold coin. They were at odds on an ideological level, but were advancing the same political campaign in support of the people of Southern Africa. The same was true of many other left formations. The crisis on the left was that, even on this level of tactical politics, there was an inability to consciously affirm what was objective: the unity of action.

Every organizational alternative that represented an extension of ALSC had a relatively short life after 1977. In fact, most left formations that were active in the 1970s soon faded from active politics. But the experience was worth the weight of the paper it created and the ideas that were advanced. Most revolutionary experiences, and the theory that developed out of that experience, can be characterized as summations of periods of struggle. Again, the slogan of the Chinese revolution is relevant: "Fight, fail, fight again, fail again, fight on to victory!"

The issues of the time of ALSC remain the issues of this time in the 21st century:

1. What is the relationship between the oppression of Black people and the class exploitation at this stage of the capitalist system?
2. How can we build a sustainable social movement from spontaneous breakouts on one or more battlefronts?
3. How to develop advanced cadre out of activists in the mass

movement?

4. How to maintain a tradition of theoretical development that is based on applying world revolutionary theory to the summation of contemporary practice?

Chapter 5
Lessons and Legacy

After examining the historical development of ALSC and its national and global contexts, we have to answer the challenging question of what lessons can be learned by current activists in the movement. It has been fifty years since ALSC was formed. These decades give us an opportunity to learn from the experience of ALSC, but not be imprisoned and disillusioned by the conflicts and factional disputes that raged within it. Great advances were made, Africa moved out of direct European colonization, and the Black liberation movement achieved a high stage of anti-imperialist action. The lessons go both ways, to the right with narrow nationalists, and to the left with dogmatic Marxists, but most important of all is the mass participation of Black people in anti-imperialist action. We have much to learn from the ALSC experience.

The first way we can learn from ALSC is from its legacy, how its work was continued after its main years of activity, 1972 to 1977.

Legacy

Divergent forces carried on the name of ALSC for a short time after 1977, but soon afterwards dropped the name, although some continued to do work supporting African liberation, mainly focusing on South Africa. The main organizational legacy of ALSC is the creation of Trans-Africa:

> [Trans-Africa] was founded in July 1977 as an African American lobby on Africa and the Caribbean. Randall Robinson was the founding Executive Director, and he remained as President of the organization until 2001. On November 21, 1984, Robinson, Congressional delegate Walter Fauntroy, and Civil Rights Commissioner Mary Frances Berry were arrested at a sit-in at the office of South African Ambassador Fourie in Washington, D.C. Similar efforts followed at demonstrations outside the South African embassy and consulates in other cities organized by what became the Free South Africa Movement. By the end of 1985, more than 3,000 people had been arrested in these protests. Trans-Africa worked closely with the Congressional Black Caucus (which had been involved in its founding) in devising legislative strategy for the Comprehensive Anti Apartheid Act of 1986. (Michigan State University n.d.)

Robinson had been an early activist in ALSC, at the national level and in the Boston local committee.

In March 1987, there was a forum and march in Harlem celebrating the fifteenth anniversary of ALD. This forum brought together ALSC veterans and others, some who had been united and others who had been involved in the conflict, but fifteen years later were still active and willing to continue to struggle and engage in joint practice to achieve agreed-upon goals. The speakers included Elombe Brath, Carl Dix, Amiri Baraka, Abdul Alkalimat, Nsia Akuffa Bea, Mario Drummonds, Chokwe Lumumba, Linda Burnham, Cecelie Counts, and Bill Sales. The theme was "Which Way Forward? A National Forum on African Liberation Support Work and the Black Liberation Movement."

As the years have gone by, many activists from the ALSC period are no longer active in the most radical sectors of the movement, but many do stay active in social justice work. They give proof of the fact that Black liberation is not a dash but a long-distance run. The comment below by Simanga, a veteran activist from CAP and RCL, applies to most of the veterans of ALSC:

Some of the people who came through CAP had a difficult time to live outside of that experience. But, most of the women and men who had been in CAP took the skills, perspective, and experience they gained into their new lives. Some joined other organizations. Some became teachers, labor organizers, and leaders; some got elected to public office or became leaders in nonprofits; they are college professors and artists, community organizers, and entrepreneurs; business executives, factory workers, and bus drivers. And with those I remained in contact with over the years, they have had a significant positive impact wherever they landed. And what remains common to us beyond the experience we shared is what I think we learned about ourselves and our country. (Simanga 2015, 159–60)

As we remember the ALSC activists from the past, it is clear that many continue to be active in their senior years. Owusu Sadaukai has worked in senior government positions and currently holds a position as distinguished university emeritus professor of education at Marquette University. After ALSC, he served as superintendent of Milwaukee Public Schools, secretary of Wisconsin's Department of Employment Relations, and director of the Milwaukee County Department of Health and Human Services. Gene Locke and Walter Searcy both got law degrees and then had distinguished careers in Texas and Tennessee, respectively. Brenda Parris stayed active and ran for political office in Montreal, Canada.

Mark Smith finished his undergraduate degree at Harvard, went on to medical school in North Carolina, then to the Wharton School for an MBA. He spent two decades as leader of the California Healthcare Foundation and was elected to the Institute of Medicine. Nelson Johnson and Dwight Hopkins both choose careers in religion. Johnson founded Faith Community Church and a faith-based community organization, Beloved Community Center in Greensboro, North Carolina. Hopkins earned a degree at Union Theological Seminary studying with James Cone. He then spent a career as Alexander Campbell professor of theology at the University of Chicago. Milton Coleman, formerly the editor of *The African World*, continued his career in journalism. He teaches journalism ethics and diversity at the Walter Cronkite School of Journalism at Arizona State University. He is the former senior editor of *The Washington Post*, former president of the American Society of News Editors, and the current president of the Inter American Press Association

Following the key slogan taken by ALSC, "Black Workers Take the Lead," several activists carried on careers in the labor movement. Saladin Muhammad, organizer for the UE Union, and Ajamu Dillahunt, local trade union officer in a union of postal workers, both collaborated in forming the Black Workers for Justice that continues to be active today. Carl Turpin became an activist in the steel industry, and Malcom Suber stayed active in New Orleans, especially after the monster storm Katrina.

Many ALSC activists kept teaching through careers in education, especially Black Studies. Bill Sales, after finishing his PhD under Charles Hamilton at Columbia University, headed the Black Studies Program at Seton Hall University. His dissertation on Malcolm X was published as an important book (Sales 1994). Sam Anderson has held multiple academic positions, being a leader in the social history of mathematics. He continues his activism as a leading activist in support of Cuba and the Palestinian struggle, and fighting racist policies in public education. Pat Wagner went into public education at the secondary school level. Abdul Alkalimat has been a leading activist in Black Studies.

This demonstrates that being a young radical activist can lead one in many directions. The main point is that our struggle is a long-distance run, a fight for changing the society with reforms, but always looking for that magic movement for a leap into massive systemic social transformation. Some of these people have maintained a revolutionary perspective and some not, but all have continued to be social justice activists in their chosen area of work.

This leads us to think about the general lessons we can glean from ALSC. This is the key result of this analysis.

Lessons

We have developed a summation of ten key lessons, based on our analysis of the historical experience of ALSC. We will cover the following points regarding each lesson: What is the lesson? How is the ALSC experience the basis for the lesson? What is the historical basis for the lesson? How can the lesson be applied to today's movement?

Lesson 1: African Americans Support the Liberation of Africa

African Americans have always identified with Africa and the African Diaspora based on culture and politics. When a struggle emerges against oppression and exploitation anywhere in Africa or the African Diaspora, Black people in the United States respond with solidarity. This is an important aspect of building anti-imperialist struggle by progressive forces in the United States. This is often linked to other national liberation battlefronts, e.g., Cuba and the Palestinian struggle.

ALSC began after the massive African Liberation Day demonstration in 1972. The struggle in Guinea-Bissau and throughout Southern Africa had sparked excitement and the spirit of freedom among African Americans, especially the youth and Black liberation activists. Apartheid in South Africa was as horrendous as segregation in the Southern United States, so people were ready to stand with the freedom struggle there based on our experience here.

A broad-based united-front coalition was formed that brought together elected officials, ministers, students, labor leaders, and community activists. The front identified the complicity of the US government in supporting the racist regimes of Southern Africa, as well as investments by US corporations helping to prop up these white minority regimes.

At the general level of support for national liberation from the European colonial rule of Africa, almost all political tendencies in the global Black community found a way to unite. Various representatives of organizations in Africa made contact and won support, both political and financial. These efforts followed upon the contact made by most of the major African American leaders during the 1960s with Africa, again in terms of cultural and political connections. This included Martin Luther King, who attended the independence ceremony of Ghana in 1957, and Malcom X, welcomed as an official representative of African Americans by the Organization of African Unity in 1964.

The longstanding tradition of Pan-Africanism was reignited, with advocates of both the Garvey and Du Bois positions getting involved. This awakened the tradition that represented the Pan-African Congress movement and the work of the Council on African Affairs, especially in places like Harlem in New York (Moore, Turner, and Turner 1988, 161–194; Smith, Sinclair, and Ahmed 1995).

At this time in the twenty-first century, there are current forces fighting for Black liberation that can re-link with the fight for freedom in Africa. We need work on strategy and tactics. The slogan of the moment, "Black Lives Matter," is a step toward confronting racist oppression,both in the United States and all over the world. But, as with the development of ALSC, the struggle is now facing class questions. It turns out that some Black lives are worth more than others, both figuratively and literally. As large sums of money are thrown at the Black Lives organizers, there seems to be a class divide related to who gets the money and what it is used for. There is a homeless struggle in both the United States and South Africa. Both face the barbarity of capital.

The example of ALSC points today's activists to link the struggle in the United States with the battles going on in Africa and throughout the African Diaspora. The Black Student Movement has a role to play here. The first task is to hold the US government accountable, from the local police department to the use of the military in AFRICOM in the service of US imperialism. The next task is to maintain close ties with political movements in Africa so full support can be given to the democratic forces who advance the well-being of the masses of African workers and poor peasants. We now face Black-on-Black class struggle in Africa, so the struggle has changed since 1972.

Chapter 5

Lesson 2: Black Studies Is a Great Asset for the Black Liberation Movement

Black Studies is an activity based on scholarship and service to implement the mission of academic excellence and social responsibility. It is a brain trust of the Black community, for research and the education of youth for leadership. Black Studies is rich with resources: space, funding, intellectual labor, and status. Black Studies was created by the Black Power Movement, and to maintain its historical identity it is expected to be an asset for the Black Liberation Movement by using resources for local, national, and international activities.

A good example of this is the ALSC Research Committee that was based in the Black Studies Program at Fisk University. The faculty and students there produced research, held conferences, and participated in ALSC forums and demonstrations. Another example is the SEEK Program in New York under the direction of Bill Sales. He facilitated opportunities for ALSC leaders to speak on campus and get honorariums that helped to fund ALSC. Also, students were mobilized for ALSC actions.

Perhaps the main way that ALSC was impacted by Black Studies was the fact that Black Studies was the educational foundation for knowledge about Africa. This impacted both students and the community at large. In the early stages of ALSC, many Black Studies faculty were active in leadership positions, e.g., James Turner at Cornell and John Warfield at the University of Texas. In addition, community-based educators, such as John Henrik Clarke and Joseph Ben-Jochannan, were hired by Black Studies programs so that they could continue their work, which had created a direct pipeline into ALSC-type activity.

Education has always been connected to the freedom struggle by African Americans (Franklin 1992). And in the context of ALSC campaigns, at a Fisk University 1975 conference on the theme "Pull the Covers Off Imperialism," the following mission statement for Black intellectuals was adopted (this is especially relevant for Black Studies faculty and students):

Therefore, we black intellectuals must organize ourselves

221

and forge unity around the historical condition of the people, and around the intellectual, moral, and political imperatives for our work:

WE DECLARE that a primary task of black intellectuals is to study the character and historical development of U.S. imperialism, especially its impact on black people, and to promote this study throughout schools, publications, conferences, and organizations;

WE DECLARE that the main objective of our study must be to expose the essence of imperialism and provide the intellectual tools necessary for combating every imperialist assault on the people;

WE DECLARE that our immediate goal is to establish a new unity between black intellectuals and the black liberation movement in which intellectuals function to serve the interests of the people with humility based on compassion, strength based on science, and a revolutionary optimism that the people will triumph over all enemies and prosper. (Alkalimat 1975)

Lesson 3: The Black Liberation Movement Needs a Black Left

The unique feature of the Black left is that it brings a strategic vision for Black liberation that is based on the end of capitalist exploitation. Many reforms have been led by and served the interests of the Black middle class, with the masses of people enjoying some of the benefits as well. However, most reforms have limited impact on the masses of Black people. The Black left is based on a process of cadre development, based on the stand, viewpoint, and method that serves the working class. These cadres are needed to serve as the reliable staff to build and sustain mass movements for social change aimed at serving Black workers and poor people.

ALSC chapters were built by cadres from national organizations: MXLU, YOBU, LEI, Peoples College, BWC, CAP/RCL, and RWC, among others. The SOP represented marching orders to all affiliated cadre organizations to sink deep roots into the masses of Black people, poor and working people, in order to build a mass anti-imperialist movement that could challenge the rule of US imperialism. This was to be accomplished through the application of theory to the practical experiences of the activists. When this happened, the movement advanced; but when theory was delinked from practice and became an abstract catechism, the movement went into decline and ALSC became an inert debate society.

The touchstone for twentieth-century revolutionary struggles was the Russian Revolution of 1917, led by V. I. Lenin. The text most often cited as a guide is his pamphlet, *What Is To Be Done?* Lenin makes a distinction between a mass organization and an organization of revolutionaries. He insists they are different and yet dialectically interconnected, meaning the revolutionaries work in the mass organization to advance it as a mass movement and to recruit and train more revolutionaries, without which the movement will devolve into reformism.

Mao Tse-tung, the leading theoretician of the 1949 Chinese revolution, clarifies the general role of the revolutionary party, the organized left:

> Who are our enemies? Who are our friends? This is a question of the first importance for the revolution. The basic reason why all previous revolutionary struggles in China achieved so little was their failure to unite with real friends in order to attack real enemies. A revolutionary party is the guide of the masses, and no revolution ever succeeds when the revolutionary party leads them astray. To ensure that we will definitely achieve success in our revolution and will not lead the masses astray, we must pay attention to uniting with our real friends in order to attack our real enemies. To distinguish real friends from real enemies, we must make a general analysis of the economic status of the various classes in Chinese society and of their respective attitudes towards the revolution. (Tsetung 2013, 11)

This is direct advice for the current activists in the Black liberation movement, indeed, all progressive forces. The challenge for the Black left is to make a class analysis of the forces in conflict at this stage of the capitalist crisis. This is a mandate for understanding the current stage of struggle in the United States as well as in every other part of the world. ALSC began this process during its last debates. Are any Black people part of the ruling capitalist class? Who are the workers? Which sections of capital are in decline and which are on the rise? The Black left has much work to accomplish in order to prepare for the next revolutionary upsurge (Alkalimat and Muhammad 2017).

Lesson 4: Black Media Is a Key Resource for the Black Liberation Movement

The Black community has developed media that has maintained an antiracist influence on Black people, mainly newspapers. This has now moved beyond mainstream forms (TV, radio, newspapers, and journals) to include digital forms (faxes, conference calls, LISTSERVs, social media, Zoom, etc.). The Black liberation movement needs to connect with community media, but also develop media of its own, both to reach out to the broad masses and to maintain discourse internal to the movement. Without media there can be no sustainable movement.

The ALSC media infrastructure was based on the newspaper *The African World,* produced by YOBU. Other important media included *The Black Scholar, Black News*, and *Unity and Struggle.* Small local newsletters, such as *the Nashville African Liberation Committee DRUM* and *Africa in Arms: News Notes from the Liberation Struggle* compiled by the Pan African Information Bureau in Stanford, California, were also key.

The template for movement media is what Lenin called the Iskra method in his essay "Where To Begin?" YOBU took Lenin's advice and developed their theory of the revolutionary press. YOBU cadres as correspondents for *The African World* both narrated the progress of the African liberation movements and organized to advance them.

We have a new situation because of the widespread use of social media facilitated by the universal use of smart cell phones. It is possible for everyone to broadcast to as large a list as they can connect with, especially using Twitter and Facebook, although this is contingent upon being able to use these tools of major capitalist corporations. One tactic that has been created by this communication technology is the flash mob, a spontaneous protest action that can be organized quickly and privately. The challenge is to develop techniques that can develop and sustain a movement.

There is a great need for digital journals. This is the format for extended discussions of key questions, the sharing of research and historical analysis, and, most important of all, the patient dialogue of ideological positions that can be shared and studied without leaping quickly to political conflict and disunity. One of the great features of a digital website is that it can be archived and accessible over time on a global basis. This is an extremely valuable advance over what was possible in the 1970s.

Finally, media is the strongest when it is created by a collective of like-minded people. The task is not to feature prominent public intellectuals, but to forge a consensus among representative activists in social movements. The goal is agreement on the path forward for the movement, a common practice of focused attack.

Lesson 5: Black Liberation Is Advanced when United with Mainstream Forces

The Black Liberation Movement is carried out by struggles on critical issues that constitute battlefronts, each with a history in geopolitical space and impacting a set of institutions, public laws, and private policies. The daily tactical struggle for change entails reforms that define the work of a mass movement. A significant measure of the power of the movement is the extent to which it can win over mainstream forces to join in the fight for reform. These include elected officials, agency leadership, ministers, journalists, educators, and trade union officials.

Black liberation activists see past the structures of oppression and exploitation, but the path to freedom is a long-distance march requiring the participation of masses of people. The march involves overturning the commanding heights of power in virtually all aspects of society, especially the state and the economy. The battles being fought are usually reforms until there is that rare and special leap to take power away from the oppressors.

This can't take place if the movement has no allies in the mainstream. The first ALSC was the best demonstration of this. The rise of Congressman Diggs to head the Subcommittee on Africa of the House of Representatives Committee on Foreign Affairs was decisive. Diggs helped advance the fight to end white minority rule in Southern Africa, both inside Congress and by working with the movement, which included state representatives and city council members throughout the country.

The church is a key resource, providing leadership, space for events, cultural solidarity with music, and congregations to be mobilized. When the movement has the blessing of the church, it is hard to stop.

Of course, this is mainly for key reform demands. Today, this includes demands such as the raising of the minimum wage to a livable standard, Medicare for all, an end to student debt, and even reparations. The movement has yet to make socialism a popular demand, although survey data demonstrates that a majority of Black people view socialism favorably:

> Nearly two-thirds of black Americans (65%) and 52% of Hispanics have positive impressions of the term socialism, compared with just 35% of whites. (Hartig 2019)

This unity with mainstream Black leaders has to be achieved by building power based on mass organization and mobilization. Otherwise, when movement activists make efforts to work with mainstream leaders, they can be coopted to serve the interests of the mainstream. Unity with mainstream leaders is necessary for reforms. Our goal must always be to get as many reforms enacted as possible, but not let success or failure stop us from fighting for our strategic goal of Black liberation.

Lesson 6: Organizational Unity Is Needed by the Black Liberation Movement

Spontaneous movements are the initial forms of resistance. They bring new forces into action on one or more battlefronts. But, they have short lives and lack clarity of purpose, tactical discipline, and agreed-upon strategic goals. Formal organizations are needed to develop and manage cadre to serve as staff for the movement in a sustainable division of labor. The main dangers facing such organizations are bureaucracy, authoritarian "grand leader" syndrome, and amateurishness. New forms of networked leadership are needed that maximize the power of digital media to maintain lines of communication and develop strategy and tactics.

ALSC had two forms of organizational unity. It was a coalition of pre-existing organizations and it was a membership organization for individuals. The process of carrying out ALSC activities was helped by both forms of organizational participation, as long as people followed through on assignments they accepted and continued to carry out the fundraising plan to support the struggle in Africa.

The ALSC decision-making process was followed by each local chapter and by the representative national leadership bodies. However, when a particular national organization played a dominant role in a local chapter or the national leadership structure, decisions were sometimes not made in an ALSC meeting and thus were imposed from the outside. People rightfully resented this avoidance of standard procedure as undemocratic, and it became the basis for dissension and conflict.

This raises the question of how cadre organization can best provide leadership in a mass movement: from above or below? "From below" means that the cadre leads by example by being the best workers for the cause, with the main tactics being discussion and persuasion. "From above" means taking top leadership positions and dominating the process, often by fiat. ALSC had cadre organization start out by leading from below, but some moved to a domineering form of commanding-from-the-top type of leadership.

We have seen this type of crisis before in the development of the Black liberation struggle. The National Negro Congress is a good example. Communist Party cadres were active here, working under the democratic leadership of Black activists such as A. Philip Randolph. However, they moved up, trying to take many of the leadership positions, which caused Randolph to withdraw and in turn led to a decline of the mass democratic character of the organization.

Organizations develop within a specific life span, the first stage being creation, the second being peak activity, and the third being dissolution. The life of an organization has a big impact on the activists involved, at the end either leading them to transition to new organizations or to drop out of the movement. It is crucial for organizations to be based on principles of democracy and respect for individuals, so that activists have positive energy to carry them on to further organizational involvement.

Lesson 7: The Highest Level of Unity Needed Is Ideological Unity

The ideology for Black liberation is composed of ideas about the past and present nature of oppression and how to overcome it. It contains a vision of the future and a strategy for how to get there. The spontaneous movement on every battlefront is usually a response to an attack or a heightened contradiction, but for sustainability a movement needs to have within it the development of ideological consensus for key activists. Ideological unity is an advanced stage of development for cadres within the movement, who support the political unity of movement activists but do not try to represent their level of unity as the standard for the entire movement.

The cadres of different organizations brought their particular forms of ideological unity into ALSC. CAP cadres were grounded in Kawaida, then Revolutionary Kawaida, and then the study of Marxism. This reflected the transition from the ideological leadership of Karenga to Baraka. YOBU and MXLU cadres were strongly influenced by Pan-African thinkers, mainly Nkrumah and Cabral, before making a change to Marxism. While these were different ideological systems, there was unity on the politics of the anti-colonial and anti-imperialist struggle.

For the activity in 1972 and 1973, the main form of unity that held ALSC together was the political goal of fighting to assist the national liberation organizations. One step in the direction of ideology was the rejection of narrow nationalists when the SOP was adopted and successfully defended, identifying imperialism as the enemy and not white people in general. This was not merely an abstract argument, because the campaigns of struggle were specific and political. Handbooks of Struggle were prepared for each campaign, demonstrating the practical reasons for what ALSC was doing.

Trying to develop ideological unity became a destructive process when the dominating activity of some Marxists tried to force ALSC to achieve a high level of ideological unity. This drove away anti-imperialist forces who desired to be activists in a mass movement united around the politics of African liberation. Abstract arguments divorced from the practical activities of ALSC took precedence. Ideological differences are best settled when operationalized into the politics of fighting for change. Abstract arguments of ideological beliefs are hard to settle with logic and reason and most often lead to a factionalism that impedes organizational progress

The future of every movement is dependent on the main activists taking up ideological study and struggle and using that to engage in and sum up the practical activities of the movement. Cadres, ideologically united and disciplined as activists, are needed for the staff of every movement to be effective as a politically progressive force. If a staff is based primarily on bureaucratic skill and being paid, a movement will be politically limited and weak.

Lesson 8: Black Liberation Requires Professional Administrative Skill

Building a movement for Black liberation has been going on for centuries, a process that has developed and declined in waves of resistance. To build a movement, one must acquire resources and then allocate them to advance progressive demands on many diverse battlefronts. It is necessary to have administrative staff operating at a professional level to accomplish this. Internal record keeping is critical, which covers minutes of meetings, summations of conferences, financial records, documentation of all activities, mailing lists, and building an archive. Democracy requires formal record keeping. This is no different than a church or a trade union—professionalism is key.

There is a big difference between being an amateur and being a professional. All movements start out with a mix of people with different levels of skill, experience, and commitment. As activities develop, there is a need for staff to coordinate and maintain continuity in planning and communication with participants. This entails a learning process that combines study with the summation of experience to identify best practices and continue to improve.

These are the same skills required for all forms of organizations, including social institutions like a church or a trade union. These are skills that need to be learned by everyone, for in that way democracy can be implemented. For far too long, such record keeping has been a gendered skill assigned to women. Furthermore, it is not only for those with the highest education. The administrative nerve center of an organization must be associated with political consciousness and all forms of cadre development. This is a matter of organizational literacy.

The memory of our struggle depends on such record keeping being archived, so that materials can be retrieved and used in any analysis of past behavior.

Lesson 9: Black Liberation Requires Unity of Forces in All Regions

The United States is a large country and Black people are in every region, mainly in cities but also the rural South. The political culture of the country has regional variations, and that includes the political culture particular to Black people. The national government sets the context for national politics, but every region has to be understood on its own terms. As Boggs has said, "The city is the Black man's land." In addition, the South is a regional foundation for Black people quantitatively and qualitatively. The Black liberation movement has a challenge to organize and develop the politics of every region in the country, especially in the South.

Black people have become an urban people, being close

to a majority in most big cities. This is true in every region of the country. Too often there is a tilt toward the Eastern and the Midwest regions. There must always be an extra effort made to include the West Coast, and with the new digital technology this can be done in a cost-effective way.

The most important silence regarding Black liberation and Black community developments in general is that of the Southern region. Yet, in terms of cities and rural areas, except for the few giant cities like New York and Los Angeles, the South is more heavily populated in general than any other region. Moreover, the exploitation suffered by Black people is often more extreme in the South than anywhere else. The Black liberation movement must always put special emphasis on organizing in the South.

As a result of the COVID-19 pandemic, the use of digital platforms like Zoom has enabled the movement to include people from all regions in an easy and cost-effective way. The use of email and social media enable each of us as individuals and organizations to be in active contact with people all over the country. This is critical, because a national movement needs activists with national contacts.

Lesson 10: Black Liberation Requires Respect and Healing for Movement Activists

Active participation in the fight for Black liberation can be a jubilation, but it can also take a heavy toll on body, mind, and spirit. We confront the barbarism of racist state power. We confront the realities of sustaining life itself, meaning those of job and family. We engage in ideological and political struggles in the movement. And we even find echoes of the barbarism around us in the ways we sometimes treat each other and ourselves. Especially without a rational health-care system in the US, healing and respect for self and others is a crucial task of our movement.

In a country with a health-care industry but no health-care system, it is rare that institutional resources are available for healing veterans of the movement. So healing has to be the work of the movement itself. And alongside healing is preventing illness. So, just as the movement requires that people study to develop their political understanding, healthy life practices must be included to guide and sustain the participation of movement activists via radical self-care.

Activists are special in terms of their political function, but that only places them in situations of greater stress, facing critical health challenges. They are likely to have little or no health insurance, even with the Affordable Care Act making health insurance more widely available. Psychological stress if overlooked can lead to serious injury to self or others. Abusive behavior is an outlet too ready at hand when a movement depends on and trusts its leaders. Since the 1970s, movements themselves have addressed all these risks, while not always having the final answers. But the resulting new knowledge has pushed mainstream health care in the right direction and activists can benefit from it too.

With these ten lessons and all that the ALSC experience can teach us, let's build and rebuild our movements.

Bibliography

Adi, Hakim. 2013. *Pan-Africanism and Communism: The Communist International, Africa and the Diaspora*, 1919-1939. Trenton, NJ [u.a.]: Africa World Press.

———. 2018. *Pan Afrikanism A History*. London: Bloomsbury.

Adi, Hakim, Marika Sherwood, and George Padmore. 1995. *The 1945 Manchester Pan-African Congress Revisited*. London: New Beacon Books.

Africa Information Service, Amilcar, ed. 1973. *Return to the Source: Selected Speeches of Amilcar Cabral*. New York: Africa Information Service.

African Liberation Day Coordinating Committee. 1972. "Statements of Endorsement." Document in the archival collection of Abdul Alkalimat.

African National Congress. 1971. "1912-1972: 60 Years of Struggle." Sechaba: Official Organ of the African National Congress South Africa 5 (12): 4–11

———. 1994. *Mzabalazo: A Pictorial History of the African National Congress*. Belville, South Africa: Mayibuye Books in conjunction with the African National Congress.

African People's Socialist Party. 2021. "About – The African People's Socialist Party." 2021. https://apspuhuru.org/about/.

Ahmad, Muhammad. 2008. *We Will Return in the Whirlwind: Black Radical Organizations 1960-1975*. Chicago, IL: Charles H. Kerr.

Alkalimat, Abdul. 1974a. *Handbook of struggle #4. African Liberation Month 1974*. Houston and Nashville: African Liberation Support Committee.

Alkalimat, Abdul. 1974b. "The Significance of the February 1st Movement: Black Students and the United Front Against Imperialism." Document in the archival collection of Abdul Alkalimat.

———. 1975. "Report from National Planning Conference: Year to Pull the Covers off Imperialism Project." *The Black Scholar* 6 (5): 54–56.

———. 1976. Interview with Elombe Brath. Document in the archival collection of Abdul Alkalimat.

———. 1986. *Introduction to Afro-American Studies: A Peoples College Primer*. Chicago: Twenty-first Century Books & Publications.

Alkalimat, Abdul, and Nelson Johnson. 1974. *Toward the Ideological Unity of the African Liberation Support Committee: A Response to Criticisms of the ALSC Statement of Principles Adopted at Frogmore, South Carolina June-July 1973*. Greensboro, NC: African Liberation Support Committee.

Alkalimat, Abdul, and Saladin Muhammad. 2017. *Three Waves of Struggle: A Discussion Paper*. Urbana, Ill.: Twenty-first Century Books & Publications. http://alkalimat.org/fmb/three-waves.pdf

Allen, James S. 1984. *The Black Question in the United States*. New York: Workers' Tribune.

ALSC. 1972a. "Minutes of African Liberation Support Committee - Greensboro." Document in the archival collection of Abdul Alkalimat.

———. 1972b. "Minutes of African Liberation Support Committee - Detroit." Document in the archival collection of Abdul Alkalimat.

———. 1972c. "Minutes of African Liberation Support Committee - Altanta." Document in the archival collection of Abdul Alkalimat.

———. 1973a. "Minutes of African Liberation Support Committee - Greensboro." Document in the archival collection of Abdul Alkalimat.

———. 1973b. "African Liberation Day - 1973." African Liberation Support Committee. Document in the archival collection of Abdul Alkalimat.

———. 1973c. "Statement of Principles of the African Liberation Support Committee." Document in the archival collection of Abdul Alkalimat.

———. 1973d. "Minutes of African Liberation Suport Committee - Frogmore." Document in the archival collection of Abdul Alkalimat.

———. n.d. "Byrd Amendment - Background Information and Present Status." Document in the archival collection of Abdul Alkalimat.

Amnesty International. 1976. "Briefing: Rhodesia/Zimbabwe." *Issue: A Journal of Opinion* 6 (4): 34–37. https://doi.org/10.2307/1166559.

Anderson, Samuel E. 1976. ALSC Interview by Abdul Alkalimat and Ron Bailey.

Austin, David. 2013. *Fear of a Black Nation: Race, Sex. and Security in Sixties Montreal.* Toronto, ON: Between the Lines.

———. 2018. *Moving against the System: The 1968 Congress of Black Writers and the Shaping of Global Black Consciousness.* London: Pluto Press.

Avakian, Bob. 2005. *From Ike to Mao and beyond: My Journey from Mainstream America to Revolutionary Communist : A Memoir.* Chicago, IL: Insight Press.

Baradaran, Mehrsa. 2019. "Opinion | The Real Roots of 'Black Capitalism' (Published 2019)." *The New York Times*, March 31, 2019, sec. Opinion. https://www.nytimes.com/2019/03/31/opinion/nixon-capitalism-blacks.html.

Baraka, Amiri, ed. 1972. *African Congress. A Documentary of the First Modern Pan-African Congress.* New York: William

Morrow & Co.

Baron, Harold M. 1971. *The Demand for Black Labor: Historical Notes on the Political Economy of Racism*. Somerville, Mass.: New England Free Press.

Bengelsdorf, Carol, and Elsa Roberts. 1971. *Building freedom: Mozambique's Frelimo*. Cambridge (Massachusetts): Africa Research Group.

Benson, Richard D. 2014. *Fighting for Our Place in the Sun: Malcolm X and the Radicalization of the Black Student Movement 1960-1973*. 1st New edition edition. Peter Lang Publishing Inc.

Bermanzohn, Paul C, and Sally A Bermanzohn. 1980. *The True Story of the Greensboro Massacre*. New York, N.Y.: C. Cauce.

Biko, Steve. 1979. *I Write What I like: A Selection of His Writings*. San Francisco: Harper & Row.

Black Workers Congress. n.d. "The Black Liberation Struggle, the Black Workers Congress, and Proletarian Revolution." Accessed December 26, 2020. https://www.marxists.org/history/erol/ncm-2/bwc-1/index.htm.

Blyden, Nemata Amelia Ibitayo. 2019. *African Americans and Africa: A New History*. S.l.: Yale University Press.

Bolling, Louis. 2017. "Birth of a New Nation: Martin Luther King on Ghana." *The Philadelphia Tribune*. January 9, 2017. https://www.phillytrib.com/birth-of-a-new-nation-martin-luther-king-on-ghana/article_01d6a859-1b2b-56e3-b619-b899f3ccdafb.html.

Boston ALSC. 1973. "Press Release on the MIddle East." Document in the archival collection of Abdul Alkalimat.

Bower, Anne L. 2007. *African American Foodways: Explorations of History and Culture*. Urbana: University of Illinois Press. https://www.press.uillinois.edu/books/catalog/38qrk5rh9780252031854.html.

Bragança, Aquino de, and Immanuel Maurice Wallerstein. 1982. *The African Liberation Reader. Volume 2, Volume 2,*.

London; Ibadan, Nigeria: Zed Press ; Progressive and Socialist Books Depot.

Brath, Elombe. 1976. ALSC Interview by Abdul Alkalimat and Ron Bailey. Document in the archival collection of Abdul Alkalimat.

Breitman, George, ed. 1965. *Malcolm X Speaks*. New York: Grove Press.

Bunting, Brian Percy. 1986. *Moses Kotane, South African Revolutionary: A Political Biography*. London: Inkululeko Publications.

Cabral, Amílcar. 1969. *The Struggle in Guinea*. Cambridge (Massachusetts): Africa Research Group.

Cabral, Amilcar. 1972. *Our People Are Our Mountains;: Amilcar Cabral on the Guinean Revolution*. Committee for Freedom in Mozambique, Angola & Guineì.

Callinicos, Alex, and John Rogers. 1978. *Southern Africa after Soweto*. London, Boulder (Colorado): Pluto Press.

Campanella Jr, Roy. 1972. *Black Unity: Breaking the Chains*. https://www.youtube.com/watch?v=xmcbne_3eFQ.

Carew, Jan R. 1995. *Ghosts in Our Blood: With Malcolm X in Africa, England and the Caribbean*. Chicago, Ill.: Lawrence Hill Books.

"Carnation Revolution." 2021. In *Wikipedia*. https://en.wikipedia.org/w/index.php?title=Carnation_Revolution&oldid=999394223.

Center for Black Education. 1969. "Our Aims." *The Pan African*, October 24, 1969.

———. 1972. *African Liberation: An Analytical Report on Southern Africa*. Washington: Drum & Spear Press.

Chaka, Malik. 1973. "ALSC in Africa." ALSC.

Chaliand, Gérard. 1971. *Armed Struggle in Africa: With the Guerrillas in "Portuguese" Guinea*. New York: Monthly Review.

Chang, Harry. 1975. *Critique of the Black Nation Thesis*. Berkeley, CA: Racism Research Project.

Chicago Committee for the Liberation of Angola, Mozambique, and Guinea, ed. 1974. *Sun of Our Freedom: The Independence of Guinea Bissau*. Chicago, IL: Chicago Committee for the Liebration of Angola, Mozambique, and Guinea.

Chilcote, Ronald H. 1972. *Emerging Nationalism in Portuguese Africa*. Stanford: Hoover Institution Press Stanford Univ.

Claude, Judy. 1976. ALSC.

"Council on African Affairs." 2020. In *Wikipedia*. https://en.wikipedia.org/w/index.php?title=Council_on_African_Affairs&oldid=985349041.

Cox, Courtland. 1972. "Position Paper on the Governing Principles of ALSC." Drum and Spear Bookstore.

Crothers, Connie. 2010. "Abbey Lincoln and Freedom Now." *Against the Current* (blog). November 2010. https://againstthecurrent.org/atc149/p3101/.

Culverson, Donald. 1996. "The Politics of the Anti-Apartheid Movement in the United States, 1969-1986." *Political Science Quarterly* 111 (1): 127149.

Davidson, Basil. 1972. *In the Eye of the Storm: Angola's People*. Garden City, New York: Doubleday.

Davidson, Carl. 1976. *In Defense of the Right to Self-Determination*. Chicago: Liberator Press.

Davies, Carole Boyce. 2008. *Left of Karl Marx: The Political Life of Black Communist Claudia Jones*. Illustrated edition. Durham: Duke University Press Books.

Davis, Joshua Clark. 2018. "The FBI's War on Black-Owned Bookstores." *The Atlantic*. February 19, 2018. https://www.theatlantic.com/politics/archive/2018/02/fbi-black-bookstores/553598/.

Diggs, Charles C. 1972. "Action Manifesto." *Issue: A Journal of Opinion* 2 (1): 52–60. https://doi.org/10.2307/1166646.

———. 1974. "Statement of Congressman Charles C Diggs, Jr: Chairman, House Foreign Affairs Subcommittee on Africa." Document in the archival collection of Abdul Alkalimat.

Dimitrov, Georgi. 1935. "The Fascist Offensive and the Tasks of the Communist International in the Struggle of the Working Class against Fascism." 1935. https://www.marxists.org/reference/archive/dimitrov/works/1935/08_02.htm#s8.

"Draft Proposal: Manifesto of the International Black Workers Congress." n.d. Accessed June 22, 2013. http://www.marxists.org/history/erol/ncm-1/bwc-manifesto.htm.

Du Bois, W. E. B. 1952. *In Battle for Peace: The Story of My 83rd Birthday*. New York: Masses & Mainstream.

Du Bois, W. E. B. 1973. "The African Roots of War." *Monthly Review* 24 (11): 28–40. https://doi.org/10.14452/MR-024-11-1973-04_3.

Elbaum, Max. 2002. *Revolution in the Air: Sixties Radicals Turn to Lenin, Mao and Che*. London; New York: Verso.

Essien-Udom, Essien Udosen. 1962. *Black Nationalism; a Search for an Identity in America.* Chicago: University of Chicago Press.

Fanon, Frantz. 1964. *Toward the African Revolution: Political Essays*. New York: Monthly Review.

———. 1967. *A Dying Colonialism*. New York: Evergreen.

———. 1965. *The Wretched of the Earth.* New York: Grove Press.

First, Ruth. 1972. *Portugal's Wars in Africa.* London: Christian Action Publications for the International Defence and Aid Fund.

Fogel, D. 1982. *Africa in Struggle: National Liberation and Proletarian Revolution*. Seattle: Ism Press.

Foner, Philip S, ed. 1982. *Paul Robeson Speaks.* Secaucus (120 Enterprise Ave., Secaucus, NJ 07094): Citadel Press.

Ford, James W., and A. W. Berry. 1938. *The Negro and the Democratic Front*. New York: International Publishers.

Forman, James. 1972. *The Making of Black Revolutionaries; a Personal Account.* New York: Macmillan.

Forsythe, Dennis. 1971. *Let the Niggers Burn!: The Sir George Williams University Affair and Its Caribbean Aftermath.*

Montreal: Our Generation Press.

Foster, William Zebulon. 1947. *The Communist Position on the Negro Question.* New York: New Century Publ.

———. 1952. *History of the Communist Party of the United States, by William Z. Foster.* New York: International Publishers.

———. 1955. *History of the Three Internationals, the World Socialist and Communist Movements from 1848 to the Present, by William Z. Foster.* New York: International Publishers.

———. 1968. *History of the Communist Party of the United States.* New York, NY: Greenwood Press.

Franklin, Vincent P. 1992. *Black Self-Determination: A Cultural History of African-American Resistance.* Brooklyn, N.Y.; Chicago: Lawrence Hill Books ; Distributed by Independent Publishers Group.

Fuller, Howard, and Lisa Frazier Page. 2014a. *No Struggle, No Progress: A Warrior's Life from Black Power to Education Reform.* Milwaukee, WI: Marquette University Press.

———. 2014b. *No Struggle, No Progress: A Warrior's Life from Black Power to Education Reform.* Milwaukee, Wisc.: Marquette University Ptress,

Garlake, Peter, and Andre Proctor. 2010. *People Making History: Book One.* Harare, Zimbabwe: Zimbabwe Publishing House.

Garlake, Peter S., and Andre Proctor. 1992. *People Making History . Book 2.* Harare: Zimbabwe Educational Books.

Georgakas, Dan, and Marvin Surkin. 1998. *Detroit, I Do Mind Dying.* Cambridge, Mass.: South End Press.

Gershon, Livia. 2015. "Divestment: The Polaroid Revolutionary Workers' Movement." JSTOR Daily. August 27, 2015. https://daily.jstor.org/divestment-the-polaroid-revolutionary-workers-movement/.

Geschwender, James A. 1978. *Class, Race and Worker Insurgency: The League of Revolutionary Black Workers.* Cambridge: Cambridge University Press.

Gordon, Larry. 2010. "UCLA Students Memorialize 1969 Black Panther Slayings." *Los Angeles Times*, May 26, 2010.

"Great Zimbabwe." 2020. In *Wikipedia.* https://en.wikipedia.org/w/index.php?title=Great_Zimbabwe&oldid=988167692.

Green, Gilbert. 1976. *Portugal's Revolution.* New York: Internat. Publ.

Griffin, Jim. 1980. *Racism and the Workers' Movement.* Philadelphia, PA: Philadelphia Workers' Organizing Committee.

Hamlin, Michael. 1973. "What Road to Building a New Communist Party." Encyclopedia of Anti-Revisionism On-Line. April 4, 1973. https://www.marxists.org/history/erol/ncm-2/g-1-bwc.htm.

Hamlin, Michael, and Michele Gibbs. 2013. *A Black Revolutionary's Life in Labor: Black Workers Power in Detroit.* Detroit, Mich.: Against the Tide Books.

Hamrell, Sven, and Carl Gösta Widstrand, eds. 1964. *The Soviet Bloc, China and Africa.* Uppsala: Scandinavian Institute of African Studies.

Harris, Robert, and et al, eds. 1992. *Carlos Cooks and Black Nationalism from Garvey to Malcolm: [Excerpts from the Lectures of Carlos Cooks.* Dover, Mass.: Majority Press.

"Harry Haywood." 2020. In *Wikipedia.* https://en.wikipedia.org/w/index.php?title=Harry_Haywood&oldid=992948369.

Hartig, Hannah. 2019. "Stark Partisan Divisions in Americans' Views of 'Socialism,' 'Capitalism.'" *Pew Research Center* (blog). June 25, 2019. https://www.pewresearch.org/fact-tank/2019/06/25/stark-partisan-divisions-in-americans-views-of-socialism-capitalism/.

Haywood, Harry. 1976. *Negro Liberation.* Chicago: Liberator Press.

———. 1978. *Black Bolshevik: Autobiography of an Afro-American Communist.* Chicago: Liberator Press.

"Herero and Namaqua Genocide." 2020. In *Wikipedia.* https://

en.wikipedia.org/w/index.php?title=Herero_and_Nam-aqua_genocide&oldid=987926798.

Herrick, Allison Butler. 1979. *Angola, a Country Study*. Washington: Foreign Area Studies, American University.

Herrick, Allison B. et al. 1967. *Area Handbook for Angola: Research and Writing Were Completed on December 31, 1966*. Washington, DC.

Herrick, Allison Butler et al. 1969. *Area Handbook for Mozambique*. Washington, DC: American University, Foreign Area Studies. https://eric.ed.gov/?id=ED033364

Heywood, Linda M. 2019. *Njinga of Angola: Africa's Warrior Queen*. Harvard Univ. Press.

Hill, Adelaide Cromwell, and Martin Kilson. 2014. *Apropos of Africa: Sentiments of Negro American Leaders on Africa from the 1800s to the 1950s*. London: Routledge,

"History of the Communist Party of the Soviet Union (Bolsheviks): Short Course." 1939. https://www.marxists.org/reference/archive/stalin/works/1939/x01/index.htm.

Hofmann, Paul. 1960. "Bunche Says '60 Is Year of Africa: Symposium Finds New Unity in Anti-Colonialism -- U.N. Membership Rise Seen." *New York Times*, February 17, 1960, p. 15.

Holloway, Joseph E. 2005. *Africanisms in American Culture*. Bloomington: Indiana University Press. http://books.google.com/books?id=UUh2AAAAMAAJ.

Holloway, Joseph E, and Winifred Kellersberger Vass. 1993. *The African Heritage of American English*. Bloomington: Indiana University Press.

Hood, Josephine. 1976. ALSC Interview by Abdul Alkalimat and Ron Bailey. Document in the archival collection of Abdul Alkalimat.

Houston ALSC. 1974. "Summary of the International Steering Committee Meeting of the African Liebration Support Committee." Houston ALSC.

James, C. L. R. 2012. *A History of Pan-African Revolt*. Oakland,

Calif.: PM Press.

Johnson, Cedric. 2007. *Revolutionaries to Race Leaders: Black Power and the Making of African American Politics*. Minneapolis: University of Minnesota Press. http://public.eblib.com/choice/publicfullrecord.aspx?p=328371.

Joseph, Peniel E. 2016. *Stokely: A Life*. New York: Basic Civitas.

Kadalie, Modibo M. 2000. *Internationalism, Pan-Africanism and the Struggle of Social Classes: Raw Writings from the Notebook of an Early Nineteen Seventies African-American Radical Activist*. Savannah, Ga.: One Quest Press.

Klonsky, Mike. 1973. "'What Road to Building a New Communist Party?'" *Encyclopedia of Anti-Revisionism On-Line*. April 4, 1973. https://www.marxists.org/history/erol/ncm-2/g-1-ol.htm.

League of Revolutionary Black Workers. 1970. *The General Policy Statement and Labor Program of the League of Revolutionary Black Workers*. Highland Park, Mich.: League of Revolutionary Black Workers.

League of Revolutionary Struggle. 1980. "The Revolutionary Community League (M-L-M) and the League of Revolutionary Struggle (M-L) Unite!" *Forward: Journal of Marxism-Leninism-Mao Zedong Thought*, no. 3 (January).

Lee, Don L. 1973. "African Liberation Day." *Ebony* xxviii (9): 41–44, 46.

Lenin, V. I. 1973. *Imperialism, the Highest Stage of Capitalism: A Popular Outline, (4. Printing)*. Peking: Foreign Languages Press.

Lenin, V. I. 1975. *What Is To Be Done?* Peking: Foreign Language Press.

Lenin, Vladimir Ilyich. 1901. "Where to Begin?" 1901. https://www.marxists.org/archive/lenin/works/1901/may/04.htm.

Lerumo, A. 1987. *Fifty Fighting Years: The Communist Party of South Africa, 1921-1971*. London: Inkululeko.

Locke, Gene. 1974a. "Report to the International Steering Committee of ALSC on Trip by ALSC Delegation to Africa in Summer of 1973." African Liberation Support Committee.

———. 1974b. "A Few Remarks in Response to Criticisms of ALSC." Lynn Eusan Institute.

Lotta, Raymond, ed. 1978. *And Mao Makes 5 [Five]: Mao Tsetung's Last Great Battle*. Chicago, Ill.: Banner Press.

Machel, Samora. 1975. *The Tasks Ahead: Selected Speeches of Samora Moises Machel*. New York: Afro-American Information Service.

Madhubuti, Haki. 1974. "The Latest Purge: The Attack on Black Nationalism and Pan-Afrikanism by the New Left, the Sons and Daughters of the Old Left." *Black Scholar* 6 (1): 43–56.

Magubane, Bernard Makhosezwe. 1989. *The Ties That Bind: African-American Consciousness of Africa*. Trenton, N.J.: Africa World.

Malcolm X Liberation University. 1972. "Information Brochure." Greensboro, NC.

Manji, Firoze, and Bill Fletcher, eds. 2013. *Claim No Easy Victories: The Legacy of Amilcar Cabral*. Dakar: CODESRIA

Mao, Zedong. 1965. *Selected Works of Mao Zedong. Volume II. Volume II*. Peking: Foreign Languages Press.

Markle, Seth. 2008. "Drum and Spear Press and Tanzania's Ujamaa Ideology." *The Black Scholar* 37 (4): 16–26. https://doi.org/10.1080/00064246.2008.11413418.

Michel, Eddie. 2018. *The Luster of Chrome: Nixon, Rhodesia, and the Defiance of UN Sanctions. Diplomatic History*. Diplomatic History. https://www.academia.edu/33172495/The_Luster_of_Chrome_Nixon_Rhodesia_and_the_Defiance_of_UN_Sanctions.

Michigan State University. n.d. "African Activist Archive." Accessed March 1, 2021. https://africanactivist.msu.edu/organization.php?name=TransAfrica.

"Mickey Jarvis - KeyWiki." 2021. Key Wiki. 2021. https://keywiki.org/Mickey_Jarvis.

Milne, June. 2000. *Kwame Nkrumah—a Biography.* London: Panaf.

Minty, Abdul S and Munazzamat al-Tahrir al-Filastiniyyah. 1990. *Israel & South Africa.* [Place of publication not identified]: Palestine Liberation Organization.

Mondlane, Eduardo Chivambo. 1969. *The Struggle for Mozambique.* Baltimore: Penguin Books.

Moore, Richard B., W. Burghardt Turner, and Joyce Moore Turner. 1988. *Richard B. Moore, Caribbean Militant in Harlem: Collected Writings, 1920-1972.* Bloomington: Indiana University Press.

Mosby, Donald, Samuel 17X, and Lonnie Kashif. 1973. "African Liberaton Day Marches, Chicago, D.C. New York, New Orleans." *Muhammad Speaks*, June 15, 1973.

Murrell, Gary, and Bettina Aptheker. 2015. *The Most Dangerous Communist in the United States A Biography of Herbert Aptheker.* Amherst: University of Massachusetts Press. http://public.ebookcentral.proquest.com/choice/publicfullrecord.aspx?p=4533230.

Mwanza. 1974. "A.L.S.C. Resignation." *Black News* 2 (18): 18,36.

National Anti-Imperialist Conference in Solidarity With African Liberation. 1973. "A Call to Afro-Americans of Every Strata: Labor, Church, Political, Student, Cultural, Civic, and Community." Document in the archival collection of Abdul Alkalimat.

National Union of Students. 1973. "10th World Festival of Youth and Students, East Berlin, 1973." Warwick University Library Modern Records Centre. 1973. https://warwick.ac.uk/services/library/mrc/archives_online/filmvideo/worldfestival.

Neto, Antonio Agostinho. 1974. *Sacred Hope.* Dar es Salaam: Tanzania Publishing House.

New York Public Library. n.d. "Black Panther Party Harlem Branch Files." Accessed December 25, 2020. http://archives.nypl.org/scm/20948.

———. n.d. "Guide to the Interreligious Foundation for Community Organization." Schomburg Center for research in Black Culture. https://tinyurl.com/ycxehd7p.

Nicolaus, Martin. 1977. "Marxism or Klonskyism?, I." *Encyclopedia of Anti-Revisionism On-Line.* 1977. https://www.marxists.org/history/erol/ncm-3/nicolaus/section1.htm.

Nkrumah, Kwame. 1970. *Class Struggle in Africa.* New York: International Publishers.

———. 1973. *Revolutionary Path.* New York: International Publishers.

October League. 1973. "For Working Class Unity and Black Liberation: Resolution of the Second Congress of the October League on the Afro-American People's Struggle." October League.

Oginga Odinga. 1967. *Not yet Uhuru. The Autobiography of Oginga Odinga. With a Forew. by K. Nkrumah.* London: Heinemann.

Padmore, George. 1956. *Pan-Africanism: The Coming Struggle for Africa.* London; Accra: D. Dobson ; Guinea Press (sole distributors of this ed. in Africa).

———. 1972. *Pan-Africanism or Communism.* Garden City, N.Y: Doubleday Anchor.

Pandya, Paresh. 1988. *Mao Tse-Tung and Chimurenga: An Investigation into Zanu's Strategies.* Johannesburg: Skotaville.

Parrott, R. Joseph. 2015. "A Luta Continua: Radical Filmmaking, Pan-African Liberation and Communal Empowerment." *Race & Class* 57 (1): 20–38. https://doi.org/10.1177/0306396815581781.

Payne, Les, and Tamara Payne 2020. The Dead Are Arising: The Life of Malcolm X. Waterville, Me: Thorndike.

Peery, Nelson. 1978. *The Negro National Colonial Question.* Chicago: Workers Press.

———. 1992. *African American Liberation and Revolution in the United States*. Chicago: Workers Press.

Peoples College. 1975. "Historical Background to the African Liberation Support Committee." Document in the archival collection of Abdul Alkalimat.

———. 1977. "Selected Documentary History of People's College in the African Liberation Support Committee." Peoples College. http://alkalimat.org/114%201973-74%20 and%201977%20selected%20documentary%20history%20of%20peoples%20college%20in%20the%20african%20liberation%20support%20committee.pdf.

Pepe, Matt. 2020. "Cuba's Operation Carlota 45 Years Later." *Counterpunch*, November. https://cuba-solidarity.org.uk/news/article/4112/cubarsquos-operation-carlota-45-years-later.

Plummer, Brenda Gayle. 2013. *In Search of Power: African Americans in the Era of Decolonization, 1956-1974*. Cambridge University Press.

Powdermaker, Hortense. 1965. *Copper Town: Changing Africa, The Human Situation on the Rhodesian Copperbelt*. New York: Harper & Row.

Progressive Student Delegation. 1974. *Viva Cuba: Down with U.S. Imperialism*. Washington, D.C.: The Delegation.

Ransby, Barbara. 2014. *Eslanda: The Large and Unconventional Life of Mrs. Paul Robeson*. New Haven, CT.: Yale University Press.

Revolutionary Communist Party. 1972. "Red Papers 5: National Liberation and Proletarian Revolution in the U.S." October 1972. https://www.marxists.org/history/erol/ncm-8/red-papers-5/index.htm.

———. 1974. "Red Papers 6: Build the Leadership of the Proletariat and Its Party." June 1974. https://www.marxists.org/history/erol/ncm-8/rp-6/introduction.htm.

Revolutionary Communist Party, USA. 1978. *Revolution and Counter-Revolution: The Revisionist Coup in China and the Struggle in the Revolutionary Communist Party, USA.* Chicago: RCP Publications.

Revolutionary Workers Headquarters. 1978. "Red Papers 8: Chna Advances on the Socialist Road: The Split in the Revolutionary Communist Party." 1978. https://www.marxists. org/history/erol/ncm-5/rp-8/index.htm.

———. 1981. *Build the Black Liberation Movement.* Chicago: Pole Publications.

Revolutionary Workers League. 1976. "Forward to the U.S. Bolshevik Party." *Bolshevik*, no. 1 (May).

Rhodesian Ministry of Foreign Affairs. 1975. "Communist Support to Nationalists in Rhodesia." November 1975. http://www.rhodesia.nl/commsupp.htm.

Rickford, Russell John. 2016. *We Are an African People: Independent Education, Black Power, and the Radical Imagination.* Oxford University Press.

Robeson, Paul. 1999. *Paul Robeson: Here I Stand.* Beacon.

Robeson, Susan. 1999. *The Whole World in His Hands: Paul Robeson—a Family Memoir in Words and Pictures.* New York; Partridge Green: Citadel ; Biblios.

Robinson, Jini M. 1972. "African Liberation Day: Festive Serious Celebration Demonstrates Black Solidarity." *California Voice*, June 1, 1972, Vol 52, No 31 edition.

Rogers, Harold. 1972. "The Upsurge of Anti-Imperialism in the Black Liberation Movement." *African Agenda*, June 1972.

———. 1973. "Special Issue: National Anti-Imperialist Conference n Solidarity with African Liberation." *African Agenda*, November 1973, Volume 2, Numbers 10-11 edition.

Sadaukai, Owusu. 1972a. "The Action of Outraged African-American Students Involving the Illegal Chomium Ore Shipment from Rhodesia Received in Burnside, Louisiana." African Liberation Day Coordinating Committee.

———. 1972b. "Speech to the African American Conference on Africa." Document in the archival collection of Abdul Alkalimat.

———. 1972c. "Text of an Address by Owusu Sadaukai, Mwalimu of MXLU." *IFCO News*, December 1972, Volume III Issue VI edition.

———. n.d. "The History of the Development of the Statement of Principles of the African Liberation Support Committee." ALSC.

Sales, Bill. 1976. ALSC Interview by Abdul Alkalimat and Ron Bailey. Document in the archival collection of Abdul Alkalimat.

Sales, William W. 1994. *From Civil Rights to Black Liberation: Malcolm X and the Organization of Afro-American Unity*. Boston, Mass.: South End Press.

Scott, Jerome. 1979. *The Struggle for Zimbabwe*. Chicago: Workers Press.

Sellers, Cleveland. 1972. "African Liberation Day Coordinating Committee Letter." African Liberation Day Coordinating Committee.

Shirokov, M and Leningrad Institute of Philosophy. 1978. *A Textbook of Marxist Philosophy*. Chicago: Proletarian Publishers.

Silber, Irwin. 1973. "'What Road to Building a New Communist Party?'" Encyclopedia of Anti-Revisionism On-Line. April 4, 1973. https://www.marxists.org/history/erol/ncm-2/g-1-silber.htm.

Simanga, M. 2015. *Amiri Baraka and the Congress of African People: History and Memory*. 2015 edition. New York, NY: Palgrave Macmillan.

Smith, Klytus, Abiola Sinclair, and Hannibal Ahmed. 1995. *The Harlem Cultural/Political Movements, 1960-1970: From Malcolm X to "Black Is Beautiful."* New York: Gumbs & Thomas Publishers.

Smith, Mark. 1975. "A Response To Haki R. Madhubuti." *The Black Scholar* 6 (5): 46–53.

"SNCC Workers Meet Oginga Odinga." n.d. *SNCC Digital Gate-*

way (blog). Accessed November 23, 2020. https://snc-cdigital.org/events/sncc-workers-meet-oginga-odinga/.

SOBU News Service. 1972. "SOBU National Assembly." *The African World*, May 9, 1972, Vol 22, No 14 edition.

South African History Online. n.d. "Rivonia Trial 1963-1964." Accessed November 10, 2020. https://www.sahistory.org.za/article/rivonia-trial-1963-1964.

South-West Africa People's Organisation of Namibia. 1987. *To Be Born a Nation: The Liberation Struggle for Namibia.* London: Zed Press.

Stalin, Joseph V. 1971. Selected Works. Davis, California: Cardinal Publishers.

Student Organization for Black Unity. 1975. "Building the Revolutionary Press." Greensboro, NC.

———. nd. "Cadre Development." Document in the archival collection of Abdul Alkalimat.

Sullivan, Joseph. 1974. "Baraka Drops 'Racism' For Socialism of Marx." *The New York Times*, December 27, 1974, sec. Archives. https://www.nytimes.com/1974/12/27/archives/barka-drops-racism-for-socialism-of-marx-special-to-the-new-york.html.

Tanzanian Publishing House. 1976, *Resolutions and Selected Speeches from the Sixth Pan African Congress.* Dar es Salaam: Tanzania Publishing House.

Tate, Florence. 1972. "ALDCC News Relese." African Liberation Day Coordinating Committee. Document in the archival collection of Abdul Alkalimat.

Teltsch, Kathleen. 1967. "S.N.C.C. CRITICIZED FOR ISRAEL STAND; Rights Leaders Score Attack on Jews as 'Anti-Semitism' (Published 1967)."

The New York Times, August 16, 1967, sec. Archives. https://www.nytimes.com/1967/08/16/archives/sncc-criticized-for-israel-stand-rights-leaders-score-attack-on.html.

Thompson, Robert Farris. 1984. *Flash of the Spirit: African and Afro-American Art and Philosophy.* New York: Vintage

Books, Random House.

———. 2011. *Aesthetic of the Cool: Afro-Atlantic Art and Music.* Pittsburgh; New York: Periscope Publishing ; Distributed by Prestel Publishing.

Tsetung, Mao. 2013. *Selected Readings from the Works of Mao Tsetung.* Peking: Foreign Languages Press.

Turpin, Carl. 1974. "Report of Information Coordinator." African Liberation Support Committee.

United Nations Association of the United States of America and Student & Young Adult Division. 1973. *Rhodesian Chrome; a Research Report by the Washington Intern Program of the Student & Young Adult Division, United Nations Association of the U.S.A.* New York.

Visser-Maessen, Laura. 2021. *Robert Parris Moses: A Life in Civil Rights and Leadership at the Grassroots.* Chapel Hill, NC: University of North Carolina Press.

Wagner, Pat. 1976. ALSC Interview by Abdul Alkalimat and Ron Bailey. Document in the archival collection of Abdul Alkalimat.

Walters, Ronald W. 1972. "Statement of Principles: The African Liberation Support Committee." ALSC. Document in the archival collection of Abdul Alkalimat.

Walton, Jeannette. 1976. ALSC. Document in the archival collection of Abdul Alkalimat.

Washington, Ron. 2009. "The Rise and Fall of the Revolutionary Workers League (RWL) Or as Was Said in the 'Bronx Tale,' There's Nothing Worse Than Wasted Potential." Document in the archival collection of Abdul Alkalimat.

Wilkins, Fanon Che. 2005. "In the Belly of the Beast: Black Power, Anti-Imperialism, and the African Liberation Solidarity Movement 1968-1975." (PhD Dissertation.) New York: New York University, 2005.

Winston, Henry. 1987. *Strategy for a Black Agenda: A Critique of New Theories of Liberation in the United States and Africa.* New York: International Publishers.

Woodard, Komozi. 1999. *A Nation Within a Nation: Amiri Baraka (LeRoi Jones) and Black Power Politics.* https://books-google-com.proxy2.library.illinois.edu/books/about/A_Nation_Within_a_Nation.html?id=itkOLfbHyEAC.

Woods, Donald. 1979. *Biko.* New York: Vintage Books.

Wright, Don. 1973. "'What Road to Building a New Communist Party?'" Encyclopedia of Anti-Revisionism On-Line. April 4, 1973. https://www.marxists.org/history/erol/ncm-2/g-1-ru.htm.

X, Malcolm, Herb Boyd, and Ilyasah Shabazz. 2013. *The Diary of Malcolm X El-Hajj Malik El-Shabazz 1964.* Chicago, Ill: Third World Press.

YOBU. 1974. "Historic ALSC Conference Discussed 'Which Road for Black People?'." *The African World*, July 1974.

YOBU News Service. 1973. "National Black College Conference Maps Out 'Survival Strategy.'" *The African World*, April 28, 1973, Vol 3 edition.

Young, Lowell, ed. 1975. *1928 and 1930 Comintern Resolutions.* Washington D.C.: Revolutionary Review Press. http://www.marx2mao.com/Other/CR75.html#s0.

Zhongguo gong chan dang and Zhong yang wei yuan hui. 1963. *A Proposal Concerning the General Line of the International Communist Movement.* Peking: Foreign Languages Press.

Appendix:

ALSC Statement of Principles, July 1973

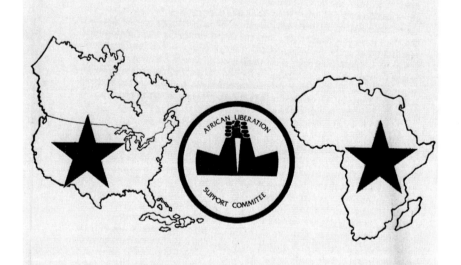

AFRICAN LIBERATION
SUPPORT COMMITTEE

P.O. BOX 14093, HOUSTON, TEXAS 77021

STATEMENT OF PRINCIPLES

of

African Liberation Support Committee

WORLD VIEW

"If there is no struggle, there can be no progress.........."

Black people throughout the world are realizing that our freedom will only be won through a protracted struggle against two forces — racism and imperialism. The world imperialist system festers in Africa and Asia and engulfs the Western Hemisphere as well. In the United States we know it as monopoly capitalism, in Africa it is imperialism in its colonial or neo-colonial form. Wherever it appears, its cornerstone is the white ruling class of the United States of America.

Imperialism is neither invincible nor invulnerable. As the blows against it increase, the crisis of imperialism heightens and leads to new levels of exploitation of Black People in the Western Hemisphere, Africa and the rest of the world.

AFRICA

In Africa, the remains of classical European colonialism is held together by Portugal (in Guinea-Bissau, Angola, and Mozambique). The United States government has been a constant supporter and ally of Portuguese oppression through direct aid (such as the $430 million Azores agreement) and gifts of planes, arms, and military training (at Fort Bragg, North Carolina) through NATO. White settler rule is based in police state South Africa, and extends to Namibia (South-West Africa) and Zimbabwe (Rhodesia) as well. There is hardly a single major U.S. or multinational Corporation, or bank that does not have investments in Southern Africa. Chase Manhattan Bank, Firestone Rubber and tires, Gulf Oil, Holiday Inn, General Motors and some 300 other firms have investments totalling over 1 billion dollars. Several major problems face the people of Southern Africa and Guinea-Bissau as a result of the present crisis:

1. Resettlement schemes to absorb unemployed European workers as new colonists in Africa; They will be expected to fight against liberation forces. An example is the Cabora Bassa Dam project in the Tete province of Mozambique, where over 1,000,000 European workers are expected to settle.

2. Increased levels of exploitation caused by the relocation of factories from advanced capitalist countries — "run'away shops." The conditions that generally accompany this new investment are no-strike laws, forced labor, slave-wages, no right-to-organize laws, and neo-facist policies of political repression against all dissent.

3. Militaristic and aggressive expansionist policies of South Africa and Israel to recolonize "independent" Africa using capital invested by multinational corporations based in the U.S., Europe and Japan.

WESTERN HEMISPHERE (U.S., Canada and the Caribbean)

Black people in the Western Hemisphere equally caught in the racist imperialist net, also face major problems in the present state of our struggle:

1. Problems on the job-unemployment, low wages, job insecurity, racism by management and union leadership discrimination in hiring and promotions (especially in skilled crafts), and super-exploitation in the shops (speed-up, compulsory overtime, etc.)

2. Continued neglect, and indeed cutbacks in the area of social services; public welfare, transporation, housing sanitation, health facilities, and education, etc.

3. Political-police-military repression with facist-type hit squads (like the STRESS squad was in Detroit), increased use of electronic surveillance and informers, a rising rate of Black Youth in prisons, and systematic introduction of heroin (or heroin substitutes) into the Black Communities.

4. Continued onslaughts on efforts to preserve and develop revolutionary culture among Black people, including the use of distorted fragments of Black history and the accomplishments of "distinguished Black Americans." These onslaughts are in fact cultural aggression. Cultural aggression, like all other forms of racism, seeks to impose the way of life, values and institutions of one culture on another culture. Culture here defined as a way of life, values, and those institutions set up to maintain and develop that way of life and its values.

FINALLY GOT THE NEWS

Black people throughout the world have finally got the news — the news that racism and imperialism the two headed monster — are our enemies. The major historical trends of the moment in Southern Africa can be summed up as:

1. The heightened struggle and increasing success of the liberation movements, which win new victories every day. Their struggle has been aided by the support of the Socialist countries, and by other anti-imperialist forces, especially the increasing support of progressive Black people in the United States.

2. The increasing support for the liberation movements by independent African countries, even conservative ones, through the OAU Liberation Committee and by direct aid.

3. The rising desperation of the Portuguese governments in the face of liberation groups marching towards total victories in the "colonies". This desperation is reflected by the cowardly assassination of Amilcar Cabral, Secretary-General of the PAIGC, on the streets of Conakry by Portuguese agents.

4. Increased co-operation between colonial and imperialist governments especially Rhodesia, South Africa, Portugal, Israel, and the United States in these areas; first, collective military arrangements; second, the wooing of governments of certain African countries in an attempt to seduce them into "dialogue" with South Africa or otherwise breach the anti-colonial unity of Africa; third, the development of schemes to hand the Portuguese colonies over the phoney "independent" Black governments — in reality puppets for the Portuguese.

5. The increasing awareness of Black workers in Southern Africa who are mounting demonstrations and strikes to prove that the system of internal oppression under which they suffer can be overthrown.

The major historical trends at the present time in the United States may be summed up as follows:

1. The international crisis of capitalism has produced effects — rising market price of gold, falling value of the dollar — that have put the U.S. economy on very shakey ground; unemployment, high food prices, run away shops are a few indications of the instability of the domestic market.

2. The increasing manifestations of frustrations and anger of people in the U.S. especially Black people-battered back and forth by forces which they do not understand.

3. The exposure of corruption in government from Nixon and Halderman to Mayors Daly and Addonizio, down to the cop on the corner. People increasingly realize that this corruption is linked to control of government by large corporations and the rich in their own interests.

4. The increasing attempts by the white ruling class of the USA and their apologists, to blame many social problems on Black People: (high taxes, welfare, unemployment for white workers; inflation)

We can clearly see that the imperialist monster has two heads — in the Western Hemisphere and elsewhere in the world. We here have the same duty as all progressive Black people — to fight imperialism in all its manifestations. To do this we must build an anti-racist, anti-imperialist United Front among Black people.

TOWARDS A UNITED FRONT

"If we do not formulate plans for unity and take active steps to form political union, we will soon be fighting and warring among ourselves with imperialists and colonialists standing behind the screen and pulling vicious wires, to make us cut each others throats for the sake of their diabolical purposes.........."

Kwame Nkumah

Black people throughout the world face a future of struggle to put together a movement with the theoretical and organizational tools and the practical experience necessary to defeat enemies and build a new world.

Theory

We must learn from the experience of other movements and other struggles experience which teaches that "there can be no revolutionary movement without revolutionary theory." We have learned rich lessons from struggles with no theory at all. Those lessons teach us two important things about unity and theory:

1. We cannot be dogmatic. Once we have rooted ourselves in certain principles, we must direct our struggle according to the concrete, changing conditions around us.

2. Real unity will come about not by ignoring differences but by airing those differences and struggling to resolve them. It is through the interplay of ideas and the testing of those ideas in practice that a correct position will be hammered out.

Organization

We must struggle to improve our organization work. Building unity means finding ways of utilizing the abilities and skills of everyone who is serious about struggling.

In order for the Black Liberation Struggle to advance there must be a dynamic and direct struggle to unite forces, and develop correct views. This unity in struggle will develop militants with experience, committed to correct views and unified with other individuals and organizations proven in the fight against imperialism. Active criticism and ideological struggle are the weapons and the way of ensuring that Brothers and Sisters within the ALSC build strong organizational unity. Non-antagonistic contradictions within the committee can only be resolved through active ideological and political struggle based on principle. The basis of such struggle will ensure us a higher unity. Such a unity based on unity-struggle, unity, will cement organizational unity and correct our political direction. If errors are left by themselves, organizational unity, strength and direction will not be achieved.

External

Our unity with other political tendencies in the Black Community must be based on a commitment to eliminate racism and defeat monopoly capitalism in the Western Hemisphere and imperialism throughout the rest of the world. For example, our view is that African people must control Southern Africa and Guinea-Bissau and the only way to really do this is by armed revolutionary struggle. Recognizing the present condition, we also support the struggles for democratic rights; for instance the right of Black workers to organize in Durham, N.C., South Africa or Detroit, Michigan. In this way we must begin to involve people of various ideological positions — ministers, elected officials, civil rights groups, etc., around the program of ALSC, not on their terms but on commonly agreed terms — on terms of the front which we can all support. This process will not happen immediately, it will have to be done step by step. Part of its success or failure will be in our ability to scientifically identify different classed and social groupings in the Black Community so that we can deal with them all effectively. The success of "unite the many to oppose the few" in any society involves knowing exactly who composes "the many" and determining what they can be united around.

Focus for Mobilization

Our anti-racist, anti-imperialist, Black united front must attempt to unite all social groups and class formations within the Black community in a common struggle. Thus our struggle must mobilize the masses but this can only be done when the specific character of this exploitation is clearly understood.

Most Black adults work in production or service jobs. It is this sector of the Black community that has the most to gain by the victory of our struggles and yet they have been the most ignored by the movement. We also consider unemployed workers, most brothers and sisters incarcerated in prisons and welfare recipients as displaced workers. We must give the highest priority to mobilizing Black workers because they have demonstrated the power to do many things, such as stopping illegal chrome shipments from Rhodesia, expose repressive use of Polaroid identification systems and stop production of cars, not only in solidarity with the liberation movements, but also as a part of the fight against their own oppression. Therefore we encourage Black workers to take the lead. It is in this area that the ALSC — the anti-racist, anti-imperialist Black United Front, must meet the challenge of showing the interrelationship of the oppression of the people of Southern Africa and the exploitation of the Black people in the Western Hemisphere.

The post World War II rise of Blacks in clerical and professional jobs provided the basis for leadership, organizational skills, and ideology during the Civil Rights Era. In turn, this struggle opened up new opportunities in government work, business opportunities, educational institutions, etc. As the crisis of imperialism causes the society to contract and cut back, the Black middle strata will be cut back. This is especially true of those jobs created by the poverty program and similar agencies in tha past nine years. In addition to the radicalization of these people, occupants of traditional middle strata "professional" jobs are increasingly feeling the squeeze of monopoly capital. Teachers, social workers, and government workers, to name a few can and must be shown the true nature of the society of the Western Hemisphere. Their struggle will ultimately not be that of saving their professional status, but rather in joining with the masses of people to defeat racism and imperialism decisively and finally.

Short life expectancy and high birth rates result in the Black community being young. Youth is also a time of struggle. We must gather together Black Youth from the plants, from the campuses, the streets, penal institutions, military reservations, and wherever else they are, to create a mass mobilization of these youth in the anti-racist, anti-imperialist struggle.

Summation

In summary we have presented three major points:

1. The new unity of the Black Liberation struggle must be anti-racist, anti-imperialist and anti-capitalist in character.

2. The struggle to unify Black anti-racist, anti-imperialist forces is our source of strength in building an ideologically advanced movement.

3. Our unity must involve all Black social groups and class formations and we propose that Black workers take the lead.

Basic Program for African Liberation Support Committee

1. Raise money for liberation groups in Southern Africa and Guinea-Bissau through the United African Appeal.

2. Conduct educational seminars and programs on racism, feudalism, imperialism colonialism and neo-colonialism and its effect on the continent of Africa, especially South Africa and Guinea-Bissau.

3. Develop and distribute literature, films, and other educational materials on racism, feudalism, imperialism, colonialism and neo-colonialism and its effect on the continent of Africa, especially South Africa and Guinea-Bissau.

4. Participate in and aid Black community and Black workers in the struggles against oppression in the U.S., Canada, and the Caribbean.....

5. Engage in efforts to influence and transform U.S. policy as regards to it's imperialist role in the world.

6. Engage in mass actions against governments, products, and companies that are involved in or are supportive of racist, illegitimate regimes in Southern Africa and Guinea-Bissau.

7. Support and spearhead annual ALD demonstrations in conjunction with the International African Solidarity Day.

THE ALSC EXECUTIVE COMMITTEE

CHAIRMAN   Gene Locke, Houston, Texas

Brenda Paris, Montreal, Canada

John Warfield, Austin, Texas

Abdul Alkalimat, Nashville, Tenn.

Nelson Johnson, Greensboro, NC

Kwadwo Akpan, Detroit, Mich.

Owusu Sadaukai, Greensboro, NC

Imamu Baraka, New Ark, NJ

Don Lee, Chicago, Ill.

Several additional persons will be added to the executive committee in the near future.

Index

A

Aaron, Walter 2

African Liberation Day (ALD)
3–4, 7–8, 33, 56–58, 61–64,
66, 69–72, 75–78, 88–89,
91–95, 97, 99, 101–102, 105,
108, 112–113, 119–120, 123,
126–127, 131–133, 135, 152,
175, 200, 207, 209–212, 216

African Liberation Support
Committee (ALSC) v–vii,
1–5, 8, 33, 52, 56, 58, 72, 75–
83, 86–123, 125, 127–130,
132, 134–136, 145–148, 152,
154–156, 158, 170–182, 191,
198–200, 202–212, 215–224,
226–229, 232, 234–238, 242,
244, 249, 251–253

African Peoples Socialist Party
(APSP) 85, 200–201

The African World 43–44, 49, 62,
76, 89, 101, 155–157, 170,
175, 198, 207, 217, 224, 250,
252

Ahmad, Muhammad (Max
Stanford) vi, 2, 61, 81,
84–85, 94, 99, 156, 160, 233

Akpan, Kwadwo vi, 61, 76,
87–88, 96, 98, 156–158

Alkalimat. Abdul   iii, viii, 2, 5,
88, 93, 98, 110, 115–120,
128, 130, 151, 152, 156, 165,
204, 207, 216, 218, 233–38,
242, 245, 247–51

All African Peoples Party (APP)
81, 85, 155, 160, 200–202

All African Peoples
Revolutionary Party (APRP)
85

Anderson, Sam 2, 57–58, 207,
209, 218, 235

Angola v, 7, 12, 16–21, 24, 63,
87, 102, 136–140, 186–188,
209, 237–238, 242

B

Baraka, Amiri vi, 2, 45, 49–50,
56, 62–63, 68, 91, 98, 109,

261

C

Index

217, 234, 243

Jones, Phyliss 2, 36, 39, 90, 96, 238, 252

L

League of Revolutionary Black Workers (LRBW) 84–85, 104, 202, 206

Lenin, V. I. 9, 44, 141, 147, 162–164, 169, 182–183, 192–193, 223–224, 239, 243

Locke, Gene 2, 56, 61, 67, 80, 88, 94, 98–100, 108, 115–116, 128, 173, 175, 177, 204, 207, 211, 217, 244

Lumumba, Chokwe 11, 20, 38, 97, 123, 207, 216

Lumumba, Patrice 11, 20, 38, 97, 123, 207, 216

Lynn Eusan Institute 98, 244

M

Madhubuti, Haki (Don Lee) 2, 68, 80, 117, 123, 147, 173, 175–176, 244, 249

Malcolm X Liberation University (MXLU) 49–53, 55–56, 62–64, 73, 78–80, 98, 146, 148–149, 156, 170, 222, 228, 249

Mandela, Nelson 14–16, 139–140

Mao Tse-Tung 166, 187, 200, 223, 246

Marxism 1, 19, 85, 135, 141, 146–148, 150–151, 176,

184–185, 194, 200, 206, 208, 228, 243, 246

Mendez, John 2, 92

Mozambique v, 7, 12, 17, 24–27, 48, 53–56, 62–64, 87, 102, 109, 136–137, 140, 236–238, 242, 245

MPLA 19–21, 76, 86–87, 96, 137–139, 187–188, 209

Muhammad, Saladin vi, 2, 37, 43, 61, 76, 81, 85, 89, 94, 110, 156, 160, 174–175, 218, 224, 233–234, 245

Muhammad Speaks 43, 76, 89, 110, 174–175, 245

N

Namibia (Southwest Africa) v, 7, 12, 31–32, 59, 102, 138–140, 250

National Anti-Imperialist Conference in Solidarity with African Liberation (NAIMSAL) 112–114

Nesbitt, Prexy 77

Newark, New Jersey 57, 62–63, 68, 91, 98, 110, 146, 153, 177, 199, 205–206

Nkrumah, Kwame 10–11, 20, 40, 52, 57, 65, 76, 91, 100, 104, 124, 137, 200, 228, 245–246

O

October League (OL, CPML) 142, 191, 194–195, 204, 243

Index

P